Philosophy, Morality, and International Affairs

Philosophy, Morality, and International Affairs

Essays edited for the Society
for Philosophy and Public Affairs

VIRGINIA HELD
SIDNEY MORGENBESSER
THOMAS NAGEL

New York
OXFORD UNIVERSITY PRESS
London   1974   Toronto

Contents

Introduction

The Society for Philosophy and Public Affairs was founded in 1969 as the natural expression of a rising interest in questions of public policy among students and teachers of philosophy. This interest was due partly to a growing conviction that the connections between abstract and practical questions could be effectively drawn, and that the failure to do so could be unfortunate for the pursuit of either interest. The task was a double one: to overcome the detachment of philosophy from concrete social issues and to challenge the widespread complacency about American institutions and practices. The formation of the Society was also due to the concern, outrage, and sense of helplessness aroused in varying degrees among philosophers by the Vietnam War. Philosophy seemed ill-equipped to handle questions raised by the war. Like many Americans, philosophers have tended to react profoundly to that event, and have felt impelled to speak about real circumstances and real policies in order to decide what to believe and how to act. The Society for Philosophy and Public Affairs, in its group meetings and in symposia held at sessions of the American Philosophical Association, has provided a forum for discussions arising from these concerns.

In 1972, the New York Group of the Society published a collection of essays entitled *Philosophy and Political Action* under the editorship of Virginia Held, Kai Nielsen, and Charles Parsons. It was drawn together from papers presented at meetings of the group or written by members and associates. In view of the response to the publication of this volume, the Executive Committee of the national Society issued a call for papers dealing specifically with philosophy and international affairs. It subsequently requested the undersigned editors to bring out the present volume, which draws on the work of members throughout the United States and Canada. All of the essays included here were written expressly for this volume. Some derive from papers originally delivered at meetings of the Society (such as the 1971 Symposium on War Crimes and Moral Responsibility).

All of the essays presented here attempt in different ways to reduce the moral and intellectual confusion that so often surrounds discussions of international conflict and international relations. When rationality and decency are absent, as they frequently are in international affairs, the rhetoric of justification may be present, but this will usually involve serious abuses of language and thought. In the attempt by all parties to corner the market in expressions of condemnation and exculpation, terms like 'genocide', 'imperialism', 'self-determination', 'freedom', 'legitimacy', 'legality', 'honor', 'justice' —even 'war' and 'peace'—are bent and distorted. Offenses against language are offenses against thought and defenses against the uncomfortable costs of knowing what one is doing, having to acknowledge it to oneself, and knowing that others know as well.

For philosophers this distortion of language is a natural target and the careful dissection and clarification of focal concepts occupy many of the contributors to this volume. But most of the essays do not limit themselves to attacking confusion brought about by the desire to manipulate or by self-deception. Some attempt to analyze terms and theories which have played important roles in social philosophy, legal discussion, and the social sciences. Others make specific proposals for international arrangements and institutions and suggest avenues for further empirical investigation. They are intended as reasoned challenges to widely held political beliefs and are written not merely to help us understand the political world but to suggest changes in it. It is a sad commentary on our situation that some of the essays have to defend the thesis that morality and justice ought to play a role in international affairs and that prudence and national self-interest (no matter how defined) ought not to be the ultimate arbiters.

It may have been blissful to have been young and philosophical at the dawn of the French Revolution. It is painful to write about international affairs in America now. The current situation reminds us that feelings of international fellowship are rare, that soldiers are willing to kill while their governments deceive, and that myopic self-regard and irrational pride and hatred have an even freer rein in international affairs than they do within national boundaries. The causal relevance of reason, to say nothing of philosophy, seems slight in international affairs. It seems pointless to detect three nonsequiturs and four evasions per dropped megaton.

But the efficacy of reasoned criticism, even if slight, cannot be neglected. Rationalization and faulty moral argument, as well as the distortion of language, play a supportive role in the execution of policies even if they do not express the true motives for those policies. People wish to have a satisfactory conception of what they are doing, and if it is denied them the cost of persisting increases. So while it is often impossible to argue people out of a political commitment by showing that it rests on a mistake, it may be possible to undermine their comfort and leave them with fewer resources for representing themselves acceptably.

Of course it is not only international terror and violence

that are being objected to in these essays. There may be a decrease of violence and also a continuation of unjust international arrangements if the powerful nations impose a peace that is satisfactory to themselves alone. But unjust arrangements induce and possibly sometimes justify violence; hence the quest for peace is at one with the quest for justice. And the delineation of alternative courses of action, the suggestion of more reasonable forms of international behavior, must precede any conscious efforts to lower the level of international violence and horror.

These essays, like many of the acts of protest against the war in Southeast Asia, are animated by the conviction that morality has a place in national conduct and international affairs, and they are guided by the experience that protest is not always futile. When people abdicate responsibility to those individuals and institutions with superior power, the door is open to terror and brutality. If, on the other hand, people commit themselves to seek sounder international arrangements, if they are encouraged to rely upon their own considered judgments and to act upon them, then just possibly we or our descendants may, after all, see the development of a humane and stable international order.

V.H.
S.M.
T.N.

Summer 1973

One
WAR AND ITS CRIMES

Introduction

The relation between law and ethics has been an active philosophical subject in recent years. There has been extensive debate about the legal enforcement of specific moral standards, about the role of moral principles in the basic structure of any legal system, and about the dilemmas arising from conflict between legal requirements and individual conscience. For a time these discussions focused primarily on domestic law. Recent events, however, have led philosophers, especially in America, to think extensively about war crimes and the laws of war: about their ethical significance, about the justice of particular charges arising out of them, and about the legal standing of individuals as well as of nations in relation to them.

The major topics have been these:

1. How do the laws of war, and laws prohibiting crimes against humanity, apply to the conduct of various governments, including the United States and its allies, during and since the Second World War?
2. Do those laws have a moral basis, or are they merely pacts of convenience between basically amoral nation-states?
3. Are there respects in which the laws as presently constituted are too stringent, not stringent enough, or incoherent?
4. What are the responsibilities of individuals, as opposed to governments, under the laws of war, and what should

happen when an actual or prospective soldier and his government differ over the legality or morality of military actions that the government requires of its citizens?

Some or all of these complex issues are discussed in each of the four essays that follow. Each is partly concerned with the Vietnam War, but all have wider implications. The current debate has led to a reconsideration of Allied actions in World War II, and it applies to possible future wars as well. The status of the laws of war themselves is part of the issue, for opinions differ as to whether they provide a basis for the development of humane standards and whether they can legitimately be appealed to by individuals who oppose the actions of their governments.

Legal debate is often philosophical. With issues like these, which are morally fundamental and conceptually difficult, philosophers of law are in a particularly strong position to contribute to the advancement of our understanding—as is evident from the essays that follow.

1

Genocide in Vietnam?

HUGO ADAM BEDAU

§1. INTRODUCTION

In 1965, shortly after the United States government had ordered regular bombing raids over North Vietnam and had landed thousands of ground troops in South Vietnam, Bertrand Russell and his Peace Foundation organized a non-governmental "International War Crimes Tribunal." Its purpose was to conduct investigations and hear evidence in order to determine whether the United States government was responsible for committing various crimes in violation of international law in its conduct of war in Indochina.[1] After considerable difficulty in securing the permission of any government to convene the Russell Tribunal within its territories, the hearings commenced in November 1966 in Sweden. A year later, the Tribunal held a second session, in Denmark. At the latter session—convened five months after then Secretary of Defense Robert S. MacNamara had ordered preparation of what have come to be known as the Pentagon Papers, and four months before the massacre at My Lai—the sixth and final question put before the Tribunal was: "Does the combination of crimes imputed to the Government of the United States in its

1. A partial record of the Tribunal's sessions may be found in *Against the Crime of Silence*, edited by John Duffett (New York: Clarion Books, 1970). A more complete text is available in French, in two volumes: International War Crimes Tribunal, *Le Jugement de Stockholm* (Paris: Gallimard, 1967), and *Tribunal Russell II: Le Jugement final* (Paris: Gallimard, 1968). For information on the organization of the Tribunal, see Bertrand Russell, *War Crimes in Vietnam* (London: Allen & Unwin, 1967), pp. 125-30.

war in Vietnam constitute the crime of genocide?"[2] Ten days later, after several presentations on genocide, including a vigorous argument in the affirmative from Jean-Paul Sartre, the Tribunal did vote unanimously that "the United States Government" is "guilty of genocide against the people in Vietnam."[3]

Within the last few years, many American critics of the Vietnam war have publicly concurred in this judgment. They have told us that the United States is guilty of "crimes against humanity,"[4] of a war against "an entire people,"[5] that our policy involves a "'final solution' to the Vietnamese problem,"[6] a "genocidal policy,"[7] and has produced "the most grotesque crime of all . . . genocide."[8] The increasing frequency with which such

2. Duffett, ed., *op. cit.*, p. 311.

3. Duffet, ed., *op. cit.*, p. 650. During June 1971 a non-governmental "International Commission of Enquiry into United States Crimes in Indochina" convened in Oslo, Norway. "At its first session, the International Commission of Enquiry concluded that the nature and scope of the crimes which are being committed by the United States and its allies can be deemed to fulfill the legal prerequisites of the 1948 UN Convention on the Prevention and Punishment of the Crime of Genocide." Hans Göran Franck, "International Law and the U.S. War in Indochina," in *The Wasted Nations: Report of the International Commission of Enquiry into United States Crimes in Indochina,* edited by Frank Browning and Dorothy Forman (New York: Harper Colophon Books, 1972), p. 300, and cf. p. 339.

4. George Wald, in *War Crimes and the American Conscience,* edited by Erwin Knoll and Judith Nies McFadden (New York: Holt, Rinehart and Winston, 1970), p. 75.

5. Hans Morgenthau, in Knoll and McFadden, *op. cit.*, p. 15. Cf. Herbert Marcuse, "Reflections on Calley," *New York Times,* May 13, 1971, p. 45 ("the war is waged against a whole people: genocide").

6. David Welsh, "Pacification in Vietnam," in *Crimes of War,* edited by R. Falk, G. Kolko, and R. J. Lifton (New York: Random House, 1971), p. 291.

7. Edward M. Opton, Jr., in Knoll and McFadden, *op. cit.*, p. 114. Cf. Anthony J. Russo, in Congressional Conference on the Pentagon Papers, *Anatomy of an Undeclared War* (New York: International Universities Press, 1972), p. 79 ("a genocidal war"); David G. Marr, *ibid.*, p. 97 ("genocidal measures"); and Frances FitzGerald, *Fire in the Lake: The Vietnamese and the Americans in Vietnam* (Boston: Little, Brown, 1972), p. 375 ("a policy . . . indistinguishable from [genocide]).

8. Richard Falk, in Browning and Forman, *op. cit.*, p. xv. The accusation of genocide in Vietnam reached the level of commonplace during 1972 with the

judgments are now seen is not owing to the delayed effect of the argument and judgment of the Russell Tribunal of 1967. Its conclusions have had little discernible effect in this country. Instead, the explanation may lie, at least in part, in the way the relatively minor incident at My Lai,[9] exposed during 1970 and discussed widely during and after the trials of Lieutenant Calley and Captain Medina in 1971, confirmed a growing uneasiness (as Sartre had charged, well in advance of My Lai) that the Vietnam war reveals a spirit of genocide in the minds of American soldiers. Few commentators actually wrote that the My Lai massacre was genocidal. Yet that unprovoked murder of hundreds of South Vietnamese civilians by a couple of dozen American infantrymen seized the imagination of many Americans in the way that years of aerial obliteration bombing had not. The revelations of the My Lai massacre, whether or not it constituted genocide, made it possible to allege that crime and to get a hearing in a way that had been impossible only a few years earlier.

Yet not every critic of American conduct in Vietnam, even in the aftermath of My Lai, has been willing to go quite this far. Hannah Arendt, who plainly opposed the war, dismissed unnamed "left-wing war critics" who called "every massacre a genocide, which obviously it was not"[10]—only to leave her readers uncertain whether she thought even one massacre in Vietnam, or possibly the whole war itself, was genocidal. The Committee of Concerned Asian Scholars, for instance, implies that the United States is guilty of "war crimes and atrocities," but they make no

---

publication of two volumes of testimony by former members of the United States armed forces in Vietnam. See Citizens Commission of Inquiry, *The Dellums Committee Hearings on War Crimes in Vietnam* (New York: Vintage Books, 1972), pp. vii, 56-57, 169 f., 196, 302; and Vietnam Veterans Against the War, *The Winter Soldier Investigation: An Inquiry into American War Crimes* (Boston: Beacon Press, 1972), pp. 1, 2, 3, 36, 171, 157, 160.

9. See Richard Hammer, *One Morning in the War—The Tragedy at Son My* (New York: Coward-McCann, 1970), and Seymour Hersh, *My Lai Four—A Report on the Massacre and Its Aftermath* (New York: Random House, 1970).

10. Hannah Arendt, "Lying in Politics: Reflections on the Pentagon Papers," *New York Review of Books*, November 18, 1971, pp. 30-39, at p. 38.

mention of genocide.[11] Telford Taylor, whose little book, *Nuremberg and Vietnam*, did so much to assault the complacency of Cold War Liberals, does mention genocide but leaves his readers unclear whether he thinks it has occurred in Vietnam.[12] The most prominent academic spokesman against the United States military adventures in Indochina, Noam Chomsky, quick and uncompromising though he has been to condemn the United States for its policy of "massacre" and its perpetration of "crimes against humanity" and "war crimes," mentions genocide only to concede hesitantly that we are not guilty of that, too.[13]

This uncertainty and confusion are understandable for several reasons. Genocide is not just another crime, not even another "war crime" or "crime against humanity." For many, it is the ultimate offense. Moreover, accusations of genocide in our time are colored by the paradigm case still very much within living memory, the treatment of European Jews and other "undesirables" by the Nazi government until its defeat in 1945. The very term 'genocide' entered our language as the designation of that holocaust.[14] Still, the concept is a general one; no one believes that only the Nazis could commit genocide, or that only Jews could be its victims. Charges of genocide have been made against many nations and governments since the end of World War II. Even so, there is a strong temptation to assert that injuries which fail to measure up to the fury of "the final solution" the Nazis designed for the Jews do not qualify under the genocidal rubric. In addi-

11. The Committee of Concerned Asian Scholars, *The Indochina Story* (New York: Pantheon, 1970), pp. 123-31.
12. Telford Taylor, *Nuremberg and Vietnam: An American Tragedy* (Chicago: Quadrangle Books, 1970), pp. 30-31; see also Taylor's comment on genocide in Knoll and McFadden, *op. cit.*, pp. 80-81.
13. Noam Chomsky, *At War with Asia* (New York: Pantheon Books, 1970), pp. 53, 56, 79, 299, 307. Cf. his most recent comment: "Whether the US will withdraw from Vietnam short of true genocide . . . is, I am afraid, still an open question." Noam Chomsky, "Vietnam: How Government Became Wolves," *New York Review of Books*, June 15, 1972, pp. 23-31, at p. 31.
14. Raphael Lemkin, *Axis Rule in Occupied Europe* (Washington, D.C.: Carnegie Endowment for International Peace, 1944), chapter IX, "Genocide," pp. 79-95.

tion, there is always the desire to repress nightmare possibilities, and simply evade or laugh off all talk of genocide in Vietnam, as though it were obviously a rhetorical exaggeration and a defamatory lie.

Despite the frequency and the gravity of the accusation of genocide in Vietnam, so far it has received no adequate analysis, much less any convincing rebuttal. The whole question is thus in danger of remaining in the half-light of journalistic charge and counter-charge. Surely, the accusation is of sufficient seriousness to warrant a more adequate response.

§2. THE CONCEPT OF GENOCIDE

Part of the uncertainty over genocide in Vietnam arises because there is not one but three relatively distinct sources for the meaning of 'genocide'. Etymology invites us to construe 'genocide' on analogy with 'homicide', 'suicide', etc., to mean the killing of an ethnically identifiable group. The United Nations General Assembly, in its 1946 resolution condemning genocide, said that genocide is "a denial of the right of existence of entire human groups," as when "racial, religious, political, and other groups have been destroyed, entirely or in part."[15] Probably most of those who assert the charge of genocide in Vietnam think of 'genocide in Vietnam' as a rough synonym for 'extermination of the Vietnamese'; and one can appeal to etymology to defend this usage. However, if genocide is to be thought of as criminal without exception—and it is fairly clear that it has been thought of only in this way ever since the term was invented—then this requires building into the concept of genocide a *mens rea* (criminal state of mind), which etymology alone fails to provide. What is wanted is an analogy between genocide and murder, not genocide and homicide. For homicide, unlike murder, is sometimes excusable and sometimes even justifiable, whereas it is unlikely that anyone

15. U. N. General Assembly Resolution 96 (I), reprinted in Nehemiah Robinson, *The Genocide Convention* (New York: Institute of Jewish Affairs, 1960), p. 121.

wants to allow for these possibilities with genocide.[16] Those who deny the charge of genocide in Vietnam undoubtedly do so because in effect they do not think United States conduct in Vietnam involves the *mens rea* of genocide, even if it obviously has involved killing many Vietnamese. The debates over genocide in Vietnam cannot really be understood if it is thought to be a debate over whether the Vietnamese people have been partially exterminated. It is not, therefore, merely the etymology of 'genocide' on which we rely when we think of this crime.

A second possible source for the meaning of 'genocide' is by association of this crime with the notion of "crimes against humanity." The idea of such crimes antedates World War II, although it is the Charter, Judgment, and Principles of Nuremberg which provide the basis for our current understanding of them.[17] As defined by the International Law Commission in 1946 and adopted by the U. N. General Assembly in that year, "crimes against humanity" consist of "murder, extermination, enslavement, deportation and other inhuman acts done against any civilian population, or persecutions on political, racial or religious

16. Suppose it was discovered that all and only persons native for several generations to a particular region of the earth carried a fatal communicable disease for which there was no known cure, and that this disease, hitherto undetected, had suddenly erupted with virulent force, and had begun to spread unchecked. Suppose that these peoples had, like ourselves, traveled and taken up residence in most countries of the world. Suppose further that it was practically ineffective to quarantine them either in their own national home or in the areas of their new residence among other nationals. Faced with this situation, suppose that the governments especially of the neighboring states combined together and, after discussion of the dreadful alternatives open to them, decided on grounds of survival to undertake immediately a systematic extermination of these people as such, wherever they might be found in the world. Such a program of extermination would be genocidal, but arguably necessary and therefore excusable. Outside of such wildly fictional assumptions as the above, however, excusable genocide plays no role whatever in the common understanding of the term.

17. See Egon Schwelb, "Crimes Against Humanity," *British Yearbook of International Law*, XXIII (1946), pp. 178-226, and Sydney L. Goldberg, "Crimes Against Humanity: 1945-1970," *Western Ontario Law Review*, X (1971), pp. 1-55.

grounds, when such acts are done or such persecutions are carried on in execution of or in connection with any crime against peace or any war crime."[18] The term 'genocide', itself, however, is not used in nor is it explained by any of the Nuremberg texts which form the basis of the international law of "crimes against humanity." On account of the Nuremberg trials, where many of the major Nazi war criminals were indicted, tried, and convicted of "crimes against humanity,"[19] we have an unusually rich source of common international law to draw upon to elucidate the *mens rea* of these crimes. But does this same source likewise provide us with the *mens rea* of genocide? For that matter, is there, in the strictest sense, any common law of genocide? Both questions must be answered in the negative. It is often believed that the infamous Adolf Eichmann was indicted, tried, and convicted of genocide,[20] but this is in error. Like the other Nazi criminals before him who were tried in Germany, Eichmann was brought before an Israeli court on charges of "crimes against humanity."[21] No doubt, in

18. The full text is reprinted in Falk *et al.*, *op. cit.*, pp. 107-8.

19. See "The Nuremberg Trial 1946," 6 *F. R. D.* 69, 76, 112-31 (1946). The text of the indictment before the Tribunal under the heading "Crimes Against Humanity" may be found in *Proceedings of the International Military Tribunal Sitting at Nuremberg Germany: The Trial of German Major War Criminals*, vol. I (London: H. M. S. O., 1946), pp. 28-30.

20. See, for example, Peter Papadatos, *The Eichmann Trial* (New York: Praeger, 1964), who says that in this case, "for the first time the genocide of six million European Jews . . . was considered by a judicial authority" (pp. ix-x).

21. Eichmann was charged under an indictment specifying fifteen counts, including four crimes "against the Jewish people," and seven crimes "against humanity." See Shabtai Rosenne, ed., *6,000,000 Accusers: Israel's Case Against Eichmann* (Jerusalem Post Press, 1961), pp. 9-26, where the indictment is reprinted in full. In the opening speech of the prosecution (*ibid.*, pp. 27-175) the crime of the accused is said to be "the crime of Genocide" (p. 31). Mention of genocide appears also in the court's lengthy judgment; see Lord Russell of Liverpool, *The Record: The Trial of Adolf Eichmann for His Crimes Against the Jewish People and Against Humanity* (New York: Knopf, 1963), pp. xvi, xxvi, 304, 320-38. An argument could be made, of course, that the crimes for which Eichmann was tried, convicted, and sentenced were in part identical with the separate crime of genocide.

some loose but intelligible sense, genocide is a crime against humanity. But the concept of genocide we have today is not in fact identical with, or included within, any of the "crimes against humanity" which international law has recognized.

The third source of definition is the Convention on the Prevention and Punishment of the Crime of Genocide, or as it is more usually called, the Genocide Convention. This Convention has been in force since 1951, after its adoption by the U. N. General Assembly in 1948. It derives ultimately from the special resolution of the General Assembly in 1946, adopted immediately on the heels of the Nuremberg Principles, in which "genocide" was declared to be "a crime under international law."[22] The Genocide Convention defines 'genocide' by giving an exhaustive enumeration of genocidal acts plus a statement of what genocidal intent is, thereby conforming to the usual division of a crime into the *actus reus* (criminal conduct) and the *mens rea*. Article II declares any of the following to be genocidal acts: "killing members of a . . . national, ethnical, racial or religious group," causing members of such a group "serious bodily or mental harm," "deliberately inflicting on the group conditions of life calculated to bring about its physical destruction in whole or in part," "imposing measures intended to prevent births within the group," and "forcibly transferring children of the group to another group." These acts become genocide, however, only if they are committed with "the intent to destroy, in whole or in part, a national, ethnical, racial or religious group, as such."[23] The record of discussion on this text makes it clear that this "intent" is "the *specific intent* of

22. For the history of the Genocide Convention, see the articles by Raphael Lemkin, "Genocide as a Crime Under International Law," *American Journal of International Law*, XLI (1947), pp. 145-71, and "Genocide as a Crime Under International Law," *United Nations Bulletin*, IV (1948), pp. 70-71; Josef L. Kunz, "The United Nations Convention on Genocide," *American Journal of International Law*, XLIII (1949), pp. 738-46; Pieter Drost, *Genocide* (Leyden: A. W. Sythoff, 1959); and N. Robinson, *op. cit.*

23. I quote here from the text of the Genocide Convention as published in *Department of State Bulletin*, XIX (1948), p. 756. Curiously, the term, 'ethnical', which is crucial to the definition of genocide, is often misread or misprinted; e.g. in the text of the Convention reprinted in Falk *et al.*, *op. cit.*, p. 51, the word appears as "ethical."

destroying the group as such, in whole or in part."[24] "It is not enough to kill persons belonging to a different race or religion, but these murders must be committed as part of a plan to destroy the given group . . . Where such specific intent is lacking there is no genocide."[25] Consequently, if the proscribed acts occur "simply as a *result* of an otherwise intentional action,"[26] that would be insufficient to constitute genocide. Whether in addition to the intent with which the crime is done, Article II includes reference to the motives for doing it depends upon how the phrase, "as such," is understood. There seems to have been no agreement in the Sixth Committee on this further question of motive.[27] Most of the controversy over genocide in Vietnam can be made to revolve, as we shall see, over just these matters of intention, specific intent, and motive.

Article III provides punishment not only for the completed crime of genocide, but also for "conspiracy," "incitement," and "attempt" to commit genocide, and "complicity" in genocide. Article IV limits those punishable under the Genocide Convention to "persons." Although the Convention nowhere explicitly allows imputation of guilt only to persons, that is the natural inference from Article IV and from the rest of the fourteen Articles of the Convention.[28] Whether this limitation in the range of punishable

24. Testimony of the deputy legal adviser to the State Department, in "Genocide Convention," *Hearings Before a Subcommittee of the Committee on Foreign Relations, U.S. Senate,* 81st Congress, 1st Session, April-May 1970, at p. 44.
25. Raphael Lemkin, "The UN Genocide Convention," printed as an Extension of the Remarks of Representative Celler of New York, 95 *Congressional Record Appendix,* A 1224 (March 3, 1949); Cf. Lemkin, *op. cit. supra* note 22 at pp. 150-51, and Kunz, *op. cit.* at p. 743.
26. Robinson, *op. cit.,* p. 58. Thus, when it is said that genocide under the Convention is "the intentional destruction of any national, ethnical, racial or religious group" (Note, "Genocide: A Commentary on the Convention," *Yale Law Journal,* LVIII (1949), p. 1144), it is left ambiguous with what intention the group was destroyed.
27. Robinson, *op. cit.,* pp. 60-61.
28. See, for example, the Report of the Special Committee on Peace and Law Through United Nations, American Bar Association, September 1, 1949, in "Genocide Convention," at p. 167; also Orie L. Phillips and Eberhard P. Deutsch, "Pitfalls of the Genocide Convention," *American Bar Association Journal,* LVI (1970), pp. 641-46.

entities under the Convention is to be regarded as a defect in the concept of genocide developed therein, or as a reflection of the inevitable limitations under which legal and political undertakings (such as this Convention) must labor, is not entirely clear. We do, after all, have the ideas of corporate or collective responsibility and guilt.[29] These ideas are on occasion given legal effect, even if punishing a collectivity or corporate body has severe constraints upon it. It is not obvious why genocide should be a crime which collectives or corporate bodies are conceptually incapable of committing, even if there is no likelihood of ever punishing such non-individuals for this crime. In any case, the Genocide Convention makes no provisions for the responsibility, guilt, or punishment of non-individuals. Consequently, even conceiving of the United States or its government as guilty of genocide in Vietnam requires some departure from the strict language of the Genocide Convention.

It is doubtful whether all those who have pondered the issue of genocide in Vietnam have relied on one and the same, or even any, definition of this crime. This poses a serious problem for the critic. It seems only reasonable to accept as the preferred meaning of the term that which is provided by the Convention. This has the advantage not only of subjecting all accusations and rebuttals on genocide to assessment under a common standard. It also forces the discussion to respond to the fact that 'genocide' is not

29. See, for example, Karl Jaspers, *The Question of German Guilt* (New York: Capricorn Books, 1947), pp. 31-32, 51-63, for an application of the idea of "political guilt" to the German people after World War II; also the provocative discussions in Peter A. French, ed., *Individual and Collective Responsibility: The Massacre at My Lai* (Cambridge, Mass.: Schenkman, 1972).

Telford Taylor implies that governments cannot be criminal in any strict sense because a nation's "'government' is not an individual and cannot be said to have intentions of its own. . . ." Taylor, *op. cit.*, p. 103. This view poses a difficulty for anyone who would take literally the judgment of the Russell Tribunal, that "the United States Government" is "guilty of genocide." No doubt, those who are ready to accept this verdict could repudiate the doctrine under which criminality presupposes the capacity to have intentions. But there is another route. They could identify as the intentions with which a government acts, the intentions with which its responsible officials act in their official capacities.

merely a term in everyone's accusatory lexicon, but that it has a specific history of international legal discussion and interpretation. Today, to talk seriously about genocide *is* to talk about the crime defined by the Genocide Convention, nothing more and nothing less. To the objection that the ensuing discussion should not be confined within a legalistic framework, it may be replied that one is not limited to what lawyers and courts would accept as *relevant argument* over acts of genocide merely by relying on what they would regard as the *standard meaning* of that term. If the objection is raised that it is this very meaning itself which is too confining, the reply is twofold. First, almost any alternative either will trivialize the issue of genocide in Vietnam (because, of course, thousands of Vietnamese have been killed there; all parties to the dispute know that) or will put it beyond resolution (because every argument over the substantive issue of genocide will be contested at the semantic level by argument over what 'genocide' really means), or it will proliferate possibilities unmanageably (because what might not constitute $genocide_1$ in Vietnam might nevertheless be $genocide_2$, or if not $genocide_2$ then $genocide_n$). Furthermore, not to rely on genocide as defined in the Genocide Convention is to leave unresolved whether there has been genocide in Vietnam in the sense of that Convention. Whatever defects there may be in the concept of genocide as embodied in the Convention, they can be brought out most effectively by relying on that concept rather than by ignoring it. Accordingly, in what follows it will be primarily genocide in the sense of that term as defined by the Genocide Convention which will be in question, and not genocide as a rough synonym for mass killings of innocent persons.

§3. THE ARGUMENT FOR GUILT

The idea that the Vietnam war might lead to genocide did not begin among Europeans, nor was it first aired at the Russell Tribunal in 1967. Early in 1966, two American professors, Edward S. Herman and Richard Du Boff, concluded that "the ultimate logic of American military policy in Vietnam appears to be genocide. . . ."[30] They argued:

> the logic of American military escalation leads to nothing less than a war of extermination against the native Vietnamese peasantry; because the guerrillas cannot be segregated from the peasantry; because the peasantry provides the necessary broad base for the guerrillas; and because the United States has the military means to eradicate this base completely, if need be, to create an "independent" South Vietnam.[31]

Two years after the judgment of the Russell Tribunal, and without evident reliance on either its verdict or the earlier argument just quoted, Townsend Hoopes, a former Under Secretary of the Air Force, deployed quite different considerations to arrive at much the same conclusion. After speculating on the grand theme of philosophical differences between Occident and Orient, he observed:

> The strategy of the weak is . . . the natural choice of ideologues in Asia, for it converts Asia's capacity for endurance in suffering into an instrument for exploiting a basic vulnerability of the Christian West. It does it, in effect, by inviting the West, which possesses unanswerable military power, to carry its strategic logic to the final conclusion, which is genocide. . . .[32]

According to these writers, the United States government need not consciously have chosen genocide, either as a means or as an end, in order to be embarked on a course which inexorably leads to genocide. On this view, a lethal dialectic is at work. The thesis of American imperialism, coupled with vast military power and the will to use it, confronts its antithesis in national self-

---

30. Edward S. Herman and Richard B. Du Boff, *America's Vietnam Policy* (Washington, D.C.: Public Affairs Press, 1966), Appendix 4, "Genocide in Vietnam?" pp. 114-23, at p. 114.
31. *Ibid.*, p. 116.
32. Townsend Hoopes, *The Limits of Intervention* (New York: David McKay Co., 1969), p. 129.

determination and anti-colonialism in Vietnam. Unlike the dialectic of Hegel and Marx, however, no higher synthesis emerges from this conflict. There is only retreat and defeat for the imperialist power or there is a Carthaginian peace, total extermination, for the peasant society.

Such arguments are misleading if they are meant to establish guilt of genocide in the sense of that term as it is defined in the Genocide Convention. The Herman–Du Boff–Hoopes argument appears to be wholly result-oriented, and that cannot be correct. Such arguments either choose to ignore that the crime of genocide requires genocidal intent, or they implicitly adopt some version of the view that the *tendency* (the "logic") of an action *is* the intention with which it is done. The former alternative involves an unacceptable departure from the Genocide Convention. The latter includes several possible alternatives, which range from obviously unintelligible identifications of an action's tendency with the agent's intention to connections between the two which are not only intelligible but are even legally and morally acceptable.[33] Precisely what Herman and Du Boff and Hoopes mean by "logic" is unclear, and for this reason alone (apart from the brevity of their remarks) it is desirable to look elsewhere for a serious development of the charge of genocide in Vietnam.

The only explicit argument known to me which is not spoiled at the start by the above dilemma is Jean-Paul Sartre's, mentioned earlier, which he presented in 1967 for the Russell Tribunal.[34]

33. It might be a person's *intention*, in pulling at the corner of the window as he is doing, to raise it; yet it might be the *tendency* of pulling it as he is doing, to jam it even more. In such cases, what is the "logic" of his action? The tendency of his act as such tells us nothing about the intention with which he does it, and vice-versa. Normally, we assume that neither ignorance nor imperceptiveness keeps the agent in the dark as to the tendencies of his actions, and on that assumption we connect them to his intentions, or even argue from them to his intentions. For the relevance of these considerations to the issue of genocidal intentions in Vietnam, see the text, *infra*, §4.B.

34. Sartre's argument before the Tribunal was first published in English (with no indication that it was a translation) in *Ramparts*, February 1968, pp. 37-42, preface by Carl Oglesby, p. 36. This text has since been reprinted, in whole or in part, in many places. The best source, and the one used here, is in Jean-

This argument, for all its superiority to its rivals and despite the fame of its author, has been almost entirely ignored (at least in this country) both by those hostile to its conclusion and by those prepared to agree with it.[35] The best way to make headway with the issue of genocide in Vietnam is to subject this argument of Sartre's to close scrutiny. Since I cannot assume familiarity with his full text, and because it is too long to quote here in its entirety, I shall set out its main themes by quoting from it selectively and transposing passages as needed to provide a smoother flow. For the sake of convenient reference later on, I have divided the argument into eight numbered parts, of which the last may be regarded as the conclusion.

> (1)   By 'genocide in Vietnam', we mean to establish that the crime of genocide as defined by The Genocide Convention has been committed by the United States in Vietnam (cf. pp. 57, 74, 79).
>
> (2)   The United States has perpetrated some or all of the acts defined and prohibited as 'genocidal', as is amply established by the evidence submitted before The Tribunal.
>
> (3)   These acts have been committed with the required intention.

Paul Sartre, *On Genocide* (Boston: Beacon Press, 1968), pp. 57-85, with "A Summary of the Evidence and the Judgments of the International War Crimes Tribunal," by Arlette El Kaïm-Sartre, pp. 3-53. Page numbers in parentheses in my text are references to this volume. Italicized portions of quotations from Sartre are italicized in the original. I have consulted the French text of his essay (see *Tribunal Russell II*, pp. 349-68), and judge the English translation adequate for present purposes.

35. Sartre's argument figures in at least two, possibly three, subsequent discussions prior to the present one. The first and briefest is in Richard A. Falk, "Six Legal Dimensions of the United States Involvement in the Vietnam War," Research Monograph #34, Center of International Studies, Princeton University, 1968, and reprinted in Richard A. Falk, ed., *The Vietnam War and International Law*, II (Princeton: Princeton University Press, 1969), pp. 216-59, at pp. 251-52. Falk only mentions Sartre. The second is Paul T. Menzel, ed., *Moral Argument and the War in Vietnam: A Collection of Essays* (Nashville, Tenn.: Aurora Publishers, 1971), pp. 51-57. Menzel reprints Sartre's essay and discusses it sympathetically. The third is Hans Göran Franck, *op. cit.*, at pp. 300-308. Franck does not mention Sartre at all, yet the two arguments have some striking parallels. For comments on their differences, see *infra*, notes 38, 57, and 60.

True, "the American government has avoided making clear statements" of any "genocidal intent" (p. 58). "It is impossible to decide . . . [whether] its authors [viz., government officials] are thoroughly conscious of their intentions" (p. 79). Nevertheless, "the government of the United States, despite its hypocritical denials, has chosen genocide" (p. 78). "The genocidal intent is implicit in the facts. It is necessarily premeditated" (p. 78).

(4) Anyone who examines "the facts" in question must reach this conclusion. These facts are to be found in the United States' foreign policy objectives in the struggle over the future of Vietnam, and in the methods used to achieve these objectives. Evidently, "the conflict has two objectives" (p. 69): (i) the "military" objective, "to encircle Communist China" (p. 69); and (ii) the "economic" objective, to show "all of the Third World . . . that guerrilla war does not pay" (p. 70). [Hereafter, (i) and (ii) will be referred to as China containment and admonitory anti-guerrilla warfare, respectively.]

(5) The first objective *"can"* be achieved by genocide, though possibly less drastic measures will suffice (pp. 71-72).

(6) To achieve the second objective, "the United States *must* carry out, at least in part, . . . extermination of the Vietnamese" (p. 72). This can be done in either of two ways: (a) by outright "massive extermination" (p. 73, cf. p. 75) of the Vietnamese in the North and the South, a policy of "physical genocide" (p. 64); the American threat, "Declare you are beaten or we will bomb you back to the stone age" is *"conditional* genocide" (p. 72) of this sort; or (b) by indirectly forcing "capitulation" on the Democratic Republic of Vietnam, and "through private investment and conditional loans, . . . the United States would destroy . . . the whole economic basis of socialism. And this too is genocide" (p. 76), "cultural genocide" (p. 63). In the South, the same kind of genocide is produced by destroying "the social structure," "family life," "religious and cultural life" (p. 74), and forcing the peasants to resettle in the "strategic or . . . 'New Life' hamlets" (p. 74).

(7) Pervading the execution of these objectives, especially the second, is "the racism of the American soldiers" (p. 79). One "proof" of the racism in American society is that "the United States government [has] refused to ratify the Genocide Convention" (p. 79). On the battlefield in Vietnam, the soldiers "often say themselves, 'The only good Vietnamese is a dead Vietnamese,' or what amounts to the same thing, 'A dead Vietnamese is a Vietcong' "

(p. 80). We have here "the truth of the Vietnam war: it meets all of Hitler's specifications. Hitler killed the Jews because they were Jews. The armed forces of the United States torture and kill men, women and children in Vietnam merely *because they are Vietnamese* . . . the spirit of genocide is in the minds of the soldiers" (p. 82). "[T]he only possible relationship between an over-industrialized country and an under-developed country . . . is . . . a genocidal relationship implemented through racism—the only relationship, short of picking up and pulling out" (p. 82).

(8)   The conclusion is inescapable. The United States in Vietnam is engaged in "neo-colonialism" (p. 67); and in neo-colonialism, "total genocide"—that is, both physical and cultural—"emerges as the absolute basis of an anti-guerrilla strategy" and even "emerges as the explicit objective," as it has in Vietnam (p. 67). "[T]he major *purpose* of 'escalation' was, and still is, to prepare international opinion for genocide" (p. 77). "[T]he true goal of imperialism . . . is to reach, step by step, the highest stage of escalation— total genocide" (p. 77). "[G]enocide presents itself as the only possible reaction to the rising of a whole people against its oppressors" (p. 83). The United States government is "guilty—according to its own admissions—of consciously carrying out this admonitory war in order to use genocide as a challenge and threat to all peoples of the world" (p. 84).

As with any argument, we must distinguish in Sartre's between its soundness and its persuasive effect. Prefaced by hundreds of pages of testimony submitted to the Russell Tribunal and by addresses from three lawyers on the concept of and evidence for genocide in Vietnam, Sartre's argument constituted the opinion of the Tribunal on behalf of its judgment against the United States. Its persuasive effect in that setting was no doubt considerable. In what follows, let us concentrate only on its soundness. This reduces to two questions: are the premises true, and is the inference to the conclusion valid? The question of validity is the question whether if the premises were true the conclusion would follow of necessity. In Sartre's argument, I think it would. To be sure, his argument as it stands in the original and in the paraphrase above, is not elegant. Some of its premises are still implicit, and others are superfluous, as anyone intent upon formalizing the argument would quickly see. But these flaws are easily repaired and typical in all actual (as distinct from textbook) reasoning. They may be ignored here.

In order to do full justice both to Sartre's argument and to all the relevant facts, a thorough examination would be required of several disputable points, e.g. his appeal to the concept of "cultural genocide" (premises (6)(b) and (8)), the anonymity of the persons in the government of the United States to whom genocidal intent is imputed, the inadequacy of confining the relevant foreign policy of the United States to China-containment and admonitory anti-guerrilla warfare (premises (4) through (6), and (8)). I do not propose to take the space here to pursue all of these important and interesting questions. Even if they were all decided in the way most favorable to Sartre's argument, the argument would fail to establish its conclusion unless it were also established that the allegedly genocidal acts were done with true genocidal intention. That is the crucial issue, to the exclusion of all else, and I propose to confine the rest of this discussion to an examination of this feature of Sartre's argument.

§4. GENOCIDAL INTENT: POSSIBILITIES

There is little doubt that a high proportion of what the United States military forces have done in Vietnam is intentional action. This is only to imply that very little of it was unintentional, i.e. involuntary, or accidental, or done for no reason or purpose at all.[36] It is to imply only that, as Professor Anscombe might put it, if we ask, "Why does the Air Force bomb those defenseless villages?", or "Why were the infantry ordered on those 'search-and-destroy' missions?", we deserve one kind of answer and not another.[37] Yet this is insufficient to assure us that the intention with

36. Cf. Stuart Hampshire and H. L. A. Hart, ". . . the whole meaning of 'intentionally' simply lies in its negation of accident or mistake. . . ." "Decision, Intention, and Certainty," reprinted in Herbert Morris, ed., *Freedom and Responsibility* (Stanford University Press, 1961), p. 209.

37. The burden of her very influential argument is to try to show why such questions as those in the text, *supra,* refer to "actions to which a certain sense of the question 'Why?' is given application; the sense is of course that in which the answer, if positive, gives a reason for acting." G. E. M. Anscombe, *Intention,* 2nd ed. (Oxford: Blackwell, 1963), p. 9.

which such actions have been done is the intention relevant to genocide. From the fact that a certain series of actions are intentional actions, it does not follow that they are done with genocidal intention;[38] in fact it does not even follow that they are done with some intention or other, though of course it is usually true that they are.[39] What is not so obvious, and for that reason all the more important to bear in mind, is that from the fact that a certain series of actions in Vietnam are deplorable, unnecessary, inexcusable, involve killing thousands and laying waste to the country, and are done intentionally, it still does not follow that they are done with genocidal intention. How, then, are we to tell whether Sartre is right, that genocide has been committed in Vietnam and that the "genocidal intent is implicit in the facts"?

Since there is no common law of genocide (*supra* §2) and since the "facts" in question are complex and ambiguous, I propose to exploit the prevailing Anglo-American views on the law of malicious intent in criminal homicide. By turning to this source of law and the related (and occasionally contrary) moral beliefs, we can obtain four models in terms of which to try to understand genocidal intent and thus Sartre's (or any other) argument. If genocidal intent cannot be understood in terms of these models, then it is doubtful whether it can be understood at all. Similarly, if an argument for genocide in Vietnam cannot be sustained on the evidence appropriate to at least one of these models, then the

38. Franck makes this error when he argues to the existence of genocidal intent in the Vietnam war from the unobjectionable premise that "the legal presumption which applies is that the natural consequences of consciously undertaken acts are intentional, insofar as the opposite cannot be proven" (*op. cit.* at p. 303, and cf. p. 306). Even if it is added to this "legal presumption" that the consequences were foreseen or foreseeable, all this entails is that the acts in question were done with *some* intention or other. It does not entail that they were done with the specific intention required for genocide under Article II of the Genocide Convention.

39. As Anscombe reminds us, "an action can be intentional without having any intention in it" (*op. cit.*, p. 1). She has in mind actions where the correct answer to 'Why did you do it?' is 'No particular reason' or 'I just thought I would.' This sort of possibility is, as she explains (*loc. cit.*, pp. 25-27), rare; since it has little or no application in the present discussion, it may be entirely ignored.

accusation is probably false. Since, as we shall see, the four models share certain affinities which makes it useful to consider them pairwise, we shall consider in the remainder of this section the first pair of these models and then, in the next section (§5), the second pair.

A. Constructive Malice

The least plausible possibility is suggested, oddly enough, by the natural way to read the verdict of the Russell Tribunal. Its verdict was in response to a question worded in this way: "Does the combination of crimes imputed to the Government of the United States in its war in Vietnam constitute the crime of genocide?" Others have subsequently used similar language in explaining the idea of genocidal guilt. The Russell Tribunal, it has been said, "wanted to determine if the totality of these [criminal] acts, committed within a war of aggression, could be clasified as genocide."[40] Most recently, it has been said of the Oslo Commission that it relied on evidence which "establishes that the battlefield tactics of high-technology counterinsurgency warfare plus the aggressive war character of the enterprise add up to . . . genocide."[41]

These ways of construing the issue of genocide in Vietnam are analogous to asking in the case of criminal homicide, Does the combination of crimes imputed to the accused constitute the crime of murder? The occasion for asking such a question with this somewhat curious wording would naturally arise only in the following kind of case. Suppose that you do *not* believe that Smith killed Brown with malice aforethought (the traditional *mens rea* of murder, as distinct from manslaughter)[42] or that he killed Brown wilfully, deliberately, and with premeditation (the traditional *mens rea* of first degree murder).[43] You do believe,

40. Arlette El Kaïm-Sartre, in Sartre, *op. cit.*, p. 50.
41. Richard A. Falk, in Browning and Forman, eds., *op. cit.*, at p. xv.
42. See J. M. Kaye, "The Early History of Murder and Manslaughter," *Law Quarterly Review*, LXXXIII (1967), pp. 365-95, 569-601.
43. See Edwin R. Keedy, "History of the Pennsylvania Statute Creating Degrees of Murder," *University of Pennsylvania Law Review*, XCVII (1949), pp. 759-77.

however, that Smith did kill Brown and that he did commit some "combination of crimes" against Brown, e.g. a breaking and entering with intent to commit a felony, and the felony of robbery, during which he did kill Brown. Long ago Blackstone declared, "If one intends to do another felony, and undesignedly kills a man, this is murder."[44] So it is, on the assumption that the *mens rea* of murder can be constituted by the intention with which the non-homicidal felony is committed and then be imputed to the felon as an irrebutable presumption of law.[45] This is the theory of *constructive malice* which underlies the familiar concept of felony murder. It is the natural way to construe how the Russell Tribunal understood its verdict of genocide, given the way it chose to word the question (quoted above) to which its verdict was the answer.

To establish the crime of genocide on this model, two basic requirements must be met. First, the argument must show that the United States government has committed in Vietnam identifiable felony-like offenses. Second, the argument must show that during the former, other acts (of the sort enumerated in Article II of the Genocide Convention) have also been perpetrated. As to the first point, the Russell Tribunal had no hesitation in judging the United States guilty of a number of war crimes.[46] Now, several years later, we can more easily imagine how such a conclusion might be reached and be correct. The by now familiar weapons (e.g. napalm) and methods (e.g. "free fire zones") of warfare in Vietnam used by the United States could be argued to be in violation of express or implied laws of war. Or one might argue that the United States is guilty of various "crimes against humanity" in Vietnam, in the sense of that term defined by the Nuremberg Principles (recall §2). Most importantly, the United States may be guilty of the crime of aggressive war in Indochina. Since the Russell Tribunal's verdicts in 1966 and 1967, other writers have

---

44. William Blackstone, *Commentaries on the Laws of England* (1765) IV, p. 200.

45. Note, "Felony Murder as a First Degree Offense: An Anachronism Retained," *Yale Law Journal*, LXVI (1957), pp. 427-35.

46. Duffett, *op. cit.*, pp. 302-9, 643-50.

canvassed all three of these possibilities, though not in order to see whether they might serve in the role presently under discussion.[47] Since the available evidence on the war surely confirms Sartre's implication that the *actus reus* of genocide had occurred in several forms in Vietnam, all that would remain to decide on this model is whether the evidence is adequate to conclude that at least one of these felony-like offenses has also occurred.

However, we are spared the need to pursue this question. As we have seen, the crime of genocide is a crime of *specific intent*. But the model of constructive malice (felony murder) can never supply such an intent; indeed, it was invented just for cases where such intent is believed to be absent or unprovable. Constructive malice gets such intention as it does for the homicidal act x by borrowing it from felony y, and grafting it onto the doing of x, and then imputing it to the agent as the intention with which he did x. That the agent did x with a criminal intention is a legal fiction of the sort guaranteed to provoke a Bentham,[48] and to enable prosecutors to obtain (first degree) murder convictions of felons who accidentally, unintentionally, unwillingly, and even unknowingly kill.[49] Is this what Sartre had in mind when he alleged "genocidal intent implicit in the facts"? If it was, and if this was how the Russell Tribunal understood his argument or their own verdict, then it represents a complete departure from what is permissible under the Genocide Convention as it stands.

Whether the Convention should be modified to permit establishing the *mens rea* of genocide on analogy with felony murder is a question which would take us too far beyond the confines of

---

47. See Taylor, *op. cit.*; Falk *et al.*, *op. cit.*; Knoll and McFadden, *op. cit.*; Ralph Stavins, Richard J. Barnet and Marcus G. Raskin, *Washington Plans an Aggressive War* (New York: Vintage Books, 1971); Leonard Boudin, "War Crimes and Vietnam: The Mote in Whose Eye?" *Harvard Law Review*, LXXXIV (1971), pp. 1940-59, esp. 1941-45; and Richard A. Falk, ed., *The Vietnam War and International Law*, III (Princeton: Princeton University Press, 1972), esp. pp. 193-487.
48. See Jeremy Bentham, *Theory of Fictions*, edited by C. K. Ogden (London: Routledge and Kegan Paul, 1932).
49. See Norval Morris, "The Felon's Responsibility for the Lethal Acts of Others," *University of Pennsylvania Law Review*, CV (1956), pp. 50-81.

the current investigation. Let it suffice here to conclude that the model of constructive malice is wholly inappropriate, whether viewed on legal or on moral grounds, as a basis for imputing any specific intent to an agent as the intent with which he did a certain (homicidal or genocidal) act.

B. Implied Malice

Suppose Smith, after an evening's drinking in the tent with Brown, gets somewhat drunk and irritable. Suddenly, he picks up a heavy ash tray and throws it at Brown. He misses, but he does hit and break the oil lamp burning overhead, causing it to drench Brown in flames, thereby burning him to death. In every ordinary sense of 'intention', we are entitled to say that Smith *did not intend* to kill Brown, that he threw the ash tray *with no intention* of killing Brown, that he did *not intentionally* kill Brown. In the circumstances supposed, we may even add that Smith had no desire to kill Brown and that he did not believe that Brown would die as a result of the ash tray's being thrown at him. Nevertheless, the courts have generally held that in this kind of case Smith did murder Brown with *implied malice*. They have held that "when no considerable provocation appears, or when all the circumstances of the killing show an abandoned and malignant heart,"[50] when the agent acts as Smith did, "recklessly indifferent as to the results of his act,"[51] thereby manifesting "a heart regardless of social duty, and fatally bent on mischief,"[52] then the law will allow these facts to be construed so that they imply the malice requisite to transform homicide into murder. After all, Smith's throwing the ash tray, however impulsive it may have been, was intentional, and anyone not an idiot or infant could be reasonably sure that if the ash tray hit Brown (or the lamp overhead) it could do serious bodily injury to him.

50. *Illinois Revised Statutes,* §140 (1874), p. 374, cited in *Mayes v. People,* 106 Ill. 306, 313 (1883).

51. Royal Commission on Capital Punishment, *Report* (London: H.M.S.O., 1953), p. 28.

52. *Commonwealth v. Webster,* 5 Cush. [Mass.] 295, 304 (1850), and cf. *Mayes v. People,* 106 Ill. 306, 314 (1883), and *Banks v. State,* 85 Tex. Cr. R. 165, 166 (1919).

Of the major alternatives in terms of which to construe a doctrine of genocidal intention in Vietnam, this one has a certain initial persuasiveness. Whatever else is true of the conduct of the United States in the Vietnam war, it has tended toward genocidal results, as many commentators have noted. It has been marked by reckless disregard of the foreseeable consequences of military policy, tactics, and weaponry. American anti-Vietnamese racist sentiments make it simply that much easier to be indifferent to the welfare of the Vietnamese, indifferent to the distinction (hard to make in the best of conditions) between a Viet Cong and a non-Communist Vietnamese peasant. The resulting state of mind of Americans in the field, like their civilian and military leaders in Washington, is consistent with "an abandoned and malignant heart," "a heart void of social duty, and fatally bent on mischief."[53] Could not genocidal intent be truly implicit in such conduct?

Characteristically, arguments over criminal guilt based on the model of implied intent revolve around questions of epistemological fact (Did the agent foresee the results of his conduct?) and conceptual questions (Does some combination of foresight, recklessness, and desire yield an intention?). As to the first sort of question, the answer we should give in the present context is somewhat uncertain. It might be argued that in the early and mid-1960s, during the step by step escalation of the war which culminated in massive aerial bombardments and ground action to halt the Tet Offensive of early 1968, the disastrous consequences of military policy and tactics upon civilian life in Vietnam were not foreseen by the civilian and military participants at the top levels.[54] The attempt to defeat the charge of genocide on this evidential ground, however, is inherently weak. It will take consid-

53. Anthony Lewis develops this sense of intent as appropriate for the criminal conduct of the United States in Vietnam—but he does not mention genocide. See "A Question of Intent," *The New York Times,* August 19, 1972, p. 23.
54. See, for example, the neglected early report by a former U.S.I.A. director in Saigon, John Mecklin, *Mission in Torment: An Intimate Account of the U.S. Role in Vietnam* (Garden City, N.Y.: Doubleday, 1965); see also Frances FitzGerald, *op. cit.,* pp. 231-400, and David Halberstam, *The Best and the Brightest* (New York: Random House, 1972).

erable time and study before one can determine whether the alleged ignorance at the highest levels in government was both genuine and sufficient so as to blunt the charge of foresight of the consequences. Even if it does, it cannot easily dispose of the objection that the ignorance was inexcusable. Nor can it cope with the objection that the conduct was excessively reckless. These unresolved issues show that if one wishes to reject Sartre's argument categorically, then one must look elsewhere for a stronger rebuttal.

A far more telling objection is available; it parallels the criticism already advanced against any attempt to use the model of constructive malice. The difficulty here, as there, turns on the requirement that genocide involves a *specific intent,* "the intent to destroy, in whole or in part, a national, ethnical, racial or religious group, as such." The doctrine of implied malice in the criminal law is designed to impute the *mens rea* of criminal conduct in light of recklessness, disregard of the foreseeable consequences, and the like. But can these "mental elements" separately or together constitute a specific intention of the required sort?

What we are considering, on the model of implied malice, is the validity of advancing a conclusion such as this:

(C) Smith killed (or gave orders which resulted in the killing of) innocent Vietnamese civilians with the intent to destroy the Vietnamese, in whole or in part, as such.

The premises at our disposal to establish this conclusion must be like these:

(P₁) Smith killed (or gave orders which resulted in the killing of) many innocent Vietnamese civilians.

(P₂) These deaths occurred as the result of a military policy, tactics, and weapons which show a reckless disregard for the lives of innocent Vietnamese civilians.

(P₃) Smith foresaw (or should have foreseen) that many innocent Vietnamese civilians would die as a result of the military policy, tactics, and weapons he used (or ordered to be used) in Vietnam.

Premises such as (P₂) and (P₃) suffice to imply that Smith's conduct was intentional, i.e. not accidental or mistaken or involuntary. Such an implication is appropriate, as we have seen, to impute to the conduct of the United States government. But do these premises also imply that Smith's conduct was done with the intent identified in the conclusion (C), the intent necessary to constitute genocidal intention? It is plain that they do not.

Whether some court of law, upon presentation of an argument of this form and of evidence sufficient to establish premises such as those above, would in fact render a verdict tantamount to the conclusion (C) is a separate and interesting question. If a court would do this, then we would have the makings of a common law of genocidal intent along precisely the lines indicated by the model of implied malice. Some might argue that in the verdict of genocide rendered in 1967 by the Russell Tribunal and in 1971 by the Oslo Commission, we already have the first steps in this direction. But as these bodies had no legal standing, it is very unlikely that their verdict contributes anything toward a common law of implied malice in genocidal intent. Since no other established legal tribunal is likely to hear and decide any cases on genocide in the near future in which the model of implied malice is relied upon to establish intent, we cannot reasonably look in these directions for ratification of this model by the common law.

In any case, the problem lies in the nature of the model of implied malice and the requirement, imposed by the Genocide Convention, of specific intent. Even in the case of murder, where the doctrine of implied malice is firmly rooted, there are major difficulties so far as the nature of the intention established by this model. It is usual to concede that the doctrine of implied malice in murder does not establish that the homicide was committed with a malicious intention. What it establishes is only something which *for legal purposes* we are entitled to regard as *equivalent* to such an intention.[55] Second, it is also conceded that the doctrine of implied malice in murder shows a plain departure from the

55. See Rupert Cross, "The Mental Element in Crime," *Law Quarterly Review*, LXXXIII (1967), pp. 215-28, at pp. 216-17. Cf. H. L. A. Hart, *Punishment and Responsibility* (Oxford: Clarendon Press, 1968), pp. 118-22.

concept of intention as it is found in ordinary life, language, and morality.[56] So, even in the crime of murder, these objections imply that *no* combination of action involving culpable foresight, culpable recklessness, and homicidal results is *identical* with action done with the specific intention to kill.

How do these reflections bear on the argument which Sartre has constructed? The central contentions of that argument lie in his theory of the nature of anti-guerrilla warfare in the Third World and of the admonitory role of the Vietnam war given the strategic policies of an imperialist United States. On such a theory, the roles of recklessness and foreknowledge, which are so crucial to the model of implied malice, are inevitably downgraded. The fact, if it is a fact, that the conduct of the United States military forces in Vietnam may best be understood in terms of reckless military adventuring with a foreknowledge of the consequences for innocent peasants throughout Indochina becomes quite irrelevant in that context. To the degree, therefore, that one finds attractive the model of implied malice, one must disagree with these central theoretical contentions of Sartre's, or at least with his emphasis upon them. Or, if one wishes to agree with them and also agree with the verdict of the Russell Tribunal, then one must develop a different argument not based on these features of Sartre's argument. The very fact, however, that it is ill-fitted to the model of implied malice may be in the end a point in its favor.[57] As we have seen, this model itself is not very helpful in interpreting the central link between Sartre's argument and the requirements of the Genocide Convention: the evidence of "genocidal intent implicit in the facts."

56. See Anthony Kenny, "Intention and Purpose in Law," in Robert S. Summers, ed., *Essays in Legal Philosophy* (Oxford: Blackwell, 1968), pp. 146-63, and especially his argument that "the principle that a man intends all the consequences of his actions which he foresees appears to the layman far too sweeping" (pp. 148-49).

57. The chief difference between the argument for genocide advanced by Sartre for the Russell Tribunal and the argument advanced by Franck for the Oslo Commission is that the latter is essentially constructed on the model of implied malice, whereas Sartre's is not. For the model which best fits Sartre's over-all argument, see the text and notes, *infra*, §5.B.

§5. GENOCIDAL INTENT: PROBABILITIES

The pair of models examined above are to be contrasted with another pair of models to be drawn from the study of how homicide is transformed into murder by the evidence of *express malice*. In murder, the *mens rea* of the crime most conspicuously appears in either of two forms. One is in the case where Smith kills Brown for no further reason (or with no further intention) at all, e.g. he hates Brown and wants him out of the way and therefore kills him. Let us call this the model of *express malice with bare intention*.[58] The other is in the case where Smith kills Brown as a means to some end (or with a further intention), e.g. Smith doesn't hate Brown but does want him out of the way so that his heirs will put up for sale the land Smith covets. Let us call this the model of *express malice with further intention*.[59] Similarly, genocide will involve express malice when it is chosen as an end in itself, as the intended result of one or another act, or when it is chosen as the means to achieve some further end.

Is there any reason to suppose that genocidal destruction of the Vietnamese is the end chosen by the United States, or the means chosen to some other end? Sartre's argument suggests that he wavers between these two alternatives. He has been quoted earlier (§3, premise (7)), as saying, "The armed forces of the United States torture and kill men, women and children in Vietnam merely because they are Vietnamese," as though the torture and killing of Vietnamese were an *end* in itself. It was in this context that Sartre drew an exact and deliberate parallel betwen our government and the Nazis. Yet he has also been quoted as saying (§3, premise (8)), that genocide "emerges as the absolute basis of an anti-guerrilla strategy," as though genocide has been of necessity adopted as the *means* to another end. Can these two different views be reconciled? One might hypothesize that killing Viet Cong troops and sympathizers began as a non-genocidal means to a non-genocidal end, and was subtly transformed by American racism

58. I borrow the term "bare intention" from Hart, *Punishment and Responsibility,* at p. 117.
59. Also suggested by Hart, *loc. cit.*

and imperialism and the exigencies of warfare into the killing of Vietnamese peasants indiscriminately as both an end and a means. Whether or not this is precisely Sartre's view, or is true, it shows that there is no strict inconsistency in arguing that genocide in Vietnam is both a chosen end and a chosen means to another end. Still, one might wish that Sartre had made it clearer whether he really wished to assert both sides of the conjunction.

Is either part of the conjunction true, however? Let us consider first genocide as the *end* chosen for its own sake.

A. *Express Malice with Bare Intention*

Sartre somewhat grudgingly admits that there is no evidence of a self-conscious United States policy in Vietnam to kill Vietnamese "merely because they are Vietnamese." He does not dwell on the possibility that such evidence may eventually appear. He makes a somewhat half-hearted attempt to convince the unpersuaded that despite the silence of the government and the absence of unambiguous evidence, genocide is the settled, even if unavowed, intention with which the government has acted in Vietnam. He does not even speculate on any of these ugly possibilities. The very idea that the United States government transported a half million-man military force into Indochina in order to commit genocide in Vietnam is appalling. At the very least, it is also implausible, because there is little or no evidence for it and considerable evidence against it.[60] Sartre's explicit parallel to the Nazis, therefore, is a groundless exaggeration and can only cause many who read his argument to distrust his perception and dismiss everything he says, which would be unfortunate. This is not to

60. In what may be an aberrant phase of his over-all argument, Franck declares that the "American attack on the Indochinese people" evidences genocidal intent because it is "directed at their nationality as such"; they are killed "in their character of representatives of their nations," and "because they refuse to renounce their national rights" (*op. cit.*, p. 302). This is parallel to the theme discussed in the text, *supra:* whereas Sartre accused the United States of pursuing genocide from anti-racial bias, Franck makes the same accusation by imputing anti-national bias. Thus their apparent disagreement is over the *motives*, not the intention, with which the (genocidal) acts have been done. Perhaps it does not need to be added that Franck gives no more evidence for his version of this argument than Sartre does for his.

deny that many Vietnamese have been killed by United States military forces, sometimes even under superior orders, "merely because they are Vietnamese." As in other wars, massacres like those at My Lai have happened several times in Vietnam.[61] But no inference to government policy or official intentions follows therefrom, not even if we add to the massacres (as, to some extent, we must) subsequent efforts by higher echelons to conceal these crimes from the public and to resist bringing the officers responsible to trial.[62] The issue before us is not whether a Lieutenant Calley committed a genocidal massacre, or whether the Pentagon's attempt at concealment is misprision of felony, but whether during the 1960's the United States government conducted a war in Vietnam in order to exterminate the Vietnamese people as such, in whole or in part. I cannot see how Sartre or anyone else could hope to prove that it did when that requires him to rely upon the model of express malice in the form appropriate to the conduct of the Nazis.

Perhaps Sartre is thrown off into this exaggeration by confusing the false proposition that the United States armed forces killed Vietnamese peasants *because they are Vietnamese,* with the true proposition that the Vietnamese peasants were killed *because they were in the way, because they were there.* The latter may be true, indeed, there is much evidence to suggest that it is true. But if it is, then either this itself is evidence of a non-genocidal intention, or it is evidence of a genocidal intention on a model quite unlike that of express malice with bare intention.

61. See, for example, Operation Speedy Express in the province of Kien Hoa, conducted some months after the Tet Offensive of 1968. According to correspondent Kevin P. Buckley, perhaps 5000 non-combatant civilians were killed by the U.S. Ninth Division troops in this one operation. See "Pacification's Deadly Price," *Newsweek,* June 19, 1972, pp. 42-43. See also "Wholesale Massacres in South Vietnam since the Son My Case," in Browning and Forman, eds., *op. cit.,* at pp. 260-81. One critic has observed, "Massacres such as that in Son My are not isolated occurrences in the course of military actions, but an integrated part of the military strategy of depopulating areas which are liberated by national liberation forces." Franck, *op. cit.,* at p. 296.
62. See Hersh, *op. cit.,* and his later book, *Cover-Up* (New York: Random House, 1972).

B. *Express Malice with Further Intention*

The final alternative to be examined is whether genocidal acts may have been committed in Vietnam as a *means* to a further end. More than any other possibility, it is this one which appears to be closest to the actual structure of Sartre's argument, as well as the model with the best fit to the evidence. It is not easy to dismiss or refute.

Sartre's major theme throughout his argument, as we have seen, is that genocide has been unavowedly adopted as the policy of the United States in order to fight a successful anti-guerrilla war under the conditions that prevail in Vietnam (recall §3, premises (4), (6), and (8)). With the usual wisdom of hindsight, many observers might now agree with Sartre's diagnosis of the nature of the Vietnam war and of United States military policy there. I propose to criticize his diagnosis and his imputation, and construct a slightly different version of the same argument which may come closer to the truth in several decisive respects.

First of all, is it not grotesque to impute Sartrean views about anti-guerrilla warfare to the succession of Presidential administrations in the United States from the end of World War II through the next twenty years, or even to the Johnson administration (1963-68)? Even if genocide was necessary for the United States to win in Vietnam, it does not follow that this necessity was both understood by our government and that our military policy and tactics in Vietnam were based on this understanding. Yet unless both are true, we cannot expect to find "genocidal intent implicit in the facts." Here, perhaps more than anywhere else in Sartre's argument, the crucial issue reduces to one of empirical evidence. Sartre himself nowhere cites any evidence that any theory equivalent to his about anti-guerrilla warfare in Vietnam was accepted in Washington, D.C., and then acted upon.[63] Moreover, is it

---

63. An examination of the position of influential members of the United States government on counterinsurgency warfare in South Vietnam indicates no belief in the necessity of genocidal measures. See W. W. Rostow, "Guerrilla Warfare in Underdeveloped Areas" (1961), reprinted in Marcus G. Raskin and Bernard B. Fall, eds., *The Viet-nam Reader* (New York: Vintage Books, 1965),

not somewhat implausible to maintain that even if his theory of anti-guerrilla warfare is among the first truths of any sound military strategy for the United States against a Third World people, that the United States civilian and military leadership knew this and acted upon it? The record of the United States involvement in Vietnam since its inception nearly twenty years ago shows with increasing clarity that all our highest leaders and those among their advisers who prevailed were ignorant of almost every fundamental aspect of Vietnamese history, society, and politics relevant to our government's policies.[64] Or, if they were not ignorant, then they were unable or unwilling to translate their knowledge into an effective policy, either to achieve their professed goals or to change those goals in light of the realities. Why should we now impute to these leaders an exact understanding of the grim necessities of successful anti-guerrilla warfare in Vietnam when it seems so unreasonable to impute to them a similar understanding in Vietnam of anything else?

But there is a stronger, more direct argument. Where is the evidence that counter-insurgency or anti-guerrilla warfare in Vietnam required genocidal means? Possibly for Sartre, the French experience in Algeria provided a lesson that anti-guerrilla warfare by an industrialized power against a colonial, Third World population, is bound to become genocidal.[65] But why is this, even if true, especially relevant to the United States involvement in Vietnam? There, it would appear, the United States leaders drew on the models of Malaya and the Philippines, not Algeria. The record is fairly clear that no genocidal means were recommended,

pp. 108-15; Robert S. MacNamara, "Response to Aggression" (1964), reprinted in Raskin and Fall, eds., op. cit., pp. 194-204. For the position of an adviser to the government, in essential agreement with the views of Rostow and MacNamara, see Frank E. Armbruster, "Guerrilla Warfare and Vietnam: A Perspective," in Herman Kahn, ed., Can We Win in Vietnam? (New York: Praeger, 1968), pp. 92-128.

64. The most recent and comprehensive survey is FitzGerald, op. cit.

65. See Frantz Fanon, A Dying Colonialism (New York: Grove Press, 1965); also Fanon, The Wretched of the Earth (New York: Grove Press, 1967), with a preface by J.-P. Sartre. In the former volume, Fanon observes that ". . . genocide . . . is rife in Algeria . . ." (p. 29).

needed or used in those two successful counter-insurgency struggles, if we may rely on the first-hand accounts of the guerrilla warfare experts involved who also advised the United States government on how to win in Vietnam.[66] This consideration by itself, if correct, may not absolve the United States leadership of genocide in Vietnam. It does suggest that if genocide has been committed there, it is not because, as Sartre argued, the government chose to fight an anti-guerrilla war with admonitory overtones, and that such a war by an industrial nation against a Third World people inevitably forces the adoption of genocidal means.

Insofar as there is an argument for genocide in Vietnam along the lines presently being explored, it requires a shift of emphasis to formulate it. The truth is that the war the United States actually fought in South Vietnam beginning in 1965 was, by and large, not conducted on any recognizable theory of counter-insurgency at all. The war—insofar as we are concerned with those events in it with possibly genocidal significance—was actually fought as a function of responses to considerations progressively incompatible with the patience and persistence required by anti-guerrilla warfare. Central to this interpretation are (a) the constraints upon the methods and tactics of warfare available to

66. On anti-guerrilla warfare in Malaya, see Sir Robert Thompson, *Defeating Communist Insurgency: The Lessons of Malaya and Vietnam* (New York: Praeger, 1966), and *No Exit from Vietnam* (New York: David McKay, 1969). For a point by point assessment of the failure of the United States strategy to follow a successful anti-guerrilla war strategy modelled on the experience in Malaya, see the latter volume, pp. 163-78. Sir Robert's assessment of 1969 was anticipated in general outline by the appraisal two years earlier by the late Bernard B. Fall. See Fall, *The Two Vietnams: A Political and Military Analysis*, 2nd rev. ed. (New York: Praeger, 1967), pp. 372-89. On anti-guerrilla warfare in the Philippines, see Edward Geary Lansdale, *In the Midst of Wars: An American's Mission in Southeast Asia* (New York: Harper & Row, 1972). See also Napoleon D. Valeriano and Charles T. R. Bohannan, *Counter-guerrilla Operations: The Philippine Experience* (New York: Praeger, 1962). For a general assessment of counter-insurgency policy in South Vietnam during the mid-1960s, and especially for General Lansdale's role, see Richard Critchfield, *The Long Charade: Political Subversion in the Vietnam War* (New York: Harcourt, Brace & World, 1968), pp. 156-70.

the Johnson administration under the exigencies of domestic politics and the military knowledge and technology in hand, and (b) the transformation of the pacification program of the early 1960's from the goal of "winning the hearts and minds of the people" in South Vietnam to the goal in the later 1960's of bringing as much of the population as quickly as possible under the control of the Saigon government, and to use almost any means to do so.

As to the first point, little needs to be said here. The availability of a large Strategic Air Force capable of delivering massive if somewhat indiscriminate destruction on short notice to any target area, with relatively little loss of American lives, has been a fixture of American military capability ever since the end of World War II. The need to keep down American casualties to the lowest possible levels for domestic political reasons, among others, needs no documentation. The resulting deployment of military equipment and manpower in order to use the maximum amount of firepower, on the ground and from the air, inevitably follows, whether or not there were suitable military targets for that weaponry and whether or not these tactics implemented the professed political aims of the war. The result, too, is well known: the intentional (and, no doubt in many cases, the unintentional) destruction of people and property through much of South Vietnam.

Why was it thought that these constraints on tactics and manpower might nevertheless suffice to win, or at least not lose the war? The answer lies in four interlocking convictions which came to dominate the thinking in the civilian and military leadership of the United States during the early years of the Johnson administration: (a) the first task of any United States policy in Vietnam is to prop up the Saigon government; (b) this cannot be done unless the Viet Cong can be kept from taking over rule of the people; (c) the only way to prevent this is to destroy the Viet Cong's political power by separating the people from them, with persuasion if possible but with force if necessary; (d) domestic constraints on United States tactics and existing superior technology and air power will still provide the necessary and sufficient force to accomplish these goals.

The documentary record to be found in the Pentagon Papers provides ample evidence of the first two and the last of the above four propositions. Here, it is necessary to notice the evidence only for the third, (c), because it is the most important for the present argument. Even before the massive build-up of American forces in Vietnam during 1965, the idea that only force would suffice to "separate the people from the Vietcong" was conceded in some knowledgeable quarters.[67] Within a few months after the bombing campaign began against the North, General Westmoreland was reported to have said that no longer will peasant farmers in South Vietnam be able to choose among three alternatives—staying put, moving into a Strategic Hamlet, joining the Viet Cong—because the first had been eliminated by "B-52 bombings." The General concluded his remarks by observing, "I expect to see a tremendous increase in the number of refugees."[68] Pacification by

67. The phrase is from an unidentified "RV [Republic of Vietnam] colonel in Kien Hoa province" sometime in 1964 or earlier, as reported in Frank N. Trager, "Vietnam: The Military Requirements for U.S. Victory," *Orbis,* VII (Fall 1964), pp. 563-83, reprinted in Marvin E. Gettlemen, ed., *Vietnam: History, Documents and Opinions on a Major World Crisis* (New York: Fawcett, 1965), p. 345.

68. Quoted in Critchfield, *op. cit.,* at p. 173. General Westmoreland's remarks were made at a news briefing attended by Critchfield in December 1965.

This was not, however, the preferred explanation of the swelling hordes of refugees. In early 1966, when specifically asked about the cause of refugees in South Vietnam, David E. Bell, then Administrator, AID, indicated no knowledge of General Westmoreland's new policy. Instead, he insisted that "the vast majority . . . are refugees from Vietcong terror and not from the incidental damage of our own military operations." *Hearings . . . on S. 2793,* Committee on Foreign Relations, U.S. Senate, 89th Congress, 2nd Session, January-February 1966, at p. 113, and cf. pp. 174-76. By 1970, a grudging concession was made by William K. Hitchcock, then Director, Refugee Directorate, CORDS, that "for a brief period in the mid-1960's, forcing people to leave the outlying areas was seen as a way of denying the Vietcong manpower they could exploit." *Hearings . . . on CORDS,* Committee on Foreign Relations, U.S. Senate, 91st Congress, 2nd Session, February-March 1970, at p. 221, and cf. pp. 229, 235-36.

The total number of refugees in South Vietnam alone has been variously reported as "over six million" (*New York Times,* November 6, 1972, p. 10) and as "8,000,000 . . . since the war began . . . almost one-half of the South Vietnamese population" (*New York Times,* October 2, 1972, p. 35). "More than 6.5

persuasion, by piecemeal efforts of small teams among the rural villagers, had not ceased. Another policy with appropriately different tactics had simply been superimposed upon it. Robert W. Komer, at the time General Westmoreland's Deputy for Pacification, is reported to have said, ". . . if we can attrit the population base of the Viet Cong, it'll accelerate the process of degrading the VC."[69] Perhaps the bluntest and most graphic statement of this new pacification policy has been attributed to an unnamed "high U.S. field commander" during the spring of 1966, when he said, "If the people are to the guerrillas as the oceans are to the fish, then . . . we are going to dry up that ocean."[70]

Given the actual methods of warfare used in Vietnam during the three years of military escalation (1965-68), with such uniform and candid avowals of policy as those recorded above, it is extremely difficult to know what to make of Secretary MacNamara's famous remark that "Above all else, I want to emphasize that . . . it [the war] is a battle for the hearts and the minds of the people

---

million [refugees are] officially listed by U.S. Agency for International Development since 1964. U.S. Subcommittee on Refugees and Escapees says 2 million more should be added to this." *New York Times,* January 31, 1973, p. 16.

One of the most interesting questions, on which there seems to be no published discussion, is the percentage at any given date during 1965-70 of the total population under "secure" control by the Saigon government constituted by its refugee population. From one source, it can be reasonably inferred that, as of mid-1966, perhaps one in eight such persons was a refugee. See Robert W. Komer, "The Other War in Vietnam—A Progress Report," *Department of State Bulletin,* LV (October 10, 1966), pp. 549-600, at pp. 558, 565.

69. Quoted in FitzGerald, *op. cit.,* at p. 344. No date or place is given for this remark; presumably it took place in the hearing of Ms. FitzGerald during 1966.

In April 1967 Komer submitted an advisory memorandum to President Johnson on future strategy in Vietnam, the final element of which was to "Step up refugee programs deliberately aimed at depriving the VC of a recruiting base." The Senator Gravel Edition, *The Pentagon Papers* (Boston: Beacon Press, 1971), IV, p. 441. Four years later, however, in an account intended for public consumption of the pacification programs which he helped devise and administer, the only "attrition" which Komer mentioned was of "the VC politico-administrative apparatus." See his article, "Impact of Pacification on Insurgency in South Vietnam," *Journal of International Affairs,* XXV (1971), pp. 48-69, at p. 60.

70. Quoted in Herman and Du Boff, *op. cit.,* p. 115.

in South Vietnam."[71] No one could believe that the methods actually being used with approval from the Pentagon by late 1965 could implement the policy of "drying up the ocean" and also win a "battle for the hearts and the minds of the people." For the government had opted for what one critic has subsequently called "a Devastation Model" of pacification.[72] But on such a model, pacification is indistinguishable from limited annihilation. Theoretically, of course, and taken in isolation of other considerations, the intention to dry up the water where the Viet Cong fish swim is not genocidal. Methods other than force, and perhaps forceful methods other than obliteration bombing, free-fire zones, search-and-destroy missions, defoliation and other essentially "scorched earth" policies could have separated the guerrilla movement even in Vietnam from its base in a dispersed, rural, peasant culture. The question, however, is that since these well-known brutal methods were used almost from the beginning and with the intention of destroying the population base of the Viet Cong, what more could be required to establish the facts of genocidal intent on the model of express malice with further intention? When General Westmoreland returned to Washington, D.C., in April 1967 and reported to the President and his advisers that the Vietnam war had become ". . . in the final analysis . . . a war of attrition in Southeast Asia,"[73] he was referring to the need to kill more North Vietnamese soldiers and Viet Cong cadres than they could afford to lose. One cannot fail to note how the same word, 'attrition', had been used a few months earlier by the Gen-

71. Quoted from a radio interview, August 9, 1965, in the Senator Gravel Edition, *op. cit.*, IV, p. 635.

72. John Lewallen, *Ecology of Devastation: Indochina* (Baltimore: Penguin Books, 1971), p. 36. Lewallen's discussion (pp. 29-37) of the development of this model against the background of the failure of earlier, less extreme models, is instructive. His argument, like mine, parallels more closely the argument developed originally in 1966 by Herman and Du Boff, *op. cit.*, pp. 114-23, than it does Sartre's argument of 1967. However, Lewallen (unlike Herman and Du Boff) is not preoccupied with the issue of genocide; and, as we have already seen (*supra* §3), Herman and Du Boff are not sufficiently preoccupied by the issue of genocidal intent.

73. Recorded in notes by the late John McNaughton, and published in the Senator Gravel Edition, *op. cit.*, IV, p. 442.

eral's chief deputy for pacification in South Vietnam in reference to destroying the population base of the Viet Cong.

It is tempting to conjecture that by the spring of 1967, coincident with the first sessions of the Russell Tribunal in Sweden, there was a growing realization and profound dismay among many American civilian and possibly even some military leaders that the truth about the war in Vietnam was to be found along essentially the lines indicated above, and that this awareness caused many of these leaders to shrink from further escalation of the war effort. Admittedly, there is little if any evidence in the Pentagon Papers or elsewhere to support such a conjecture.[74] If it is at all correct, however, it would have the effect of absolving those concerned from acting with genocidal intent. For on this conjecture, we would join the fact of a scaled-down war effort after 1968 to the hypothesis that the quasi-Sartrean claims above about the Devastation methods of anti-guerrilla warfare were accepted by many high officials in the government, and then infer that these officials had been acting with non-genocidal intentions all along: When confronted with the belief that to continue to use the tactics and strategy they had initially supported in Vietnam on non-genocidal grounds would force them to accept genocide as the means to pursue their original ends, they lost their stomach for the war itself. Where this leaves their successors, who four years later (December 1972) continued to carry out ever more destructive daily bombing raids throughout Laos, Cambodia, and Vietnam North and South, is another matter. The ignorance and intentions I think it not implausible to impute to the highest officials of the United States government through the early and mid-1960s are, on almost any theory, either not plausibly imputable or not much of an excuse in the early 1970s.

74. Those who, like Under Secretary of State George W. Ball, were never persuaded of the policy to enlarge the Vietnam war in 1964-65, seem to have opposed that enlargement mainly on cost benefit grounds. See Ball, "The Lessons of Vietnam: Have We Learned or Only Failed?" *The New York Times Magazine,* April 1, 1973, pp. 12 ff. Perhaps the nearest one can come to finding evidence for the view suggested in the text, *supra,* is in Hoopes, *op. cit.* His allusion to "genocide" as the "strategic logic" of United States policy in Vietnam carried "to its final conclusion" (p. 128) is offered in the context of explaining his own disenchantment with the war (pp. 119-34).

Against all this, there is only one line of defense which seems adequate. This defense might concede that many of the acts in question were acts of the sort enumerated in and prohibited under Article II of the Genocide Convention, and so in that sense were genocidal acts. The defense would also concede that these acts were done as the means to a certain end, as instruments of policy, and thus were done intentionally (by and large). But they were not truly genocidal acts, it would be contended, because they were not done in order to "destroy, in whole or in part, a national . . . [or] racial group, as such." That they were not done to destroy the group *as a whole* is shown by many considerations, not least the efforts to house and feed the refugees once they were under the nominal control of the Saigon government. That these acts were not done to destroy the group *in part* is more difficult to prove. The acts, of course, *did* destroy the group in part; but that does not prove the point in contention. Almost *any* methods of counter-insurgency warfare used on behalf of the Saigon government would have had that result.[75] The methods used were undertaken as a last resort, and would never have been used at all if the people of South Vietnam had shown both a nominal loyalty to Saigon and some sustained resistance to the blandishments and threats of the Viet Cong. In any case, the

75. By far the best defense available of the morality of counter-insurgency operations conducted against guerrilla "fish" in a neutral population "ocean" is in Paul Ramsey, "How Shall Counter-insurgency War be Conducted Justly?" in Menzel, ed., *op. cit.*, pp. 93-113. Ramsey argues that the acts of the insurgents, which involve conducting their war from "inside" the civilian population, legitimates what under other conditions would be the unjustifiable destruction of the non-combatant population. Ramsey does not explicitly consider whether such destruction could ever become truly genocidal; presumably, he would think it could not. On his analysis, even if an entire racial or national population were exterminated in order to destroy the guerrillas diffused throughout and shielded within (whether by consent or coercion of) that population, it would be no crime under "just war theory," and a fortiori, not the crime of genocide. Yet it is quite clear that genocide could be adopted as a means of counter-insurgency warfare; and, that under certain unlikely distributions of the guerrillas through the whole population, it might even be the only method of successful counter-insurgency warfare. If, therefore, Ramsey's analysis of "just war theory" is correct, that theory is incomplete, for it fails to prohibit the crime of genocide as a permissible strategy in warfare.

genocide-like acts were not genocidal, because they were not done with the intention of killing *any part* of the people of South Vietnam "as such." These acts were done with the intention of killing people who were simply in the way, simply there, because, in the judgment of field officers, they might at a later point prove to be Viet Cong or because they were in a zone or area of South Vietnam where one could not be sure that any of the natives were loyal to the Saigon government. Finally, the people who were killed, wounded, and caused to become refugees were not caused to become these things in order to destroy the people, *as such*. All the peoples resident in South Vietnam were to be ruled by the Saigon government, hopefully a government of their own choosing (whether by formal elections or other consensual devices) but in any case not a government consisting of an anti-Western pro-Communist minority who had seized political power away from the anti-Communist pro-Western minority centered in and around Saigon. This was the intention of the United States government throughout the 1950s and 1960s for the peoples of South Vietnam as such; and no methods used or other policies pursued by the United States provided intentions which supplanted that one. Actions from this intention, and actions done with an intention to commit genocidal acts (in the strict sense of that term) in order to accomplish intermediate or alternative goals, are strictly incompatible.

This defense, only sketched in the preceding paragraph, is not offered as a parody. It is meant as a genuine rebuttal on all fours with the genocide charge as developed in the early paragraphs of this section. Whether it persuades, is not for me to say. Much hinges on the evidence and on how the troublesome notions of the destruction of a people "in part" and "as such" are to be understood.

§6. CONCLUSION

The charge of genocide in Vietnam against the United States has an undeniable rhetorical appropriateness. No other single word so well captures the magnitude of the offensiveness of the war in light of the methods used to fight it, the purposes advanced as its justification, the facts of the political and social realities in Southeast Asia, and the complex but not entirely elusive intentions of the Johnson (and Nixon) administrations in fighting it as they did. Our vocabulary and our history give us no better single term than 'genocide' with which to express our horror at the decade of warfare our government has conducted in Vietnam. The newly minted word, 'ecocide',[76] may possibly do more justice to all the facts. But it lacks a paradigm historical antecedent, in contrast to 'genocide'. Moreover, genocide is not only morally wrong, it is a crime which has been recognized for a generation under international law.

In the final reckoning, is the fit between the facts and the conception of genocide under the Genocide Convention close enough to justify the charge of genocide in Vietnam, as Sartre and others have alleged? The crime of genocide as defined under that Convention is not invulnerable to criticism. With the Vietnam war hopefully behind us, we may have a new opportunity to assess the limitations of this definition of that crime. But what the future may hold in this direction is of no avail in the present setting. If, as we have seen, the issue of genocide in Vietnam were simply the issue whether the United States military forces have killed thousands of innocent Indochinese peasants, there would be nothing to discuss. If the issue were simply whether this killing, in its mode and circumstances, evidences a reckless and dangerous disregard for the life and limb of the innocent, in the pursuit of objectives which do no honor to those in our government who sought them, there would be, again, nothing to discuss. But, as we have also seen, what is chiefly at issue is the intention with which

76. 'Ecocide' has been defined as the intentional destruction of the physical environment needed to sustain human health and life in a given geographical region. See Barry Weisberg, *Ecocide in Indochina* (San Francisco: Canfield Press, 1970), p. 35; Lewallen, *op. cit.*, note 121, p. 128. See also J. B. Neilands *et al.*, *Harvest of Death: Chemical Warfare in Vietnam and Cambodia* (New York: The Free Press, 1972), and Anthony Lewis, "Scorch Their Earth," *New York Times*, May 8, 1972, p. 35. The most recent materials on ecocide in Vietnam are to be found in International Commission of Enquiry into U.S. Crimes in Indochina, *The Effects of Modern Weapons on the Human Environment in Indochina*, Documents Presented at a Hearing Organized by the International Commission in Cooperation with the Stockholm Conference on Vietnam and the Swedish Committee for Vietnam, Stockholm, Sweden, 2-4 June 1972, especially John H. E. Fried, "War by Ecocide," pp. 2:1-2-26.

these things have been done, and whether that intention coincides with the requirements of genocidal intention under the Genocide Convention.

Of the four models canvassed to this end, two of them—the model of implied malice (§4.B) and the model of express malice with further intention (§5.B)—will continue to have special aptness for interpreting the idea of genocidal intent in the Vietnam war, and *horribile dictu,* in any future warfare by an industrial power against a Third World nation such as Vietnam. The merits of these two models differ, however, in complementary ways. The model of implied malice has the edge so far as the evidence presently available is concerned. But this model places the greatest *conceptual* strain on the imputation of genocidal intent. The model of express malice with further intention provides a perfectly intelligible notion of genocidal intent, but it puts the argument under *evidential* strain. Consequently, if the accusation of genocide in Vietnam against the United States is to be taken in the strictest sense, in terms of the Genocide Convention, it can be sustained, if my analysis is correct, only by further conceptual argument or evidential researches. The gap between the results of the present discussion and a verdict of genocide in Vietnam, by any measurement, is not very wide. There is no way to give any assurance that this gap cannot be altogether closed.[77]

By stressing the issue of genocide in this discussion to the complete exclusion of any consideration of other war crimes or crimes against humanity committed by the United States, it is not my in-

77. Among those in government associated with planning and managing the Vietnam war, few have commented on the genocide issue at all. Probably most of those who shared responsibilities in the Kennedy, Johnson, and Nixon administrations would agree with Robert W. Komer's tart remark that the charges of "genocide and war crimes . . . will look silly in a few years' time," because all that "buttress[es]" them is "a new mythology." Letter of July 23, 1971, to Congressman William Morehead, and reprinted in *Hearings Before a Subcommittee of the Committee on Government Operations,* 92nd Congress, 1st Session, August 2, 1971, at p. 289. Whether the charges of war crimes and genocide are sound is one thing. Whether those who advance such charges do so on nothing more substantial than "mythology" is another. If the present analysis proves anything, it proves that the charge of genocide against the United States in Vietnam has an arguable, not mythological, basis in fact and theory.

tention to imply that no such crimes have occurred in Indo-China, or that if they have, then it is of slight importance. By dwelling on the issue of genocide, in this way, one does not necessarily encourage (much less exhibit) the "mentality" which is "quite willing to condone massacre and other war crimes so long as they [are] not genocide."[78] Nor is it correct to agree with those who endorse the verdict of genocide, only to go on and add: "In a sense, it does not really matter whether American action in Vietnam is fixed with the term 'genocide'. That action is, in any case, just what it *is*: that particular pattern, sequence, and aggregation of deeds. Its meaning is intrinsic, beyond the need for clarification, beyond the power of abstract thought to alter. What it is called has little to do with its character as concrete human experience."[79] This reflection is no doubt true. But if it has any point as a counsel, then it should make us specially cautious *before,* not after, rendering a judgment either way.

A difficulty which dogs every step of the discussion is the irreducibly forensic nature of the issue. Given the realities of American power and the frailty of international legal tribunals, there is no likelihood that the charge of genocide in Vietnam will ever be brought before any judicial body with the power to bring in a true verdict or acquittal. Yet the issue is not the less forensic if it is assessed chiefly in an extra-legal setting. For those who are not convinced beyond a reasonable doubt by Sartre's argument (or by similar arguments), as I admit I am not, the problem is, as the lawyers are fond of saying, the impossibility of proving a negative. To prove that the United States is *not* guilty of genocide in Vietnam, it is either clear that the available evidence does not suffice, or unclear what evidence would. About all one can do is to appraise the charge on the available evidence. My appraisal leads me to render a Scottish verdict, Not proven, not quite.[80]

78. Hannah Arendt, *op. cit.,* at p. 38.
79. Carl Oglesby, in *Ramparts,* February 1968, p. 36, in his preface to the first publication of Sartre's *On Genocide.* Oglesby was one of the four Americans who served on the Russell Tribunal; see Duffett, ed., *op. cit.,* at p. 17.
80. For encouragement, helpful suggestions, references to the literature, and the correction of plain errors in an earlier draft, I am indebted to Noam Chomsky, Marshall Cohen, Richard A. Falk, John H. E. Fried, Virginia Held, Thomas Nagel, and Constance Putnam.

2

The Responsibility
of the Individual for War Crimes

RICHARD WASSERSTROM

I

One way to think about the responsibility of the individual for war crimes is to divide the topic up in two different ways. On the one hand, problems relating to the *substantive* laws of war can be distinguished from problems relating to the *mens rea* requirement for the commission of war crimes. On the other hand, different classes of individuals can be held responsible for war crimes: the *soldiers* in the field who directly commit war crimes, and the *military and civilian leaders* under whose guidance, direction, or control these soldiers serve.

In this paper I consider a variety of problems arising under these headings. More specifically, I concentrate upon three things. First, I consider the substantive laws of war. I elucidate one conception of the laws of war that I take to be a very common one, and then seek to delineate two respects in which this system of rules and prohibitions is seriously flawed. Second, I consider some aspects of the *mens rea* requirement of a war crime as that requirement relates to soldiers in combat. I examine a number of factors which serve to diminish, if not to excuse, the culpability of such soldiers for the commission of what are ostensibly war crimes. Finally, I consider some problems of the *mens rea* requirement for war crimes as that requirement relates to military and civilian leaders. I concentrate primarily upon one common argument for the non-culpability of the military and civilian leaders of the United States vis-à-vis Vietnam, and try to show that that agreement is neither sound nor persuasive.

I am concerned with a particular view of the character of the laws of war and the related notion of a war crime.[1] I believe it to be the case that this account constitutes an accurate description of the existing laws of war and the dominant conception of a war crime. I am not, however, interested in insisting that it is the only possible explication of the nature and character of the laws of war. It is sufficient for my purposes to claim, as I am prepared to, that it is what many if not most lawyers, commentators, military tribunals, and courts have had in mind when they have talked about the laws of war and the responsibility of individuals for the commission of war crimes.

The system I am concerned to describe and discuss has the following features. There are, to begin with, a number of formal agreements, conventions, and treaties among countries that prescribe how countries (chiefly through their armies) are to behave in time of war. And there are, as well, generally accepted, "common law" rules and practices which also regulate behavior in warfare. Together they comprise the substantive laws of war. For the most part, the laws of war deal with two sorts of things: how classes of persons are to be treated in war (e.g. prisoners of war), and what sorts of weapons and methods of attack are permissible or impermissible (e.g. the use of poison gas). Some of the laws of war—particularly those embodied in formal documents—are narrow in scope and specific in formulation. Thus, Article 4 of the Annex to the Hague Convention on Land Warfare, 1907 provided in part that all the personal belongings of prisoners of war, "except arms, horses, and military papers," remain their property. Others are a good deal more general and vague. For example, Article 23(e) of the same Annex to the Hague Convention prohibits resort to ". . . arms, projectiles, or material calculated to cause unnecessary suffering." Similarly, Article 3 of the Geneva Convention on the Law of War, 1949, provides in part that "Persons

1. For my purposes I treat all violations of the laws of war as war crimes, and do not, therefore, make distinctions between the laws of war and the notion of a war crime that in other contexts would be necessary. See, for example, Richard Falk, Gabriel Kolko, and Robert J. Lifton (eds.), *Crimes of War* (New York: Random House, 1971), p. 33.

taking no active part in the hostilities . . . shall in all circumstances be treated humanely. . . ." And at Nuremberg, war crimes were defined as follows:

> . . . violations of the laws or customs of war. Such violations shall include but not be limited to, murder, ill-treatment or deportation to slave-labour or for any other purpose of civilian population of or in occupied territory, murder or ill-treatment of prisoners of war or persons on the seas, killing of hostages, plunder of public property, wanton destruction of cities, towns or villages, or devastation not justified by military necessity.[2]

One very important feature of this conception of the laws of war is that the laws of war are to be understood as in fact prohibiting only violence and suffering that are not connected in any direct or important way with the waging of war. As one commentator has put it, the laws of war have as their objective that "the ravages of war should be mitigated as far as possible by prohibiting needless cruelties, and other acts that spread death and destruction and are not reasonably related to the conduct of hostilities."[3]

This is reflected by the language of many of the laws themselves. But it is demonstrated far more forcefully by the way, even relatively unambiguous and absolute prohibitions, are to be interpreted. The former characteristic is illustrated by that part of the Nuremberg definition of war crimes which prohibits the *"wanton destruction of cities, towns or villages."* The latter characteristic is illustrated by the following commentary upon Article 23(e) of the Hague Convention quoted above. That article, it will be recalled, prohibits the resort to arms calculated to cause unnecessary suffering. But "unnecessary suffering" means suffering that is not reasonably related to any military advantage to be derived from its infliction. "The legality of hand grenades, flame-throwers, napalm, and incendiary bombs in contemporary warfare is a vivid

2. *The Charter of the International Military Tribunal,* Article Six (b).
3. Telford Taylor, *Nuremberg and Vietnam: An American Tragedy* (New York: Quadrangle, 1970), p. 20.

reminder that suffering caused by weapons with sufficiently large destructive potentialities is not 'unnecessary' in the meaning of this rule."[4]

Another way to make the same point is to indicate the way in which the doctrine of "military necessity" plays a central role in this conception of the laws of war. It, too, is explicitly written into a number of the laws of war as providing a specific exception. Thus, to quote a portion of the Nuremberg definition once again, what is prohibited is "devastation not justified by military necessity."

The doctrine of military necessity is, moreover, more firmly and centrally embedded in this conception of the laws of war than an illustration of the preceding type would suggest. The doctrine does not merely create an explicit exception, i.e. as in "devastation not justified by military necessity." Instead, it functions as a general justification for the violation of most, if not all, of even the specific prohibitions which constitute a portion of the laws of war. Thus, according to one expositor of the laws of war, Telford Taylor, the flat prohibition against the killing of enemy combatants who have surrendered is to be understood to permit the killing of such persons where that is required by "military necessity." There may well be times in any war when it is permissible to kill combatants who have laid down their arms and tried to surrender.

> Small detachments on special missions, or accidentally cut off from their main force, may take prisoners under such circumstances that men cannot be spared to guard them or take them to the rear, and that to take them along would greatly endanger the success of the mission or the safety of the unit. The prisoners will be killed by operation of the principle of military necessity, and no military or other court has been called upon, so far as I am aware, to declare such killings a war crime.[5]

4. Georg Schwarzenberger, *The Legality of Nuclear Weapons* (London: 1958), p. 44.
5. Taylor, *op. cit.*, p. 36. There is an ambiguity in this quotation that should be noted. Taylor may not mean that the laws of war permit an exception in this kind of case. He may mean only that the law is uncertain, that he knows

Similarly, most forms of aerial warfare are legal because of the importance of aerial warfare. Once more I take Telford Taylor's analysis to be illustrative of the conception I have been trying to delineate. The bombing of cities was, he observes, not punished at Nuremberg and is not a war crime. This was so for two reasons. Since it was engaged in by the Allies—and on a much more intensive level than by the Germans or the Japanese—it would have been improper to punish the Germans and the Japanese for what we also did. But more importantly, the bombing of cities is generally permissible because bombing is an important instrument of war.[6]

---

of no court decision which authoritatively declares this to be either a war crime or a permitted exception. It is sufficient for my purposes if he means the weaker claim, that it is an open question.

A more serious objection to my assertion that I am accurately characterizing the existing laws of war would call attention to the following quotation from the U.S. Army Field Manual, *The Law of Land Warfare*, Chapter I, Section I, 3.

> "The law of war places limits on the exercise of a belligerent's power in the interests mentioned in paragraph 2 and requires that belligerents refrain from employing any kind or degree of violence which is not actually necessary for military purposes and that they conduct hostilities with regard for the principles of humanity and chivalry.
>
> "The prohibitory effect of the law of war is not minimized by 'military necessity' which has been defined as that principle which justifies those measures not forbidden by international law which are indispensable for securing the complete submission of the enemy as soon as possible. Military necessity has generally been rejected as a defense for acts forbidden by the customary and conventional laws of war inasmuch as the latter have been developed and framed with consideration for the concept of military necessity."

I do not know exactly what this means. It seems to anticipate, on the one hand, that the laws of war and the doctrine of military necessity can conflict. It seems to suppose, on the other hand, that substantial conflicts will not arise either because the laws of war prohibit militarily unnecessary violence or because they were formulated with considerations of military necessity in mind. In substance, I do not think that the view expressed in the quotation is inconsistent with the conception I am delineating.

6. Taylor makes the same points in respect to the London Naval Treaty of 1930. The treaty required that no ship sink a merchant vessel "without having first placed passengers, crew and ship's papers in a place of safety." The provi-

The general test for the impermissibility of bombing is, says Taylor, clear enough. Bombing is a war crime if and only if there is no proportionate relationship between the military objective sought to be achieved by the bombings and the degree of destruction caused by it.

Two potentially relevant considerations are explicitly ruled out: the fact that bombs are the sorts of weapons that cannot discriminate between combatants and non-combatants and the fact that bombing is an inherently inaccurate undertaking. These are not relevant to the question of whether bombing is a war crime because bombs are important weapons of war.

The foregoing constitutes a brief sketch of the collection of specific prohibitions, accepted conventions, and general excusing and justifying conditions which comprise that conception of the laws of war with which I am concerned. I want now to discuss more fully two characteristics of this conception which seem to me to flaw the substantive laws of war in genuinely fundamental ways.

The first of these is the failure of the laws of war to regard as impermissible almost all cases of the resort to aerial warfare and the use of weapons of mass destruction. I think this is a very serious defect because it obliterates rather completely the distinction between combatants and non-combatants.

Some people would doubtless argue that the distinction be-

---

sions of the treaty were regularly violated during the Second World War. Nonetheless, these violations were not punished as war crimes at Nuremberg. Here, too, Taylor gives the same two reasons. First, the doctrine of military necessity made the treaty unworkable. And second, even if considerations of military necessity were not decisive, violations of the treaty would not have been war crimes because the treaty was violated by both sides during the Second World War. And nothing is properly a war crime, says Taylor (at least in the absence of a genuine international tribunal) if both sides regularly engage in the conduct in question, see for example, Taylor, *op. cit.* p. 39.

This latter point is ambiguous. Sometimes the point seems to be that it is procedurally unfair for the victor to punish the loser but not himself for the same act. This I find a quite unobjectionable principle. But sometimes the point seems to be that there is a different principle at work, one that *legitimizes* a practice which was previously proscribed once the practice becomes widespread. This principle I find far less attractive and not obviously appropriate.

tween combatants and non-combatants is neither an important distinction in theory nor a meaningful one in practice. This seems to me to be a mistake. For the distinction reflects, I believe, a concern for two basic considerations: the degree of choice that persons had in getting into the position in which they now find themselves, and the likelihood that they are or are about to be in a position to inflict harm on anyone else.

To be sure, the distinction between combatants and non-combatants is a relatively crude one. Some non-combatants are able in reasonably direct ways to inflict harm on others, e.g. workers in a munitions factory. And some non-combatants may very well have knowingly and freely put themselves in such a position. Concomitantly, many combatants may have been able to exercise very little choice in respect to the assumption of the role of a combatant, e.g. soldiers who are drafted into an army under circumstances where the penalties for refusing to accept induction are very severe, and difficulties such as these would make is plausible to argue that the laws of war cannot reasonably be expected to capture perfectly these distinctions. For this reason, it would, I think, be intelligible to argue that it is unreasonable to expect anyone or any weapon to be able to distinguish the conscripts from the volunteers in the opponents army. It would, perhaps, even be plausible to argue (although less convincingly, I think) that civilians who are engaged in activities that are directly connected with the prosecution of the war can reasonably be expected to understand that they will be subject to attack. If the laws of war even preserved a distinction between soldiers, munitions workers, and the like on the one hand and children, the aged, and the infirm on the other, one might maintain that the laws of war did succeed in retaining—at a low level and in an imprecise way—these distinctions of fundamental moral importance. But, as I understand them, the laws of war that relate to aerial warfare and the use of weapons of mass destruction do not endeavor to preserve a distinction of even this crudity. What is perhaps ruled out (although it is by no means certainly so after Dresden and Hiroshima) is the deliberate bombing of wholly civilian populations for the sole purpose of destroying those populations. What is

clearly permissible is the knowing destruction of civilian populations—women, children, and the like—provided only that a military objective is sought to be achieved by the bombing mission.

I do not think that a plausible justification can be found for
continuing to regard this kind of behavior as permissible. I do
not see any rational ground by which to distinguish the knowing
destruction of non-combatants with bombs dropped from a B-52
from shooting them at close range with a machine gun. If the latter is wrong because it does violence to the distinction between
combatants and non-combatants, then the former is too. I find
quite unpersuasive the two grounds for differentiation which are
sometimes advanced.

The first of these is that a bomb is the kind of weapon that cannot discriminate between combatants and non-combatants whereas
a machine gun, when properly aimed, can. This is doubtless true,
but only seems to me to be a good reason for prohibiting the use of
weapons like bombs—at least in those cases where the relevant distinctions cannot be made.

The second of these is a particular illustration of a more pervasive defect in the laws of war; namely, that a general exception
to almost all of the laws is permitted on grounds of military necessity. In the case of aerial warfare, this way of thinking gets
reflected in the view that bombs and other weapons of mass destruction cannot be proscribed because they play too central a
role in the prosecution of modern warfare. But this is, as I have
said, only a particular version of a more pervasive defect that at-
tends the doctrine of military necessity.

That doctrine, it should be noted, is typically employed in an
ambiguous and highly misleading fashion. "Necessity" leads us
naturally to think of various sorts of extreme circumstances which
excuse, if they do not justify, otherwise impermissible behavior.
Thus, one exception to the rule about taking prisoners is, perhaps, a case where necessitarian language does fit: if the prisoners
are taken by the patrol deep in enemy territory the captors will
themselves almost surely be captured or killed. They cannot, in
such circumstances be held to the rule against killing prisoners
because it is "necessary" that the prisoners be killed.

Now, one may not be convinced that necessitarian language is appropriately invoked even in this case. But what should nonetheless be apparent is the inappropriateness of describing the doctrine that justifies aerial warfare, submarine warfare, or the use of flame-throwers as one of military *necessity*. Necessity has nothing whatsoever to do with the legitimacy of the aerial bombardment of cities or the use of other weapons of mass destruction. To talk of military necessity in respect to such practices is to surround the practice with an aura of justification that is in no way deserved. The appeal to the doctrine of military necessity is in fact an appeal to a doctrine of military utility. On this view, the laws of war really prohibit (with only a few minor exceptions) some wrongful practices that also lack significant military value. The laws of war permit and treat as legitimate almost any practice, provided only that there is an important military advantage to be secured.

The more that *this* doctrine of military necessity permeates the conception of the laws of war, the less intelligible and attractive is the claim that the laws of war are a coherent, complete, or admirable code of behavior—even for the jungle of warfare. For given the pervasiveness of this doctrine of military utility, the laws of war are reducible in large measure to the principle that in war it is still wrong to kill (or maim or torture) another person for no reason at all, or for reasons wholly unrelated to the outcome of the war, but that is all. On this view the governing principle is that it is legitimate and appropriate (and sometimes obligatory) to do almost anything to anybody, provided only that what is done is reasonably related to a perceived military objective. It is, in short, to permit almost all possible moral claims to be overridden by considerations of military utility. Whatever else one may wish to claim for such a system of the laws of war, one cannot claim that they deserve either preservation or respect because of the connection these laws maintain with the idea of how persons ought to behave toward other persons.

Nor is it just a matter of relatively abstract, semi-aesthetic concerns for coherence that are at stake. Much that is claimed for the laws of war must, I think, be abandoned under this conception of them.[7] In addition, if any persons under any circumstances are to be held to answer for the commission of war crimes, it is important that they be held to answer under a scheme of substantive law that is not fundamentally unfair. This means that they should not be held liable for actions which are indistinguishable in the significant, relevant respects from actions which are not proscribed. Thus, if the bombing of cities cannot be distinguished from other ways of killing civilians, it is hard to justify the punishment of persons who do the latter while people who do the former go unpunished (and even receive medals). Finally, as I shall try to demonstrate in the section of this paper that follows immediately, this conception of the laws of war makes it very difficult to formulate and apply a defensible *mens rea* requirement to the typical combat soldier.

II

The case that many people think is the easiest case in which to justify judgments of culpability and decisions of punishment is that of the soldier in combat who violates the laws of war. As I have indicated, I do not think it is at all an easy case. This is so because I do not believe that the *mens rea* requirement that ought to be satisfied before culpability attaches is often satisfied in the case of the ordinary soldier.

There are several considerations that ought to make us uneasy about the application of judgments of criminal responsibility to soldiers in combat, and the most prominent of these is the problem of superior orders. Nuremberg[8] is illustrative of some of the difficulty.

7. For example, that there is a rationale, based on moral considerations, for such things as the prohibition upon the bombing of hospitals or the prohibition upon the use of poison gas. I have offered a more detailed examination of these and other problems concerning the morality of behavior in time of war in "The Laws of War," *The Monist,* Vol. 56 (1972), pp. 1-19.
8. Although I tend to draw upon the proceedings at Nuremberg, per se, I mean in some of my references to Nuremberg to include all of the war crimes trials that took place after the Second World War.

The Charter of the International Military Tribunal took what is certainly a hard line in respect to the problems of superior orders. "The fact that the defendant acted pursuant to order of his government or of a superior shall not free him from responsibility, but may be considered in mitigation of punishment if the Tribunal determined that justice so required."[9]

The Tribunal, in its Judgment, modified (without indicating that it was doing so) the position of the Charter by only half-accepting the Charter's rejection of the plea of superior orders as an excuse. The Tribunal did this by introducing some sort of a defense of duress. Here is what the Tribunal said:

> It was . . . submitted on behalf of most of these defendants that in doing what they did they were acting under the orders of Hitler, and therefore cannot be held responsible for the acts committed by them in carrying out these orders. . . .
>
> The provisions of . . . Article [Eight] are in conformity with the law of all nations. That a soldier was ordered to kill or torture in violation of the international law of war has never been recognized as a defense to such acts of brutality, though, as the Charter here provides, the order may be urged in mitigation of the punishment. The true test, which is found in varying degrees in the criminal law of most nations, is not the existence of the order, but whether moral choice was in fact possible.[10]

It is difficult, I think, to imagine a more obscure way of characterizing the nature of the defense that the Tribunal was prepared to allow, but what is clear is that the Tribunal accepted superior orders as an excuse (provided "moral choice" was not possible) whereas in the Charter they were at best a mitigating circumstance.

The idea of *moral choice* is not a clear one, so it will be worthwhile to consider a bit more carefully what the Tribunal might have meant. At least two interpretations come to mind. One would go something like this. The mere fact that an actor had

9. *The Charter of the International Military Tribunal,* Article Eight.
10. "Judgment of the International Military Tribunal," *Trial of the Major War Criminals* I, pp. 223-24.

been ordered to do something does not by itself excuse the actor from responsibility for his actions. This is as it should be because, at a minimum, we must know something about both the stipulated consequences for disobedience and the likely consequences of disobedience before we can decide whether someone who acts in obedience to orders should be excused for his obedience. This is what the talk about the existence of "moral choice" comes to. Suppose, for instance, that there is a general standing order that soldiers are to kill rather than capture all enemy prisoners. At the very least, we would not want to excuse completely a soldier who complied with that order and who shot all his prisoners until we knew a good deal more about such things as the announced penalty for disobeying that order, the probable penalty for disobedience, the typical soldier's reasonable beliefs about the penalty, and this soldier's belief as to what the penalty was. If the announced, probable, and understood penalty for disobedience was summary execution the case would be a very different one from that where the penalty was demotion in rank. Thus, one interpretation of "moral choice" would focus heavily on the degree of choice exercisable by the actor. Where the penalty for disobedience is very great, and believed to be such, then one rationale for permitting the defense is that of excuse: in such circumstances a person will naturally, and perhaps inevitably, act so as to avoid the penalty. He does not, we might say, "really have any choice" and so he is for this reason to be exempted from punishment.

A somewhat different rationale would not focus upon the absence of choice so much as upon the poignancy of the dilemma in which the actor finds himself. It is not that he cannot help himself when he seeks to avoid the punishment; it is rather that human beings, when caught up in such circumstances, simply ought not be blamed for opting so as to save their own lives at the cost of other lives. People are not to be blamed, in other words, for failing to behave heroically, or with such altruism that they bring consequences of a severely detrimental character upon themselves.

In either case, as I have said, the defense of superior orders would be a defense provided the accused could show that the choice involved was an illusory or unduly difficult one.

But to say that a soldier in combat is only excused from liability where the consequences of disobedience were perceived by him to be very severe does not, I think, do full justice to the plight of the ordinary combat soldier. For what this account leaves out is the context within which he will surely have been trained and within which he will find himself once in combat. His training will consist very largely in a process designed to inculcate within him habits of obedience to command. And this is, I think, an inevitable part of military training because an army functions successfully only if habitual, unquestioning obedience is forthcoming on the part of the ordinary soldier. Thus, even if a portion (and it will invariably be a small portion) of basic training is devoted to a discussion of (say) the laws of war, even if a soldier is instructed that he ought not obey any order that is illegal on its face, the dominant thrust of his training will have consisted in efforts directed toward transforming him into a person who will obey without question and without hesitation. Thus, it is not sufficient to excuse him when moral choice was not present; he ought, perhaps, to be excused whenever he does what he is told to do because this is what he will have been trained to do.

But, suppose that a soldier's training is not as monolithic in respect to obedience to orders as I have supposed it to be. Suppose instead that a genuine and serious attempt is made to inculcate only habits of limited obedience. Suppose soldiers are earnestly encouraged to believe that while obedience to orders is important it is not all that is important; and suppose in particular, that soldiers are convincingly taught that an order that is clearly or obviously illegal, one that requires the soldier to do what it is manifestly wrong to do, ought not to be obeyed. Even if we had such a system of training (and I do not think that we do) there is still a powerful argument that obedience to orders ought to be a complete defense. The argument turns upon the character of the existing laws of war and, concomitantly, upon the soldier's capacity to assess what is and is not a violation of the laws of war. More specifically, I want to call attention here to two related characteristics of the system of the laws of war that are of particular significance. In the first place, although war crimes are thought to be the most clearly defined of the three sorts of activities in respect to war for which persons are held responsible, they are, as we have seen, often extremely vague and imprecise. Thus, to revert once again to Article 23(e) of the Annex to the Hague Convention of 1907, it seems to me to place an ordinary soldier in an extremely difficult position to require him to decide when he is using a weapon calculated to cause unnecessary suffering. In a more systematic way, moreover, the doctrine of military necessity (conceived of as a general justifying condition) makes it virtually impossible for the soldier to determine from his limited perspective whether an ostensible war crime in fact comes under this exemption. It is, in short, often a fiction that the soldier in the field is in any position to ascertain to which situations the laws of war apply and to which they do not.

In the second place, the problem of knowledge is compounded by the fact that the laws of war are not a rational, coherent scheme of rules and principles. Were there an intelligible rationale to the laws of war, recourse to this rationale might assist the soldier in his attempt to determine which of his actions were war crimes and which were not. For reasons that I have already endeavored to make clear, I do not believe that such a rationale can be derived from the existing laws. As a result, unless the soldier happens to get ordered to do one of those few, unambiguously proscribed acts, like firing a projectile filled with glass, there is no readily applicable general principle to which he can appeal for guidance. As the laws of war are presently constituted, he cannot, for instance, appeal in any simple, straightforward way to the idea that the intentional killing of non-combatants is a prohibited act.

So far I have discussed primarily the problem of the soldier who is ordered to do an action that may be a war crime. I have tried to explain why, in such cases, there are serious problems of duress and knowledge that ought to be dealt with before criminal liability is fairly imposed. But still, it might be urged, all of this leaves unaffected cases of the gratuitous commission of war crimes—cases where there were no direct superior orders and where soldiers on their own behaved in ways that were clearly proscribed by the laws of war, and known by them to be such. My Lai is, arguably, one such case; no one ordered the soldiers involved to line up the unarmed women, children and elderly people and machine gun them. The laws of war do make it plain that such behavior is forbidden. What are we to say about this kind of case?

There is no question in my mind that there is genuine culpability in such cases. However, the culpability is diminished, I think, by a variety of factors typically present. At the very least I can, I believe, understand why the ordinary soldier regards this sort of behavior as reasonable and appropriate, even though it is not.

To begin with, all that I have said about the uncertainty and irrationality of the laws of war applies regardless of whether the soldiers in question did what they did because they were ordered to do it or for some other reason. Similarly, as has already been indicated, the typical combat situation is hardly conducive to a reflective consideration of the application of the laws of war to particular situations.

In addition, contemporary ideas about warfare have certain consequences of their own. In the first place, in combat it is certainly more plausible than it would be in any other context to regard everyone who is not clearly on your side as your enemy. Because so many things are permissible in war that are not permissible elsewhere, and because even more things are practiced which would never be practiced elsewhere, it certainly makes it reasonable to be extremely suspicious of anyone who is not unquestionably your friend or who is not utterly and completely helpless. If the threat to your life as a foot soldier can so easily and permissibly come from so many sources against which you are defenseless (e.g. airplanes), apparent cruelty and wanton barbarism often turn out to be nothing more than moderately pursued self-defense. Such is one consequence one might say of the logic of contemporary war.

In the second place, and closely related to what has just been said, modern war is, I think, extraordinarily corruptive of the capacity to behave morally. If the distinctions between what is obligatory and what is prohibited appear to rest on no intelligible grounds or persuasive principles, if one is encouraged in war to neglect as morally uninteresting just those distinctions which in any other context are of utmost moral importance, and if one has no reasonable assurance (as one cannot in time of war) that others will behave with a careful regard for the moral point of view, then it is not surprising if persons lose interest in and concern for even the minimum demands of morality. They are somewhat excusable, even when they do terrible things, because war has, in some important ways, made psychopaths of them all.[11]

Once again, the dominant conception of the laws of war has, I submit, a good deal to do with this state of affairs, because it is the laws of war that define what is and is not permissible for the soldier to do in time of war. If we had a different, more rigorous conception of the nature of war crimes, if we had a conception that corresponded more convincingly with fundamental principles, then it would be easier than it now is to expect consistent behavior from combatants.

III

When we turn to the leaders—both civilian and military—we come to those persons to whom many principles of responsibility most obviously and plausibly apply, and to whom culpability most

11. I find quite unconvincing the claim that the laws of war enhance persons' capacities to be moral. Thus, Telford Taylor argues that the laws of war are

". . . necessary to diminish the corrosive effect of mortal combat on the participants. War does not confer a license to kill for personal reasons—to gratify perverse impulses, or to put out of the way anyone who appears obnoxious, or to whose welfare the soldier is indifferent. War is not a license at all, but an obligation to kill for reasons of state; it does not countenance the infliction of suffering for its own sake or for revenge.

"Unless troops are trained and required to draw the distinction between military and non-military killings, and to retain such respect for the value of life that unnecessary death and destruction will continue to repel them, they may lose the sense for that distinction for the rest of their lives. The consequence would be that many returning soldiers would be potential murderers" (Taylor, *op. cit.*, pp. 40-41).

I find this unconvincing because the laws of war do not, as I have tried to show, embody and reflect in a coherent way important moral distinctions or truths.

It is possible, of course, to make the claim on another ground; namely, that teaching persons to obey orders, or even laws—whatever their content may be —is an important constituent of the curriculum of moral education. This is not a view I share.

fairly and appropriately appears to attach. For these are the persons who are least subject to formal military discipline; they have substantially more discretion in respect to their own behavior; they are the ones who give orders and formulate battle plans and objections; they are in a position more accurately to assess the consequences of their action; they are removed from combat and can, therefore, reflect and deliberate. To the degree to which various *mens rea* requirements ought to depend upon the presence of just these conditions, these requirements are satisfied here in a way in which they are seldom satisfied in the case of combat soldiers.

This truth is, of course, reflected in the principles and the practices of Nuremberg. It was the leaders—both civilian and military —whose culpability seemed easiest to establish and most difficult to deny. In terms of what was done at Nuremberg, as well as what was said, it was leaders and not ordinary soldiers who were held most responsible for the commission of war crimes as well as for the commission of crimes against peace and crimes against humanity.

I do not, however, mean to suggest that there are no problems with the standards and principles of responsibility that were applied at Nuremberg to the various leaders. To take just one example, the already described vague and elastic properties of the substantive laws of war create some of the same difficulties for leaders that they do for all other persons. Nonetheless, the problems in respect to culpability often seem to me too greatly exaggerated.[12] More specifically, as I shall indicate later, the only major issues seem to me to center upon any particular leader's knowledge of and causal connection with the actual commission of war crimes by others under his supervision, direction, or control. But this is not the way the topic is sometimes discussed.

12. I should make it plain, too, that I am not at all interested in this paper in considering arguments that it would be impractical, nationally divisive, or generally unwise to try to hold the leaders of the United States criminally responsible for their respective roles in the Vietnam war. These, too, seem to me to be often exaggerated, but they are beyond the reach of this paper. Here, I am only concerned with the question (or a part of the question) of whether they satisfy the conditions of culpability.

In particular, it is sometimes claimed that there is a special *mens rea* requirement that must be satisfied in addition before leaders can be held responsible. This I think to be false. One reasonably well known version of this claim is to be found in an article by Townsend Hoopes entitled, "The Nuremberg Suggestion." The relevant passages are these:

> The tragic story of Vietnam is not, in truth, a tale of malevolent men bent upon conquest for personal gain or imperial glory. It is the story of an entire generation of leaders (and an entire generation of followers) so conditioned by the tensions of the Cold War years that they were unable to perceive in 1965 (and later) that the communist adversary was no longer a monolith, but rather a fragmented ideology and apparat . . .
>
> Lyndon Johnson, though disturbingly volatile, was not in his worst moments an evil man in the Hitlerian sense. And his principal advisers were, almost uniformly, those considered when they took office to be among the ablest, the best, the most humane and liberal men that could be found for public trust. No one doubted their honest, high-minded pursuit of the best interests of their country, and indeed of the whole noncommunist world, as they perceived those interests. Moreover, the war they waged was conducted entirely within the framework of the Constitution, with the express or tacit consent of a majority of the Congress and the country until at least the autumn of 1967, and without any press censorship. . . .
>
> . . . [S]hould we . . . establish a war crimes tribunal . . . and try President Nixon and Dr. Kissinger as 'war criminals'? The absurd questions answer themselves.
>
> . . . above all [we must avoid] the destructive and childish pleasure of branding as deliberate criminals duly elected and appointed leaders who, whatever their human failings, are struggling in good conscience to uphold the Constitution and to serve the broad national interests according to their lights.[13]

There are a number of respects in which the argument is an interesting one; for my present purposes, though, what I want to

13. Townsend Hoopes, "The Nuremberg Suggestion" reprinted in Falk, Kolko, and Lifton, *op. cit.*, pp. 235-37.

concentrate upon is the insistence that there is something about the state of mind of the leaders of the United States which makes it obvious that their conduct in respect to Vietnam is not culpable.

We might, I think, be tempted to reject the argument out of hand on the ground that the author has confused two notions that the criminal law tries very hard (admittedly with only moderate success) to keep straight; namely, motive and intention. That is to say, one way to regard what Hoopes has to say is to see it as depending upon the claim that a person whose motives are good cannot be (or, perhaps, should not be—or, perhaps typically, is not) held accountable by the criminal law. Thus at Nuremberg, what was punished was the doing of proscribed acts by persons who had despicable motives in so acting.

Now it is plain, I think that in any simple form this is not an accurate account of the requirements of the criminal law generally, nor is it an obviously attractive view of the way the criminal law ought to operate. We might, for example, think that a person who robs a poor widow of her life savings in order to have a wild week in Monaco is worse than a person who robs the same widow in order to give the money to the cancer fund. We might even think it appropriate that the punishment of the two persons should be different. But we would reject, I take it, the claim that a person ought not be held liable at all merely because his motive in robbing the widow is, in the abstract, a commendable one.[14] What we would say in the law is that we are not interested primarily in his motive or in his purpose in doing the act. What we want to know is whether he intended to do the act in question; whether he regarded himself as taking by force the money that did not belong to him. If he did, then he has committed the crime of robbery. Similarly, for Nuremberg to be applicable, it would be sufficient for the leaders to intend (in this sense of intend) to do those actions that are in fact prohibited by Article Six of the

14. Or, to give the example a more contemporary bite: would a proponent of this argument also concede the nonculpability of a black militant who selflessly risks his life to assist other black militants escape from prison when he sincerely believes (doubtless reasonably) that they were unjustly convicted and confined there?

Charter; it is not of central importance that we inquire into their motives (in this sense) for acting.

But this is not, perhaps, to put an end to the matter. Someone might reply that the distinction I have proposed is not always a clear one. Nor, someone might add, is it obvious that motive ought to be as irrelevant as the criminal law appears at times to make it. Moreover, it might still be claimed, there does seem to be something to be said for the original argument that the American leaders do seem different from the leaders of the Nazi regime in ways that are of moral, if not legal, significance.

Thus, there is, I think, a somewhat more sophisticated defense that might be made of Hoopes's position, although it, too, does not succeed. To begin with, it might be argued that at least some of the crimes established at Nuremberg did mean to include motive (in the sense I have been using it) as a part of the definition of the offense. Thus, it could be maintained that the waging of aggressive war means not simply the initiation of war (whatever the motive or purpose) but rather the initiation of war provided there is a certain objective or end in view, namely, to achieve personal gain or the imperial accession of territory. Even more to the point, given the way the definition of war crimes encompasses the notion of military necessity, the separation of motive and intention seems less easy than appeared at first. Up to a point, this does seem to me plausible and I want to consider the matter further. However, it is also essential to observe that there is nothing about the Nuremberg principles and the judgment of the Tribunal that supports in an unqualified way this sort of interpretation. While it may be true that the German motives for doing some of the things that were done were especially despicable, it is certainly a mistake to identify the Nuremberg rationale with a condemnation of those motives.

Yet, as I have indicated, there may be something to be said for this point of view. I think the most attractive interpretation is this. Perhaps the truth to be extracted is that culpability is and ought to be limited to those actions that the actor knows to be wrong. This is not quite the same as insisting upon the presence of a malevolent motive. Rather it is to emphasize that serious liability ought not attach unless the actor had a certain conception of what he was doing—unless he knew or should have known that what he was doing was wrong. And this is a principle that we do —at least to some degree—embrace in the operation of our own municipal legal system.

Of course, it must immediately be observed that what I have just said is ambiguous. The principle that the actor must know that what he is doing is wrong can be the principle that the actor must know that what he is doing is legally wrong—that it is forbidden by the legal system. Or, it can be the very different principle that the actor must know that what he is doing is morally wrong—that he is doing what one who is concerned to be moral ought surely not to do.

In our own legal system the principle that is generally regarded as the operative one is that it is sufficient if the actor knows, or ought to know,[15] that what he is doing is legally wrong. Although there are numerous qualifications that must be made, the general point is clear enough. In our own legal system it is regarded as appropriate to impose criminal liability upon an actor who intended to do an action that he knew to be proscribed by the law, and in such case the actor is not absolved of liability by his belief that it was morally right to do the action.

It is also surely the case that the conception with which the Nuremberg Tribunal worked was one in which intending to do an illegal act was sufficient to justify liability. For the Tribunal was concerned to establish that the actions of the accused were violations of international law and in some cases known to be such by them. The Tribunal took appreciable pains to demonstrate the pre-existing illegality of the acts denominated as crimes against peace and crimes of war. It did so, I take it, because it deemed it sufficient to justify the imposition of criminal liability that these acts were illegal and either known or capable of being known by the defendants to be such.

It is possible, I admit, to fall back to still another position: that

15. There are clearly differences between the requirement that the actor *know* and the requirement that he *ought to know*. For the present, I wish to ignore those differences, but I return to them at the very end of the paper.

in respect to the kinds of crimes dealt with at Nuremberg, persons are only to be held liable if they knew or ought to have known that they were violating the relevant law and had bad motives for doing so. At this stage it is not clear how one ought to reply. This is not the requirement that was applied at Nuremberg. It is, indeed, quite possible that some of the leaders convicted at Nuremberg did not have bad motives at all, for example, Speer. Perhaps the claim is that if this is so, such persons ought not to have been convicted. I do not know. What is plain is that the case for such a new, more stringent *mens rea* requirement has yet to be made out. I, for one, do not see why the motives of United States leaders ought to be taken to be the decisively relevant aspect of the question of their culpability for war crimes in Vietnam.

If we reject the idea that bad motives are an essential requirement for responsibility, we are left with the question of what is the appropriate test for the responsibility of leaders. Anyone thinking about this topic is led sooner or later to the Yamashita case.[16] For it deals with the two significant factors of knowledge and causal connection.

As recent discussions of the Yamashita case have brought out, there are two rather different ways in which the case can be thought relevant. One approach is to concentrate upon the situation in which General Yamashita found himself, to focus upon the harshness of holding him responsible for the behavior of his troops in the circumstances of that case. The other approach is to emphasize the criteria for culpability elaborated in the majority opinion without worrying about whether those criteria were in fact satisfied vis-à-vis General Yamashita.

There is something to be said for the former, quite draconian approach, but not, I think, a great deal. If it is the case that General Yamashita was unaware of the brutalities committed by his troops, was not even responsible for having encouraged them to behave as they did, and was in no position to have prevented them from so behaving, then we are tempted, surely, to conclude that he was unjustly held criminally liable for their con-

16. *In re Yamashita*, 327 U.S. 1, 66, S.Ct. 340 (1945).

duct. As a result, we are also led to conclude that it would be equally unjust to hold American leaders responsible if they are in a similar position in respect to the commission of war crimes in Vietnam.

However, it is not quite as easy as that. For we can surely find intelligible the claim that now is not the time to engage in a scrupulous re-examination of the fairness of the treatment by the United States of the German and Japanese leaders after the Second World War. The point is not that precedents ought or must be mindlessly applied without regard to the fairness of the rule. Rather, the point is that, having ourselves applied rules and principles to others in a certain way, we are now in a poor position to object to the fairness of those rules and principles.

As I have indicated, we can, I think, acknowledge the force of this argument without being wholly convinced by it. If General Yamashita was treated as badly as he appears to have been, I am inclined to think that this is a good reason for trying to make certain that no one is treated in a similar fashion in the future—even those from the country responsible for his mistreatment.

But to reject this application of the Yamashita case is not, of course, to dismiss the problem with which the case dealt. For there is still the question of the appropriate test for the culpability of leaders for war crimes committed by forces in the field. I will conclude with some remarks about only one of the main *mens rea* problems in this area.

No one, I take it, would question the appropriateness of holding the military and civilian leaders of the United States responsible for those acts which they ordered United States and South Vietnamese troops to perform and which they knew to be violations of the laws of war. The live issues concern, rather, their culpability in less clear cases. The chief issues, as I see them, can be framed thus by: (1) Is it sufficient if the leaders simply adopted or knowingly permitted the adoption of policies and objectives the realization of which were likely to lead to the commission of war crimes? Under this test, if it is the case that an emphasis upon "body counts" leads to the killing rather than the capture of enemy soldiers who wish to surrender, then the leaders who knowingly encouraged or permitted this emphasis are properly held liable for the ensuing war crimes. (2) Is it necessary, as an addition to (1) that the leaders should have known that such a policy was likely to have such consequences? That is to say, is it necessary to ask whether the leaders should have known that an emphasis upon body counts would have this effect? Or, (3) is the test more stringent, still? Must we inquire into the actual state of mind of the leaders to see whether they in fact knew that such a policy was likely to have such consequences?

Similar questions can be asked about policies or programs, the implementation of which may in fact constitute the commission of war crimes. Thus, if the use of anti-personnel bombs is a war crime, is it sufficient that the leaders directed or knew of the use of this weapon? Or is it necessary to establish that they ought to have known that the use of such a weapon was a war crime? Or is it necessary to establish that they in fact knew that the use of such a weapon was a war crime?

As far as I can tell, actual knowledge in either of these kinds of cases has not usually been required, and was certainly not required in respect to the leaders prosecuted after the Second World War. On the other hand, strict liability is hardly a more attractive notion for war crimes than it is in our own legal system. The appropriate test in this regard appears, therefore, to be what the leaders ought to have known or foreseen about the policies and programs under their authorship, direction, or control. It is upon this question, and not the question of their motives, that our attention ought to focus far more intensely than it has thus far.

3

Morality and the Laws of War*

MARSHALL COHEN

I wish to discuss two distinguishable, but related, problems concerning the laws of war. One concerns the interpretation of these laws, and particularly the interpretation of the crucial concept of military necessity. The other problem has to do with an appraisal of these laws from a moral and a practical point of view. Telford Taylor,[1] for instance, finds certain persistent inadequacies in the laws of war and in the crucial concept of military necessity. He believes, nevertheless, that the laws of war and the principle of military necessity serve moral and practical purposes and that they ought to be preserved and enforced. Richard Wasserstrom[2] appears to accept Taylor's interpretation of the laws of war. He notes, however, that it is not the only one possible, and argues that so understood the laws of war are "morally unattractive" and have "no special claim upon our attention or energies." I want to argue that some of the "ambiguities" that Taylor finds in the laws of war, and that some of the "moral unattractiveness" Was-

* An earlier version of this essay appeared in *The Yale Law Journal*, Vol. 80, No. 7, pp. 1492-1500. At a symposium subsequently held at the Yale Law School, December 10, 1971, Professor Taylor replied to that essay and I have attempted to take account of his comments in the present version. I am also grateful to Professor Richard A. Falk, to members of the Society for Ethical and Legal Philosophy, and especially to Mr. Pierre N. Leval for assistance.

1. T. Taylor, *Nuremberg and Vietnam: An American Tragedy*, 33 (1970) [hereinafter cited to page number only].

2. R. Wasserstrom, "The Laws of War," *The Monist*, Vol. 56, No. 1, pp. 1-19.

serstrom finds in them, are illusory. This is, I believe, important to understand, for unless one sees that the laws of war may be construed in something like the manner I suggest the main argument that Taylor offers in favor of the view that they help to preserve civilized values will be weakened, if not actually undermined. And when the laws are properly interpreted it will be easier to defend them against the kinds of charge that Wasserstrom brings. In any case, it will be useful to note that they need not be defended in the way that he supposes.

It will be helpful, then, to turn to the account of the laws of war that Taylor provides in his important book *Nuremberg and Vietnam* for, as I have suggested, this account is in danger of being taken as authoritative. First of all it will be helpful to try to understand the crucial "dilemma," or the central "ambiguity," that Taylor finds in the laws of war, and this is not, in fact, an easy thing to do. For it is unclear, to begin with, whether Taylor means that some statements of the laws of war give unbridled sway to the principle of military necessity while others, in apparent contradiction, restrict it, or whether he means that some statements of the law are simply unclear or ambiguous on the matter. Thus, Taylor illustrates the ambiguity he finds in the laws of war by comparing two passages from the Army's field manuals, one from the 1917 version, the other from the 1956 version. According to the 1917 version the laws of war are determined by the following principles:

> *First,* that a belligerent is justified in applying any amount and any kind of force which is necessary for the purpose of the war; that is, the complete submission of the enemy at the earliest possible moment with the least expenditure of men and money. *Second,* the principle of humanity, which says that all such kinds and degrees of violence as are not necessary for the purpose of war are not permitted to a belligerent.[3]

3. U.S. Dep't of War, *Rules of Land Warfare,* para. 9 (1917) (War Dep't Doc. No. 467, Office of the Chief of Staff, approved April 25, 1914) (emphasis in original), quoted at p. 34. The 1917 version also lists a rather vaguely worded "principle of chivalry," which I have not quoted, as a principle of the laws of war.

This, according to Taylor, "is a plain statement of the rule of military necessity; if the use of force is necessary, it is lawful, and if unnecessary, it is unlawful."[4] It should be observed that, so defined, the principle of humanity places no limitation on the principle of military necessity, since the former is concerned only with violence which is "not necessary." Given these definitions, it is erroneous to speak of the laws of war as a compromise between the principle of military necessity and the principle of humanity; for, so conceived, these principles cannot come into conflict. To speak as though the laws of war are the result of a compromise between them must mean that there are military interests more ambitious than those specified by the principle of military necessity, and humane interests more comprehensive than those guaranteed by the principle of humanity, and that it is these interests which are compromised. At the level of principle, however, no further compromise is effected. Thus, on this conception of the laws of war, justification on grounds of military necessity is always sufficient since there is no competing principle forceful enough to rule it out.

If the 1917 passage is "plain" so, I think, is the 1956 version[5] which is also, I believe, plainly inconsistent with it. The 1956 version says that

> The prohibitory effect of the law of war is not minimized by "military necessity" which has been defined as that principle which justifies those measures not forbidden by international law which are indispensable for securing the complete submission of the enemy as soon as possible. Military necessity has been generally rejected as a defense for acts forbidden by the customary and conventional laws of war inasmuch as the latter have been developed and framed with consideration for the concept of military necessity.[6]

Now, sometimes Taylor appears to mean by the ambiguity of the laws of war that the two passages do not mean the same thing

4. P. 34.
5. P. 35.
6. U.S. Dep't of Army, *The Law of Land Warfare*, para. 3 (1956) (Dep't of Army Manual FM 27-10), quoted at pp. 34-35.

and sometimes that the second passage itself incorporates the two inconsistent views. I would agree that the two passages are inconsistent, but not that there is any important "ambiguity" internal to the second passage which, as I see it, gives the correct rationale for the laws of war. It is, of course, possible to find a verbal ambiguity here. For, when the passage states that the laws of war have been framed with consideration for "the concept of military necessity," it must mean with consideration for the military interest (or possibly with consideration for the principle of military necessity). But, when it says that "military necessity" had been "defined as that principle which justifies those measures *not forbidden by international law* which are indispensable for the complete submission of the enemy as soon as possible,"[7] it is referring to neither of them. Rather, it is invoking what may be called the Lieber-Hague (henceforth the Hague) conception of the laws of war.[8] This conception permits the interests of humanity to carry enough weight so that they can sometimes inhibit the operation of the principle of military necessity. On this conception, therefore, the appeal to military necessity is by no means always a legitimate one; indeed, it is sometimes plainly ruled out. Certainly, then, it is at least misleading to characterize the very conception that results in restrictions on the principle of military necessity by the term 'military necessity' itself. But, confusing as this may be, there is nothing essentially ambiguous about the passage

7. *Ibid.* (emphasis added).
8. According to Taylor, in "the Lieber rules of 1863, military necessity was defined as 'those measures which are indispensable for securing the ends of war, *and which are lawful* according to the modern law and usages of war'." P. 33 (emphasis added). Hence, under the Lieber doctrine, an action had to be *both* indispensable to the ends of the war *and* otherwise permitted by the laws of war to be covered by the principle of military necessity. The scope of that principle is also restricted by the Hague Convention of 1907, under which it is "especially forbidden" to "kill or wound an enemy who, having laid down his arms, or having no longer means of self-defense, has surrendered at discretion." That Convention also forbade a declaration "that no quarter will be given." (Quoted at p. 35.) If such acts are forbidden without qualification, no principle of military necessity can endow them with a permissible character which they have otherwise been stated to lack.

which Taylor quotes. The verbal ambiguity in no way weakens the impact of the 1956 passage, which, as I read it, unequivocally endorses the Hague conception of the rules of war. What really bother Taylor are not, I think, the putative ambiguities so far examined ("no form of words can resolve the essential difficulty"), but his doubt that any restrictions of the sort the Hague conception places on the principle of military necessity can in fact survive as valid law given the changing conditions of war, the vagueness of the conception of "military necessity," and the very imperiousness of necessity's demands.

So, immediately after his discussion of the ambiguity of the 1956 passage, Taylor proposes to illustrate the dilemmas and difficulties inherent in the laws of war by offering some "pragmatic"[9] examples. They will show, he says, that "necessity" is a matter of "infinite circumstantial variation,"[10] and later he extracts the "lesson of all these examples, which is that the laws of war do not have a fixed content, but are constantly reshaped by the exigencies of warfare."[11] But, in fact, the difficulties that Taylor alleges do not invalidate a Hague conception of the laws of war nor show that they cannot resist the pressures of military necessity. For, whatever may be meant by saying that the concept of military necessity is capable of "infinite circumstantial variation," all that is required to sustain a Hague-like conception of the rules of war is that in certain of these circumstances the claims of military necessity should be denied. Now it sometimes appears that what bothers Taylor is not so much the variety or instability of military circumstances as it is the vagueness of the concept of military necessity itself. But the concept of military necessity is much like the concepts of due process and fair price; commanders are as capable of taking guidance from the rules employing this concept as courts are of applying similarly vague judicial concepts. Often enough the killing of survivors, the torture of prisoners, and the plunder of captured cities are not justified, and are not thought to be justified, by the principle of military necessity. In any case,

9. P. 35.
10. *Ibid.*
11. P. 38.

even if the concept of military necessity is vague, its vagueness is less damaging to a Hague conception whose rules do not always permit its invocation than it is to a "plainer," more "realistic" conception of the laws of war that can never avoid appealing to it.

In the end, Taylor relies on the simple fact that rules which attempt to restrict the operation of the principle of necessity are ineffective. But, in addition to the fact that he moves too easily from the alleged ineffectiveness of rules to their lack of validity,[12] Taylor's own examples are not persuasive here. Often when he claims that the courts have acceded to demands of military necessity, it is far from clear that they have done so; and even if they had done so in the specific cases he mentions, this is far from showing that they do so whenever the demand arises. Indeed, the International Military Tribunal was notable for the firmness with which it rejected pleas of military necessity.[13] Besides, as we shall see, Taylor's own "realism" in this matter, if consistently pursued, would take him farther in the direction of legalizing crime than I think he would care to go. Before pursuing that issue, however, let us confirm these observations by considering Taylor's own examples.

A crucial rule of war requires that an enemy soldier who surrenders is to be spared further attack, and, upon being taken prisoner, is to be conducted as soon as possible to safety in the rear of the capturing force. But, Taylor points out, in certain circumstances this rule is violated.[14] Sometimes in the heat of battle soldiers are killed even though they might have been taken prisoner—a circumstance which, of course, shows nothing about the validity of the rule. Sometimes, too, they are killed in cold blood

---

12. On the distinction between validity and efficacy, see, *e.g.*, H. L. A. Hart, *The Concept of Law*, 100-101 (1961). Nothing Hart says suggests that this distinction cannot be applied in the area of international law. One might, of course, argue that in international law efficacy is in fact the criterion of validity. But, if I have interpreted Taylor correctly (*see* pp. 1499-1500 *infra*), he cannot rely on such a view. In any case, I should reject it.

13. *See, e.g., United States v. List*, reported in *11 Trials of War Criminals*, 1230, 1255-56, 1272 (1950) ("The Hostage Case"). *See generally*, M. McDougal and F. Feliciano, *Law and Minimum World Public Order*, 676-78 (1961).

14. P. 36.

on the orders of "humane" commanders when "[s]mall detach-
ments on special missions, or accidentally cut off from their main
force . . . take prisoners under such circumstances that men cannot be spared to guard them or take them to the rear, and that to
take them along would greatly endanger the success of the mission or the safety of the unit."[15] Taylor says that these prisoners
will be killed in accordance with the principle of military necessity and that no military court has been called upon, so far as he
is aware, to declare such killing a war crime.

To begin with, the vulnerable position of a small squad cut off
from its main force has all the makings of a special case, and
would not show that in more typical cases prisoners may be sac-
rificed if doing so will lead to what the principle of military necessity describes as "the complete submission of the enemy at the earliest possible moment with the least expenditure of men and
money."[16] But even in the special case, commentators are virtually unanimous in maintaining that when such killings are
undertaken to guarantee the success of a mission they violate the
laws of war.[17] Moreover, it is far from clear what follows from the
fact, if it is a fact, that no court has been called upon to declare
such killings criminal. It surely does not follow that they are not
criminal. Where the killing of prisoners has been undertaken not
to secure the success of a mission—the case most favorable to Taylor's view—but to secure the safety of a force that is critically
threatened, or in cases where the state's principal forces cannot
detain prisoners and where their release would so reinforce the
enemy as to make defeat inevitable there has, to be sure, been
controversy about the proper rule. Some have suggested that the
requirement is absolute and that, after being disarmed, the prisoners should be freed;[18] others have argued that in such circum-

15. *Ibid.*
16. See p. 1492 *supra.*
17. See, for example, M. Greenspan, *The Modern Law of Land Warfare,* 103
(1959); 2 L. Oppenheim, *International Law,* 339 n.3 (7th ed. H. Lauterpacht
1948).
18. *See,* for example, W. Hall, *International Law* 474 (8th ed., A. Higgins,
1924); Albéric Rolin, *Le Droit moderne de la guerre,* 286-88 (1920); 2 H.
Wheaton, *International Law,* 179-80 (7th ed., A. Keith, 1944).

stances they may, in fact, be killed.[19] But, and this is crucial, even those who say that the prisoners may be killed are not necessarily relying on the principle of military necessity—a much narrower principle of (state) self-preservation will suffice. If this narrower principle is also described as the "principle of military necessity," an ambiguity has indeed been introduced and this time it is a crucial and even vicious one.

Similar objections apply to Taylor's other major example, drawn from the development of naval warfare. The London Naval Treaty of 1930 forbids warships from sinking merchant vessels "without having first placed passengers, crew, and ship's papers in a place of safety."[20] Soon after the outbreak of the Second World War, however, it became apparent that due to the development of "[r]adar, sonar, convoys and long-range aircraft" it was "virtual suicide" for a submarine "to surface anywhere near its target, let alone to remain in the vicinity for rescue operations."[21] These rescue provisions were, as a result, generally ignored. When Admirals Raeder and Doenitz were charged with violating the London Treaty, Admiral Nimitz testified that in respect to the rescue provisions the Germans had done nothing that the British and Americans had not also done. Taylor observes that the "Nuremberg Tribunal therefore ruled that, while Raeder and Doenitz had indeed violated the London rescue stipulations, they would not be subjected to any criminal penalties on that account. The plain rationale of this decision was that the London rescue requirements were no longer an effective part of the laws of naval warfare, because they had been abrogated by the practice of the belligerents on both sides under the stress of military necessity."[22] He also observes that the scope of application of the laws of war must be limited by the extent to which they had been observed by the enforcing party. "To punish the foe—especially the vanquished foe—for conduct in which the enforcing nation has en-

19. J. Bluntschli, *Das moderne Völkerrecht der civilisierten Staten*, § 580 (1878); 3 Emmerich de Vattel, *The Law of Nations*, § 151 (1758 ed., C. Fenwick transl., 1916).
20. Quoted at p. 37.
21. P. 37.
22. Pp. 37-38.

gaged, would be so grossly inequitable as to discredit the laws of war themselves."[23]

In fact, however, the Tribunal was far from relaxing the requirement. It said: "If the Commander cannot rescue, then under the [terms of the international law] he cannot sink a merchant vessel and should allow it to pass unharmed before his periscope."[24] Certainly, then, the Tribunal did not take the practice of belligerents to undermine the validity of the rule. All it said was that in consequence of the breach on both sides "the sentence of Doenitz is not assessed."[25] The Tribunal appears to have invoked a doctrine of estoppel, and its reliance on this doctrine does not entail that the rule is no longer valid law. The Tribunal did not acquiesce in the principle of military necessity, but plainly upheld the validity of a rule that was meant to limit the force of that principle.[26]

The examples examined above do not show that the laws of war cannot or, indeed, that they do not, restrict the principle of military necessity. But Taylor's discussion of the aerial bombardment of civilian populations suggests that, given his own line of reasoning, the laws of war are not subject even to the limits imposed by the principle of military necessity. Thus, in one passage Taylor remarks that there was "not much law left"[27] governing the bombardment of civilian populations at the end of World War II. He claims, in consequence, that there was "no basis for criminal charges against Germans and Japanese"[28] after World War II and that there is no basis for such charges in connection with our own bombings in North Vietnam today.[29] On the other hand, he believes that the bombings of Dresden and Nagasaki

---

23. P. 39.

24. 22 *The Trial of German War Criminals*, 509 (H.M.S.O. 1950).

25. *Ibid.*

26. Of course, it could be argued that the rule should be applied to victor and vanquished alike. In any case, invoking this doctrine does not preclude applying the rule to other parties or in other circumstances. The point being made in the text is simply that there is no inconsistency in the Tribunal's invoking this doctrine and still professing the validity of the rule.

27. P. 140.

28. P. 141.

29. P. 142.

were, in fact, criminal, as he believes that some of our own bombing practices in South Vietnam are today. (The bombing of Hiroshima can, he thinks, perhaps be justified,[30] although the *Shimoda*
court judged it in violation of international law.)[31] Now, if Taylor believes that the Germans and the Japanese engaged in bombing practices comparable to those the Allies engaged in at Dresden and Nagasaki, he ought not to say (whether because the
rules against such bombing were no longer effective, because cus-
tomary practice had changed, or because practices that both sides
engage in cannot be illegal) that the bombing of Dresden and
Nagasaki was criminal. Furthermore, since he apparently believes
that the bombing of Dresden and Nagasaki violated the "proportionality" requirement implicit in the principle of military necessity,[32] he ought to conclude, if efficacy is the criterion of validity,
that at the end of World War II the laws of war no longer imposed even a requirement of military necessity. Unfortunately,
Taylor does not speak to the issue of German and Japanese practice regarding proportionality in aerial warfare and follows his
observations about Dresden and Nagasaki with the morally pertinent but legally unhelpful observation that they are "tolerable in
retrospect only because their malignancy pales in comparison to
Dachau, Auschwitz and Treblinka."[33] He does try to avoid the
consequence that even the principle of military necessity was in-
validated at the end of World War II by saying that to "a degree"[34] the proportionality principle was observed in World War
II—Oxford and Heidelberg were not bombed. But the crucial
point would seem to be that London, Coventry, and Rotter-
dam were. Taylor attempts to salvage the vitality of the principle

30. P. 143.
31. I refer here to *Shimoda v. Japan*, 355 Hanrei Jiho 17 (Tokyo Dist. Ct. Dec.
7, 1963), in which a Japanese civil court, while denying damages to survivors
of Hiroshima and Nagasaki, characterized the bombings as "contrary to the
fundamental principles of the laws of war." The case is mentioned by Taylor
at p. 141 n.12. It is discussed and the opinion reproduced in English in 1 R.
Falk and S. Mendlovitz, *The Strategy of World Order*, 307-54 (1966).
32. P. 143.
33. *Ibid.*
34. *Ibid.*

of military necessity by making it an article of faith that violations of that principle are illegal. Were he to continue applying
his dubious principles about effectiveness, current practice, and
reciprocity, he would have to conclude that the principle of military necessity was inefficacious and so invalid at the end of the
Second World War. And, if he should argue that Axis bombing
practices never in fact violated the principle of military necessity
he would still have to face the same theoretical question. If both
sides violated the principle of military necessity would even it remain a legally valid restraint on the conduct of war?

But if he is willing to ignore, or to subordinate, these arguments when they jeopardize the validity of the principle of military necessity, why does he not do so at a point more favorably
disposed to the interests of humanity? If he waived them at a different point, he could give more weight to the principle of humanity. This would not only permit Taylor to give a more accurate
account of the laws of war (reflecting the Hague conception which
underlies many of them), but would also strengthen his own arguments in favor of preserving and enforcing these laws. Indeed,
Taylor's own arguments in this matter are weakened, and perhaps
even undermined, by his failure to give sufficient weight to the
prohibition on the deliberate killing of innocent persons. Taylor
takes the most important argument for preserving the laws of war
to be that they diminish the corrosive effect of mortal combat on
the participants. Thus he writes: "Unless troops are trained and required to draw the distinction between military and nonmilitary
killings, and to retain such respect for the value of life that unnecessary death and destruction will continue to repel them, they
may lose the sense for that distinction for the rest of their lives."[35]
Many returning soldiers would be, he is inclined to think, potential murderers. Surely, however, the distinction between military
and nonmilitary killings is substantially irrelevant to civilian life.
A distinction between necessary and unnecessary killings is, to be
sure, sometimes invoked in civilian life. For example, a homicide
which would otherwise be criminal or immoral may be neither if

35. P. 41.

a person is attacked and finds it necessary to kill his assailant in order to preserve his own life. But this is not the distinction that a soldier learns when he learns the distinction between killing that is necessary from a military point of view and that which is not. And that distinction, like the distinction between military and nonmilitary killing, is irrelevant to civilian life. Taylor's argument will have to be, then, that the value of the laws of war is that they teach soldiers the distinction between legitimate and illegitimate killings. No doubt this will be of value to those—presumably there will not be very many—who would return to civilian life having forgotten that there is one. Unfortunately, however, given the laws of war as Taylor understands them, ex-soldiers will have learned that the deliberate killing of innocent persons may be "necessary" in many circumstances that moral principle would condemn. Learning this lesson, if it has any effect at all, can only increase the chances that these men will be potential murderers—and legalizers of murder. There is no safety here.

In fact, however, although the laws of war are far from satisfactory, they do give far greater weight to the prohibition on killing innocent persons than Taylor allows (and they "reflect" the distinction between combatants and non-combatants much more pervasively than Wasserstrom acknowledges). They are, then, capable of a much stronger defense than Taylor is able to provide. For instance, the distinction between combatants and non-combatants is in fact embodied in various protections that the law extends to neutrals, civilian populations, prisoners of war, the wounded, and those who tend them. It can also be observed in the protection offered to schools, churches, temples, shrines, hospitals, and private houses. We have seen how Taylor's interpretation of the laws of war deprives them of much of their humane content—in the case of the rule against denying quarter, and in the case of the rule guaranteeing the safety of the passengers and crews of merchant vessels. And this is, as has been suggested, also true in the case of aerial bombardment. If we agree, however, as Taylor agrees, that the laws of war are not exhausted by formal agreements, conventions, and treaties but incorporate an international "common" law as well, it will be possible to mitigate the alleged defects in the treaty law by relying on the principles and policies that are embodied in the laws of war. Indeed, it can be argued that precisely this effort is demanded by the Hague Conventions themselves. For the well-known De Martens clause requires that

> Until a more complete code of the laws of war has been issued, the high contracting Parties deem it expedient to declare that, in cases not included in the Regulations adopted by them, the inhabitants and belligerents remain under the protection and the rule of the principles of the law of nations, as they result from the usages esablished among civilized peoples, from the laws of humanity, and the dictates of public conscience.

So, if we reject Taylor's view that *tu quoque* considerations dissolve international legal obligations and especially if we understand the prohibition on the killing of innocent persons to be supplemented by the traditional doctrine of double-effect or by some variant or descendant of it,[42] we can argue that much of the aerial bombing of World War II, certainly much more of it than Taylor concedes, was illegal, and that the moral and legal prohibitions in these areas are not so discrepant as he suggests. A similar conclusion is reached in the very cogent opinion of the *Shimoda* court which, as we have noted, did not agree with Taylor's view that at the end of World War II "there was not much law left" in this area. The *Shimoda* court argued that the bombing of Hiroshima, as well as the bombing of Nagasaki, was forbidden by the laws of war. It claimed that international law forbids an indiscriminate or blind attack on undefended cities like Hiroshima and Nagasaki. And it argued, too, as Richard Falk summarizes it, that "International law only permits, if at all, indiscriminate bombing of an undefended city if it is justified by military necessity; no military necessity of sufficient magnitude could be demonstrated here."[43] Falk's inclusion of the phrase "if at all"

42. Thomas Nagel, "War and Massacre," *Philosophy and Public Affairs*, Vol. 1, No. 2, p. 130 ff.

43. Richard A. Falk, "The Shimoda Case: A Legal Appraisal of the Atomic Attacks upon Hiroshima and Nagasaki," in his *Legal Order in a Violent World* (Princeton, 1968), p. 393.

reflects his appreciation of the fact that the court, for well-understood jurisprudential reasons, is resting its holding on narrow grounds. The court is, therefore, not to be understood as endorsing the view that broader principles protecting civilian populations cannot be elicited from the laws of war. It is only suggesting that they are not needed to provide that protection here (although one might argue that they are implicitly invoked in Falk's phrase "no military necessity *of sufficient magnitude* could be demonstrated here" and that they provide the foundation for some of the restrictive rules that the court extends by analogy). In the main, the opinion suggests as against Wasserstrom, that the principle of military necessity, far from obliterating the distinction between combatants and non-combatants cannot even be understood without appealing to the distinction. In addition, it suggests that even that principle, not to mention more specific rules and other, more humanitarian principles afford far greater protection to non-combatant and civilian populations than Taylor's analysis allows.

If something like the interpretation of the laws of war suggested here is accepted, Taylor's defense of the laws of war and particularly his claim that the laws diminish the corrosive effect of mortal combat on combatants, will be far more powerful than it is on his own interpretation of them. Similarly, attacks on those laws like Wasserstrom's will be far weaker. It will be useful, therefore, to consider that attack, and some of the related defenses, in detail.

Wasserstrom argues, to begin with, that a criminal code may be criticized for being incomplete or, worse still, for being morally incoherent. A code that punished "a variety of harmful acts against property" but permitted and treated as in this sense legitimate, all acts of violence against persons, would be not only incomplete, but incoherent. "The code would be incoherent in that it could not be rendered intelligible either in terms of the moral principles that ought to underlie any criminal code or even in terms of the moral principle that justified making theft itself illegal."[44] A criminal code with this feature would have "a very

44. Wasserstrom, p. 8.

serious defect" and would in fact be "odious." (Whether this odiousness is thought to be an inevitable consequence of this kind of "incoherence" or whether it is simply a feature of Wasserstrom's particular example is not entirely clear.) In addition to having these moral defects a code such as this would be dangerous—not only because under it "what is not forbidden is in some sense legitimate" but because we may "concentrate our energies and our respect upon its enforcement."

Much that Wasserstrom says about the properties of a criminal code that is incoherent in this sense is, it seems to me, highly questionable. Indeed, incoherence in his sense would seem to be a ubiquitious, and not always a regrettable, feature of criminal codes. Consider, for instance, the treatment of various forms of lying in our own legal system. The criminal law does not prohibit certain lies which nevertheless form the basis for liability in the law of contracts or the law of torts. Nor does it prohibit many lies that are nevertheless condemned by professional codes of ethics or by moral opinion quite generally. Surely, some of the conduct not prohibited by the criminal code (such as the telling of gratuitous and malicious lies to family and friends) is condemned by the very moral principles that apply to lying that is criminal (such as the falsification of customs declarations or of income tax returns). These omissions in the criminal law are not necessarily "defects," however, and there may be excellent reasons why the criminal code does not attempt to regulate some of this conduct: it may better be regulated by the procedures and penalties of the civil law; it may be that the costs of bringing the criminal process to bear, or simply the inherent difficulties of bringing it to bear, are prohibitive; it may be that the attempt to regulate and control certain activities by the criminal code would constitute a serious threat to personal privacy, to individual liberty, and to the development of a mature appreciation of the fact that man is not "ague-proof." But even where we feel that despite the difficulties involved, an incoherence in the criminal law is a regrettable defect (as, for instance, in its general failure to prohibit the intentional infliction of non-physical forms of suffering and injury) or even where we judge illegitimate and sinister interests to be responsible for the incoherence (as in the failure of the criminal law to control safety conditions in mines and in industrial plants more strictly) it does not follow that the criminal code which displays these "defects" must itself be regarded as odious or dangerous. Even if we take the sort of case most favorable to Wasserstrom's view, for instance, the failure of our criminal law, at one time, to forbid the owning of slaves, it does not seem plausible to argue that the entire criminal code must be characterized as odious, or that the enforcement of its central features constituted a dangerous concentration of "energies" and "respect." For the most part, abolitionists did not find it necessary to abolish the protection that the criminal law provided to the principles of liberty and equality in order to extend them further. *Reculer pour mieux sauter* is, in general, a dangerous social tactic. And it would be an especially dangerous one, I believe, in the area under discussion.

Wasserstrom supposes that if one is going to support the present laws of war the "chief" argument offered in their defense is likely to be that the present laws of war constitute a complete and coherent, although a perhaps "lower," standard of behavior (appropriate to the morality of war). Thus, he says, "the argument might conclude [that] the laws of war are not like a criminal code that only punishes theft. Rather, they are like a criminal code that only punishes intentional homicides, rapes, and serious assaults and thefts."[45] It is, of course, possible that Taylor believes the laws of war, understood simply to prohibit killing which is not a military necessity conform to some minimal, but "coherent complete, or admirable code of behavior."[46] At least some utilitarians appear to maintain a position of this sort—although they would not characterize the standard of morality as a "lower" one (the distinction between "higher" and "lower" moralities having no clear meaning in utilitarian terms). But it is not inevitable that someone like Taylor should claim that the laws of war embody a morality (either "higher" or "lower") completely and coherently. Such a person might simply argue that the laws of war, which prohibit (militarily) unnecessary suffering, constitute a compromise between an utter lack of restraint and the princi-

45. Wasserstrom, p. 9.
46. Wasserstrom, p. 12.

ples of humanity, and that this compromise, although morally incoherent in Wasserstrom's sense, nevertheless provides the best
available way to mitigate the corrosive effects of mortal combat
and to save lives. Given the current realities of international politics this is better than nothing and it may provide an important
basis for future progress. If, however, one adheres to a Hague conception of the laws of war it will be possible to argue that in addition to maintaining the "lower" standard which forbids unnecessary killing, the laws of war "reflect" (if only obliquely) and
"embody" (if only incompletely and incoherently) a "higher"
standard forbidding the intentional killing of innocent persons.
So understood, arguments like Taylor's for supporting the laws
of war are greatly strengthened. In addition, the more perspicuous
the moral content of the laws of war becomes, the more persuasive
it will be to urge their value as a basis of criticism, and as a rally-
ing point for domestic and international opinion. For this kind of
effect, although not a formally legal one, may nevertheless be the
most important power this body of law possesses. All this, and
more, can be urged without appealing to the sort of argument
that Wasserstrom supposes to be the "chief" one.

Even if it does not follow from the fact that the laws of war are
"incomplete" or "incoherent" that they are odious or dangerous it
may nevertheless be the case that they are so. Consider, for instance, Taylor's argument that the laws of war are valuable because, if nothing more, they save lives. Aside from whatever objections Wasserstrom may have to the truth of this argument, it is
less attractive than it seems, for if, as is arguable, the laws of war
save guilty lives at the expense of innocent ones, or belligerent
ones at the expense of pacific ones, they would, in fact, be odious.
But, even if we waive this argument, it is necessary to assess Wasserstrom's argument that because what is not forbidden by the
law is in some sense permitted the laws of war are dangerous. As a
general matter, there is little to be said for the claim that what is
not legally forbidden is in an appropriate and significant sense
"legitimate." If an act is not legally forbidden we may allow (for
the sake of argument—Kelsen's view that there are no "gaps" in the
law is far from persuasive) that there is a sense in which it is "legally" legitimate. But it is certainly not imagined that, in general,

a form of conduct is acceptable simply because it is legally "permitted" or "legitimate." No one supposes that because the criminal code does not forbid the telling of gratuitous and malicious lies to parents and friends that it is acceptable to tell them. When, therefore, Wasserstrom writes that "the laws of war inescapably permit as well as prohibit; they make some conduct criminal and other conduct legitimate,"[47] it is important to see that in itself this observation is not telling, but trivial. On the other hand, it is the case that while the inference from that which is legally legitimate to that which constitutes an acceptable form of conduct is neither valid nor in general tempting, it is frequently thought to be appropriate in the areas of economic relations and in the conduct of war. And where this is so, as appears to be the case with many of those who control the engines of war, the "incoherence" of the laws of war will contribute to, or at least not mitigate, the danger that morally outrageous conduct will be thought "legitimate." It may be that in consequence of this fact the laws of war do encourage more killing than they discourage. I do not know whether this is so although I am inclined to doubt it. However that may be, the problem is, on either Wasserstrom's view or on the view defended here, to persuade those who need persuading that moral relations do in fact govern the conduct of war. It must come to be understood that the principles of morality are not one among a number of competing interests and that they cannot be subordinated to other interests. They are, rather, the principles that govern the pursuit of all interests. Once this is understood the generally obnoxious inference from legality to legitimacy will appear as obnoxious in the case of warfare as it does elsewhere. And until this is understood it is unlikely that the laws of war will take the form that Wasserstrom desires in any case. However that may be, it is the failure to appreciate the requirements of morality rather than any "incoherence" in the laws of war that constitutes the main impediment to civilized conduct in this area. Unfortunately, it is more than dubious whether this impediment can be overcome at a time when so many believe, as Malraux has sensed, that not to have killed is to be a virgin.

47. Wasserstrom, p. 18.

4

Reasons and Conscience: The Claims of the Selective Conscientious Objector

ALAN GEWIRTH

Should selective conscientious objectors be exempted from military service? This question asks about the justification of imposing a certain limit on the legal obligation of all draft-age male citizens to perform military service as required by the conscription law. The criteria used in answering this question of justification may be of different kinds, including especially the legal and constitutional standards applied by the Supreme Court in reaching its decisions on the issue. But ultimately the criteria must be moral ones by which those standards and decisions are themselves evaluated. This is true not only on various grounds deriving from the concept of morality, but also because the selective conscientious objector bases his claim to exemption from military service on moral reasons bearing on what he believes to be the moral wrongness of the particular war in which he is asked to fight. Now moral criteria and reasons may themselves be of different kinds. In the following inquiry into the moral justification of the selective conscientious objector's claim, I shall confine myself for the most part to various middle-level principles or criteria on which there is considerable agreement, although some of the main problems arise from conflicts among these criteria. In dealing with such conflicts I shall implicitly appeal to what I have elsewhere called the Principle of Categorial Consistency, which requires, in its individual application, that an agent respect his recipients' freedom and welfare as well as his own, and in its social application, that policies and institutions serve to foster equal freedom and mutual accommodation of wants and purposes among human beings.[1]

I

In order to be clear about the nature and merits of the selective conscientious objector's claim that the law's failure to exempt him from military service in some particular war is morally unjustified, we must distinguish this claim from the claims of three other sorts of social protesters or dissidents: the anarchist, the revolutionary, and the civil disobedient. Although selective conscientious objectors may be anarchists, or revolutionaries, or civil disobedients, in these cases their claims are of a more general nature than those which characterize the selective conscientious objector as such. All four of these types of dissident may be defined in terms of moral opposition to the law, but they differ in respect of the specific reasons on which they ground this opposition, and this difference is reflected in the distinct aspects of law to which they object. To see this, we must note that the word 'law,' even when confined to municipal law, is used with three different kinds of reference which must be carefully distinguished.[2] 'Law' is used to refer (1) to a general social institution which is common to all societies which have even minimal legal systems; (2) to one or another specific legal system which may differ from other legal systems in its contents and procedures; and (3) to some particular legal rule or rules which may exist within the same or different legal systems. I shall indicate these three kinds of reference of 'law' by using the subscripts 1, 2, and 3. Thus, in the first reference ('law$_1$') we talk of law as against, for example, religion or etiquette as a kind of social institution and as a method of social

1. For arguments toward and analyses of this principle, see my "Categorial Consistency in Ethics," *Philosophical Quarterly,* vol. 17 (1967), pp. 289-99; "Obligation: Political, Legal, Moral," *Nomos,* vol. 12 (1970), pp. 55-88; "The Justification of Egalitarian Justice," *American Philosophical Quarterly,* vol. 8 (1971), pp. 331-41; "Moral Rationality," The Lindley Lecture for 1972, University of Kansas.

2. I have previously discussed these distinctions in "Obligation: Political, Legal, Moral" (cited above, note 1), at pp. 74 ff.

regulation, namely, that institution and method which consist in coercively binding and publicly promulgated general rules for regulating violence and other socially important situations. In the second reference ('law_2') we talk of United States law, Soviet law, and the like. And in the third reference ('law_3') we talk of the United States income tax laws, the conscription law, and so forth.

Now the anarchist, the revolutionary, and the selective conscientious objector are morally opposed, respectively, to law_1, to a certain law_2, and to a certain law_3. Confusion results when these three different bases of opposition are indiscriminately intermingled, as they sometimes are even by otherwise quite intelligent supporters of exempting selective conscientious objectors from military service. Some such supporters, in their zeal to defend selective exemption, take the anarchistic position that there is no moral justification for imposing any legal obligations at all in the sense of coercive requirements set by law_1: they hold, indeed, that no governments have any moral right to force people to do things against their will. For example, one writer asserts that "a democratic society should not require its citizens to violate their deeply held principles."[3] If the writer meant this literally, he would not be able to say, as he does a few pages later, that "committed racists" should be forced to pay their taxes even though they object strongly to some uses to which the taxes are put.[4] Since, then, he recognizes that a democratic society is at least sometimes justified in requiring its citizens to violate their deeply held principles, he cannot use an anarchistic opposition to law_1 itself as a basis for supporting the exemption of selective conscientious objectors from military service.

Other proponents of such exemption seem to base their views on a revolutionary opposition to our law_2 insofar as this consists in the American constitutional system. They hold that the legal compulsion to perform military service is not justified within our present constitutional system because that system is itself morally

3. Michael Harrington, "Politics, Morality, and Selective Dissent," in *A Conflict of Loyalities: The Case for Selective Conscientious Objection* edited by James Finn (New York: Pegasus, 1968), p. 227.
4. *Ibid.*, p. 232.

unjustified. In support of this charge they point, in particular, to the severe inequalities which the system permits in the distribution of economic and political power; and they assert that these are intimately connected with our repressions of foreign national liberation movements in general and with the Vietnam War in particular. (The iniquities of the Vietnam War have, of course, provided the greatest impetus to selective conscientious objection.) While there is, I think, much that is sound in this contention, it is important to be clear about whether one's support of the selective conscientious objector is based on advocacy of revolutionary change of our whole legal system, i.e. our law_2, including its Bill of Rights and its provisions for equal protection of the laws and so forth; or whether one opposes only some $laws_3$ or particular institutions within the whole system. If one opposes our law_2, this would indicate at least a severe qualification of whatever support one might seek from the constitutional provisions for religious freedom, due process, and equal protection which undergird many arguments in support of the selective conscientious objector. This point can be accepted even if one recognizes, as surely one must, the serious gaps between formal constitutional provisions and institutional realities. On the other hand, it is possible, without contradiction, to regard our law_2, or at least basic parts of it, as morally justified while regarding as morally unjustified some particular law_3, such as that which denies exemption from military service to the selective conscientious objector. One obvious reason why there is no contradiction here is that the relation of law_3 to law_2 is not a deductive one: at least our law_2 gives leeway for many different $laws_3$, none of which follow logically from the general framework set by our law_2.

Let us now look briefly at the relation between the selective conscientious objector and the civil disobedient. There are two main potential differences between them, one bearing on what they oppose, the other on how they carry out their opposition. While the civil disobedient, like the selective conscientious objector, is usually morally opposed to a particular law_3, the targets of his opposition may also be broader. They may extend from the whole law_2 of his society to certain official policies or $laws_3$ which he contends are basically illegal because unconstitutional. In the latter case, the civil disobedient, unlike the selective objector, holds that what he opposes is not a valid law_3 at all; familiar examples of this were the segregation ordinances in the South. To be sure, some selective objectors similarly criticized the conscription laws related to the Vietnam War on such grounds, maintaining that the war itself was unconstitutional because not declared by Congress. Still, the basic issues of selective conscientious objection go beyond this particular contention. Moreover, even when the civil disobedient's target is some particular law_3 which he admits to be valid, this may be something other than the law_3 bearing on military service in a particular war which is the specific target of the selective conscientious objector. Examples of these other $laws_3$ include ordinances requiring school attendance and setting school boundaries, income tax laws, eviction orders, civil rights laws, and many others.

In addition to these potential differences as to the laws or policies to which they are respectively opposed, the civil disobedient also differs from the selective conscientious objector with respect to the way in which he carries out his opposition. The civil disobedient, by definition, disobeys either the law to which he objects or some other law, but this is not necessarily true of the selective conscientious objector. The latter may, indeed, refuse the induction into the armed forces which he is legally obligated to accept. But unlike the civil disobedient, he may refrain from making a public issue of this refusal and of the grounds for it; he may also seek to evade the penalty by hiding, emigrating, or other nonpublic methods; and he may even, with a heavy heart, accept induction. Objection, then, may but need not go so far as disobedience; and when it does, it need not be civil in the sense of accepting the legally prescribed penalty.

Beside these differences in the objects and the methods of the respective protests of the civil disobedient and the selective conscientious objector, there is also frequently a difference in the main justificatory question which is raised about each of them. With respect to the civil disobedient, the main question raised is whether and when his disobedience is itself justified; it is usually taken for granted that the state will proceed to punish him, although recently the justification and degree of this punishment have also been discussed. With respect to the selective conscientious objector, on the other hand, the main question raised has been not whether he is justified in his objection to serving in the particular war he opposes and in carrying out his objection by refusing to serve, but whether the government and the law are justified in not exempting him from this requirement of military service. In other words, in the case of civil disobedience the main justificatory question bears on the protester himself, while in the case of selective conscientious objection the main justificatory question bears rather on the law's requirement about the protester. The chief reason for this difference is that, on the one hand, it is usually held that there is a *prima facie* obligation to obey the law, at least in a constitutional democracy, so that the civil disobedient's refusal to do so requires justification. But on the other hand, it is usually held, at least in our tradition, that conscientious objection to military service deserves respect because of the high value placed on the individual conscience, so that the law's failure to grant this objection is what requires justification. One result of this tradition, however, has been that the specific reasons or grounds for conscientious objection have received very little justificatory scrutiny on their own account. But in the case of the selective conscientious objector, it is precisely these reasons that assume central importance.

Hence, while recognizing that the claims of the civil disobedient, like those of the anarchist and the revolutionary, point to serious problems, I shall focus primarily on the specific issues raised by the selective conscientious objector in respect of a particular law_3. Our chief question, then, is this: even if there is a moral justification for the obligations set both by law_1, or law in general, and by our law_2, the American constitutional system, is there also a moral justification for the obligation set by the particular law_3 which requires that selective conscientious objectors not be exempted from military service? At the appropriate point, I shall also consider whether the objector is justified as to his reasons for opposing some particular war.

In order to cope with the issues posed by this question, we must distinguish four main variables that enter into the general area where some person conscientiously objects to performing some legally obligatory action. These variables are, first, the nature of the *action* which persons are legally obligated to perform, and which they object to performing; second, the *conscientiousness* of their objection; third, the *grounds or reasons* on which they base their objections to performing that action; and fourth, the *consequences* of whatever policies are followed in this area, including especially the consequences of legally granting the objection, that is, of legally allowing persons to be exempt from performing the actions which they are otherwise legally obligated to perform, where these consequences are of two main kinds: distributive, involving the distribution of various goods and evils among individual persons, and aggregative, involving the summing of goods or utilities for the society as a whole. I shall refer to these four variables, respectively, as the Action Variable, the Conscience Variable, the Reason Variable, and the Consequence Variable.

The dispute over selective conscientious objection most directly concerns the Action Variable. With respect to this variable, the question is: Is it morally justified that conscientious objectors be exempted from military service only if the actions they object to performing comprise *all* military acts, that is, all participation in war; or is it sufficient if the actions they object to performing comprise only *some* military acts, that is, participation only in some particular war or wars? I shall now develop my answer to this question by considering it within two distinct contexts, one relative or comparative, the other absolute.

II

The relative or comparative context involves the comparison of the selective conscientious objector with the universal conscientious objector. My point here is that if the universal conscientious objector's exemption from his legal obligation to perform military service is morally justified, then so too is the selective conscientious objector's exemption. All the grounds for exempting the former tell also in favor of exempting the latter.

In order to come to somewhat fuller grips with this thesis and with some of the controversial issues it raises, let us look at one of the chief arguments presented by persons who support the universal objector's exemption while opposing the selective objector's exemption. Justice Thurgood Marshall, speaking for the Court in the 1971 Gillette decision, cited the 1967 Report of the National Advisory Commission on Selective Service which opposed exempting the selective objector on the ground that "legal recognition of selective pacifism could open the doors to a general theory of selective disobedience to law, which could quickly tear down the fabric of government," and thus "jeopardize the binding quality of democratic decisions."[5] This argument, it will be noted, focuses on what I have called the Consequence Variable, i.e. on the consequences of exempting the selective objector from military service. And as can be seen from the argument's reference to a "general theory of selective disobedience to law," there is an implicit appeal here to a universalization principle. In terms of this principle, the argument may be stated as follows: If it is right that one person be exempted from some legal obligation on the ground that he is conscientiously opposed to fulfilling it, then it must be right that every other conscientious opponent be exempted on this ground. But if such general exemption from legal obligations were permitted, this would make it impossible to have a society regulated by law. For it is a necessary condition of such a society that laws have universal coercive force in the society, i.e. that all persons in the society be required to obey legal rules even when they conscientiously disapprove of them or oppose them, so long as the rules in question have been established as laws by the constitutionally prescribed procedures. Hence, to drop this requirement of obedience for certain individuals in the face of their conscientious opposition would mean that laws would no longer have universal coercive force: there would be only *selective* obedience to law, and hence also selective *disobedience*. But, the argument continues, this would mean that there would be no law

5. Report of the National Advisory Commission on Selective Service, *In Pursuit of Equity: Who Serves When Not All Serve?* (Washington, D.C.: U.S. Government Printing Office, 1967), p. 50; *United States v. Gillette*, 401 U.S. 459 (1971).

at all, since there would no longer remain the element of coerciveness, the requirement of obedience even in the face of vehement personal opposition or disapproval. But this would be anarchy. Consequently, it cannot be right that any person be exempted from his legal obligation on the ground that he is conscientiously opposed to fulfilling it. Therefore, the selective conscientious objector should not be exempted from his legal obligation to perform military service.

The usual replies given to this argument by proponents of exempting the selective conscientious objector comprise two main contentions. First, they point out that the argument tells just as much against the universal conscientious objector to military service as against the selective objector. For the universal objector also claims, and the conscription laws and the Supreme Court have upheld his claim, that he should be exempted from fulfilling a certain legal obligation—that of rendering military service—on the ground that he is conscientiously opposed to fulfilling it. Hence, those who present the universalization argument just cited ought logically to admit that the anarchic consequence they fear from exempting the selective conscientious objector applies just as much to the case of exempting the universal conscientious objector.

How can this contention be dealt with by persons who present the universalization argument? They can, and do, try to distinguish in various ways between the cases of the universal and the selective objector to military service, and this primarily in terms of further aspects of the Consequence Variable. They assert that it would be more difficult to administer fairly a provision exempting the selective objector than one exempting only the universal objector; that military morale would suffer much more if selective as well as universal objectors were exempted; and in general that many more persons would be exempted, thereby weakening much more the whole coercive structure of democratic law. Thus, with respect to the antecedent of the universalization argument as originally stated—"If it is right that one person be exempted from some legal obligation on the ground that he is conscientiously opposed to fulfilling it, . . ."—those who present the argument insist that the antecedent, in order to be cogent against the selective but not the universal objector, must be filled out in such a way as to take account of these differences, so that the argument must be stated somewhat as follows: If it is right that one person be exempted from some legal obligation on the ground that he is conscientiously opposed to fulfilling it, *and* if the exemption can be granted with no unfortunate consequences bearing on the difficulty of fairly administering the exemption, the lowering of military morale, and the weakening of the whole coercive structure of democratic law from an undue increase in the number of persons exempted, then it must be right that every other conscientious opponent be exempted on this ground *so long as* the unfortunate consequences just mentioned are not likely to ensue.

This attempt to distinguish between the cases of the universal and the selective conscientious objector focuses on important considerations, and must be taken seriously. But I think that, by and large, it does not succeed.[6] There is no reason to think that it would be more difficult to administer exemptions for the selective than for the universal objector, or that military morale would suffer, or that the number of persons exempted would be unduly increased. The example of Britain, which provides for selective exemptions, affords confirming evidence for this.[7] In addition, it must be noted that an increase in the number of persons exempted from the legal obligation of military service would not, strictly speaking, entail any increase in persons exempted from the coercive structure of democratic law. The assertion of this entailment rests on a confusion between law_3 and law_2. The selective objector's exemption from military service would be made by a particular law_3 which qualifies an antecedent law_3; but such qualification would itself be in accordance with law_2.

6. Thus I agree with David Malament's arguments in "Selective Conscientious Objection and the *Gillette* Decision," *Philosophy and Public Affairs*, I, 4 (Summer 1972). See also the valuable discussion of this question in Ralph Potter, "Conscientious Objection to Particular Wars," in Donald A. Gianella, *Religion and the Public Order*, No. 4 (Ithaca, N.Y.: Cornell University Press, 1968), pp. 92-95.

7. See Denis Hayes, *Challenge of Conscience: The Story of the Conscientious Objectors of 1939-1949* (London: George Allen & Unwin, 1949), ch. 5.

One point should be added, bearing on the difficulty of administering exemptions for selective objectors—and this concerns the Reason Variable. By comparison with the universal objector, the selective objector will often have more complex reasons for objecting to military service, based on his specific analyses of particular aspects of our foreign policy, including its history and purposes. These are usually subjects of intense political partisanship, and it may often be difficult for the members of a draft board to hear them out dispassionately. It is this point, among others, that leads opponents of exempting selective objectors to refer to the latter's reasons as being "political," as against "religious" or "moral." But there are at least two confusions in the way in which the Supreme Court has drawn this distinction between the political and the moral. First, it confuses the nature of the *subject-matter* in question—in this case, political or governmental policies and institutions—with the nature of the *judgments* that are made about that subject-matter—in this case, moral judgments. A judgment may be moral, or for that matter, religious, with respect to its motivation or the reasons on which it is based, bearing on considerations of justice and welfare, regardless of whether its subject-matter—that about which it judges—is political, social, or economic institutions, or individual actions, or many other things. In a parallel way, a judgment may be a political one in two quite different respects: first, with respect to the governmental subject-matter about which it makes a judgment; second, with respect to the personal motivations or reasons for which it is itself made. I can make a judgment about a political, i.e. governmental subject-matter without having a personal political motivation in that sense of 'political' in which it refers to partisan purposes of obtaining power or influence over other persons.

A second confusion in the Supreme Court's way of distinguishing between moral and political judgments bears on the interpretation it gives of the moral. The Court, influenced strongly by past traditions of universal objectors, seems to hold that for a judgment about the wrongness of war to be genuinely a moral one, it must be intuitionist or deontological in some very simple way. So soon as reasons for opposing war are introduced of a greater degree of complexity than "my church—or my conscience

—tells me it's wrong," the Court finds that the resulting judgments become political rather than moral. This ignores, of course,
the fact that a moral judgment may often be based on a careful
examination of facts bearing on the subject-matter which is
judged.

I conclude, then, that the opposition to selective exemption
which is based on the above universalization argument fails in
its attempt to dispose of the first reply given to the argument by
proponents of exempting selective conscientious objectors—the reply, namely, that the argument tells as much against the universal as against the selective conscientious objector. But this point,
far from leaving the selective objector in the clear so far as concerns the justification of his being exempted from military service, rather puts both him and the universal objector under the
anarchic suspicion emphasized by the above universalization argument. For the selective objector is now in the position of placing
both himself and the universal objector under the same principle:
that it is right that persons be exempted from fulfilling some legal obligation insofar as they are conscientiously opposed to fulfilling it. To ward off the potentially anarchic implication of this
principle, proponents of selective conscientious objection offer a
second reply, which focuses on the Action Variable—that is, the
specific kind of action which they are legally obligated to perform
and which they object to performing. They emphasize that there
is a drastic difference between the kinds of actions which the legal
obligation of military service requires and the kinds required by
other legal obligations, including the paying of taxes, the obeying
of civil rights laws, and so forth. Military service involves, at least
potentially, killing other persons. Nothing of comparable seriousness is involved in the actions required by other legal obligations.
Hence, the universalization argument fails, for it does not take
account of this decisive difference. Properly stated, the argument
should say: If it is right that one person be exempted—not from
some or any legal obligation to which he conscientiously objects,
but—from the legal obligation to perform military service with its
potential killing of other persons to which he conscientiously objects, then it must be right that every other conscientious oppo-

nent of performing military service be exempted. Since the exemptions from legal obligation which are here in question are limited in this way to military actions, they do not have the anarchic implications stressed by proponents of the above universalization argument.

This second reply to the universalization argument is sound, but it raises at least three difficulties for the selective objector. First, persons opposed to various other laws, such as civil rights laws, could argue, emphasizing both the Conscience and the Action Variables, that the actions which these laws require of them offend against their conscience as vehemently as military killing offends against the selective objector's conscience. The latter could perhaps answer this by holding that the issue concerns not merely the subjective impact of actions on conscience but rather the objective status of actions. However much racists, for example, are horrified by having to act in accordance with civil rights laws, their horror does not remove the fact that military killing is an infinitely more serious kind of action.

This point raises, however, a second difficulty for the selective objector. If military service involves potential killing, then it also involves potentially being killed. How fair is it, then, that some qualified persons be exempted from this danger while others are not? So far, this difficulty applies, of course, to the universal conscientious objector as well as to the selective objector. In addition, however, it has been held that to make exemptions from military service available to selective objectors would wrongly favor one stratum of the population over other strata, since it would introduce a serious "class bias." For only better-educated young men have the greater specific knowledge and perhaps greater articulateness that would be required in order to make good their claim to exemption on grounds of objecting to a particular war.[8] The implication here is that no comparable expertise or favorable cultural background enters into the exempting conditions for universal conscientious objectors. Now this consideration of fairness is indeed very important. But it applies in a

8. See Michael Walzer, *Obligations: Essays on Disobedience, War, and Citizenship* (New York: Simon and Schuster, 1971), pp. 142 ff.

parallel way to those universal objectors whose consciences have been formed under the influence of a particular religious up-bringing not available to other persons. In addition, improving the level of education in the country at large should serve to equalize the abilities relevant to arguing for exemption on grounds of objection to a particular war.

It still remains the case, however, that, by the admission of both the universal and the selective objector (as conveyed by their dis-tinction between killing and other actions), they seek exemption from a danger that goes beyond all others. The universal objector could, of course, meet this point by emphasizing his universal pacifism: he advocates that all military killing cease. The selective objector, however, does not have this way out—and this raises a third difficulty for him. For, unlike the universal objector, he does not object to all wars or to all military killing but only to such killing in certain wars to which he is opposed for moral rea-sons. Hence, he cannot make opposition to military killing as such the decisive factor in his claim to exemption from military service; this opposition figures only in combination with the rea-sons for which he objects to the particular war in question. It is this emphasis on more specific reasons which especially distin-guishes the selective from the universal objector. Hence, the Ac-tion Variable, bearing on the sort of legally obligatory action which he objects to performing, must here be supplemented by consideration of the Reason Variable.

III

It will be best to deal with this point in connection with my sec-ond context, the absolute one. I call this context absolute because it does not, like the relative or comparative context, focus pri-marily on comparing the cases of the selective and the universal objector; it is rather concerned directly with the moral justifiabil-ity of exempting the selective objector, especially as this is affected by the moral quality of the war to which he is opposed and of the reasons on which he bases his opposition. In this context, I shall consider two main alternatives: one where the war in question is morally wrong or unjust, the other where it is morally right or just.

It may be contended that these alternatives are too simple, because all wars involve many moral ambiguities, so that it is a matter of more or less rightness and wrongness, not all of one or all of the other. While there is much truth to this, the fact still remains that because of the violent impact of war on human life and liberty, any particular war is morally justified only if there is overwhelming evidence that the most basic rights of freedom and well-being will be jeopardized unless the war is undertaken. Any war for which such overwhelming evidence is not available is not morally justified. Thus, despite all its moral ambiguities, I should hold that World War II was a morally justified war, while on the same ground the Vietnam War was not morally justified.

This criterion of a war's being morally justified bears on the question of intended end, the sort of consideration invoked when one says, "The war is being fought in order to secure x," or "The purpose of the war is to secure x." I am aware of the great complexities which these simple locutions may obscure. There are such questions as: Whose purpose is it? How enlightened, factually and morally, is the reasoning which adopts this war as the means to this purpose? How likely is it that the war will secure x as against some quite different outcome? Should the moral quality of the war be evaluated by reference to the end intended by the ruling authorities or by reference to the probable outcome of the war, especially if these diverge sharply? In addition, where "x" consists, as in my above criterion, in protecting the most basic rights of freedom and well-being, there arise such questions as: Whose freedom and well-being? What if the freedom and well-being of only a small proportion of the inhabitants will be jeopardized? To what degree must they be jeopardized? What is, or must be, the relation between this jeopardy and the preservation of the state as such? How much evidence for such jeopardizing is required? This question of evidence raises the serious issue of who is to determine whether some particular war is morally wrong. If the official procedures of a democratic state are deemed inadequate for such determination, should the convictions of individual citizens be trusted more? The specter of anarchy again arises here.

In reply, I must reiterate the extreme seriousness of war and the consequent requirement that overwhelming evidence be supplied of its necessity to safeguard basic freedom and well-being. This evidence must be intellectually sound, and objective means must be provided for checking this soundness, so that propaganda may be differentiated from fact.

All these questions bear on the crucial relation invoked by the selective conscientious objector: the relation between the moral quality of a particular war, evaluated as suggested above, and his reasons for opposing that war. In order to understand this relation in the present context, we must give further consideration to the connection between the Conscience Variable and the Reason Variable. Originally, the conscription law required that in order to be exempted from military service a conscientious objector had to base his objection on a specific kind of reason, namely, that he was a member of a recognized church or religious sect which explicitly prohibited any resort to physical violence against other persons. This requirement as to the reason for objection was progressively broadened by court decisions so as to consist, first, in belief in God, then in belief in a Supreme Being, then in religious belief, then in "a sincere and meaningful belief which occupies in the life of its possessor a place parallel to that filled by the God of those admittedly qualifying for the exemption . . . ;"[9] and finally, in the 1970 Welsh decision, the Supreme Court held that one's reason for objecting to military service could consist in "deeply and sincerely [held] beliefs that are purely ethical or moral in source and content but that nevertheless impose upon [the individual] a duty of conscience to refrain from participating in any war at any time. . . ."[10]

It is important to note one point about this broadening of the reasons or grounds which conscientious objectors may successfully adduce in claiming exemption from military service. Although the Welsh decision characterizes the exempting beliefs or reasons

9. *United States v. Seeger*, 380 U.S. 176 (1965).
10. *United States v. Welsh*, 398 U.S. 340 (1970).

by the words "purely ethical or moral in source and content," it lays down no specifications as to what that content must consist in, other than an opposition to participating in any war. In particular, normative considerations as to the truth or falsity, or the moral rightness or wrongness, of the objector's beliefs have been explicitly disavowed as a basis for exempting the conscientious objector from military service. As Justice Clark put it in the Seeger decision: "The validity of what he believes cannot be questioned . . . the 'truth' of a belief is not open to question. . . ."[11] This was reiterated by Justice Black in the Welsh decision when he wrote that " 'intensely personal' convictions which some might find 'incomprehensible' or 'incorrect' come within the meaning of 'religious belief' in the Act."[12] On the other hand, Justice Marshall in rejecting the selective objector's exemption in the *Gillette* case, wrote that "under the petitioners' unarticulated scheme for exemption, an objector's claim to exemption . . . might be predicated on a view of the facts that most would regard as mistaken."[13] But Marshall then went on to repeat the words of Clark that "the 'truth' of a belief is not open to question. . . ."

What this means, then, is that exemption from military service is in no way to be affected by the question of the validity or correctness of the Reason Variable, that is, of the factual or moral beliefs which constitute one's grounds or reasons for conscientiously objecting to military service. Indeed, the Reason Variable as having a content distinct from the Conscience Variable has been given up as a requirement for exemption. The only requirement, in addition to an opposition to participating in any war, is that this opposition, whatever the beliefs or reasons on which it is based, must be conscientious. This latter requirement, bearing on what I have called the Conscience Variable, was enunciated by the Supreme Court in what seem to be primarily psychological terms: the emphasis is on the intensity and sincerity with which beliefs are held and on the way in which these beliefs

11. *United States v. Seeger*, 380 U.S. 184, 185.
12. *United States v. Welsh*, 398 U.S. 339.
13. *United States v. Gillette*, 401 U.S. 456-457.

function in the objector's life. Thus the Welsh decision puts the requirement as involving that the individual "deeply and sincerely holds" his beliefs; it says the decisive question "is whether these beliefs play the role of a religion and function as a religion in the registrant's life"; it asserts that the relevant section of the draft law "exempts from military service all those whose consciences, spurred by deeply held moral, ethical, or religious beliefs, would give them no rest or peace if they allowed themselves to become a part of an instrument of war."[14] In his concurrence, Justice Harlan said: "The common denominator must be the intensity of moral conviction with which a belief is held."[15]

This development, in which the requirement of a specific religious content has been dropped, a concern with validity or truth has been disavowed, and a purely psychological requirement has been substituted, has usually been hailed as a strong move in the direction of libertarian enlightenment; and I agree that in many important respects it is. But it has implications which are potentially quite serious for the issue of the moral justifiability of exempting the selective conscientious objector from military service. The point emerges clearly in connection with my absolute context. For this context, like the selective objector himself, views the moral justifiability of exempting him from military service in terms of reasons which determine whether the war in which he is asked to fight is morally right or morally wrong. Thus, where the selective objector emphasizes not only the Conscience Variable but also the Reason Variable as a distinct normative consideration justifying his opposition to a particular war, the Supreme Court emphasizes only the Conscience Variable. Moreover, the selective objector, unlike the Supreme Court, does not have a purely psychological conception of a belief's being a moral one. On the contrary, the objector distinguishes between the moral rightness and the moral wrongness of beliefs, actions, and policies, including wars, in terms of reasons bearing on certain specific contents of each of these. To put it otherwise, for the selective objector moral utterances have not only illocutionary

14. 398 U.S. 339 ff.
15. *Ibid.* 358.

force and perlocutionary effects; they have also certain specific criteria of application which determine for him whether he will apply the words 'morally right' and 'morally wrong' to various objects. But this criterial or objective aspect of moral words is completely rejected in the Supreme Court's test for conscientious objectors because it merges the Reason Variable into the Conscience Variable.[16]

This means that my absolute context, like the selective objector himself, focuses on a variable which is omitted from the Supreme Court's doctrine, namely, the Reason Variable. I shall now go on to consider the two alternatives of my absolute context with due consideration for this variable.

The first alternative is where some particular war is morally wrong, in that the purpose for which it is being fought, as established by the most adequate available evidence, is not to protect basic rights of freedom and well-being but rather to promote national aggrandizement or some similar objective. The thesis I wish to present here is that in such a case it is morally justified that everyone refrain from participating in the war, and *a fortiori* that the selective conscientious objector be exempted from participating in it. I am aware of the problems raised by this position: the war may have been voted for by constitutional democratic procedures, the conscription machinery may be set up by legal processes, and so forth. Nevertheless, as we saw above, the fact that there is a just law$_2$, i.e. a just constitutional system, does

16. This rejection may in fact be less complete than the Court's explicit statements suggest. The Court seems implicitly to incorporate into the meaning or criteria of "religious" and "ethical" or "moral" various conceptions of universalist beneficence, as against their opposites. See, for example, the passage from *Berman v. United States,* 156 F. 2d 381 cited in the Seeger decision: "Surely a scheme of life designed to obviate [man's inhumanity to man], and by removing temptations, and all the allurements of ambition and avarice, to nurture the virtues of unselfishness, patience, love, and service, ought not to be denounced as not pertaining to religion when its devotees regard it as an essential tenet of their religious faith" (380 U.S. 184). See also the passages from letters by Seeger and Welsh cited in the Welsh decision (398 U.S. 338, 342, 343). Nevertheless, directly after citing the passage from the Berman case, Justice Clark went on to say: "The validity of what he believes cannot be questioned . . . the 'truth' of a belief is not open to question. . . ."

not entail that all the particular laws₃ made in accordance with that system or law₂ are themselves morally right or just. Now in the case of many morally wrong laws₃ made within a morally right law₂, such as the Prohibition amendment or the income tax laws with their loopholes for the very rich, it may be expedient to obey them for various familiar reasons. But in the case of something as profoundly serious as war, such expediency is overridden because of its drastic impact on basic rights of life and liberty.

The relation of the selective conscientious objector to a morally wrong war is hence of two convergent sorts. Simply as a citizen of the nation engaged in the war, his participation therein is not morally justified. But in addition, since he opposes participating in the war for the reason that the war is morally wrong, and since the war is indeed morally wrong, the selective objector's reasons for claiming exemption from military service are morally correct ones, while the reasons of those who oppose his exemption and who support the war are morally incorrect. The moral rightness of his reasons for refusing to participate hence reinforces the moral rightness of his refusal to participate.

IV

I turn now to the second alternative of my absolute context, where a particular war is morally right in that it is fought in order to protect basic rights of freedom and well-being. Since the selective conscientious objector refuses to participate in the war on the ground that it is morally wrong, this means that he is mistaken so far as concerns his reasons. What we have here, then, is the problem which Aquinas and other scholastics referred to as the "erroneous conscience."[17] It may seem obvious that the selective objector's position here cannot be morally justified, on the principle that it cannot be morally right to oppose what is mor-

17. See Thomas Aquinas, *Summa Theologica*, II, I, qu. 19, art. 5-6. For a recent discussion, see Eric D'Arcy, *Conscience and Its Right to Freedom* (London: Sheed and Ward, 1961). Justice Douglas referred to the concept of the "erroneous conscience" in his dissent from the *Gillette* decision, 401 U.S. 471, n. 5.

ally right. Whatever be the case as to the soundness of this simple principle in general, however, it fails to take account of the specific sort of opposition which is in question. One may, for example, oppose assisting in the implementation of a morally right end because one regards the means of implementation as morally wrong. In the case of the selective conscientious objector, the simple principle may lead one to ignore the specific nature of his reasons for opposing the war and the relation of these reasons to his own moral character. Two possible aspects of these reasons must be distinguished, one empirically factual, the other moral. The selective objector may oppose a morally justified war because he is mistaken about certain empirical facts; he may think, for example, that the war is being fought in order to suppress further some submerged people (a purpose which he correctly holds to be morally wrong), although it is in fact being fought for the opposite purpose. On the other hand, he may oppose the war because he upholds a morally wrong principle; he may, for example, be a racist who holds that the enslavement of black persons is morally justified (and he holds the correct empirical belief that the war is being fought in order to prevent the enslavement of blacks). Now if the objector's opposition to the war is based, as in the first situation, on a reason which is factually false but morally right or at least neutral, then it may still be correctly said that he is here morally good (in respect of his moral character) even though his acts of opposition are morally wrong (in respect of their objective relation to the principles of moral rightness). If, however, the selective objector's opposition to the war is based, as in the second situation, on a reason which is itself morally wrong, then it is the case both that he is morally bad and that his acts of opposition are morally wrong. The moral quality of the selective objector's opposition to the war is hence affected by the quality of his reasons for opposing it.

There are, of course, further possible alternatives here. At one extreme, the selective conscientious objector may be constitutionally incapable of making a morally correct judgment about the war. At the other extreme, he may deliberately uphold a morally wrong principle while knowing or believing that it is morally wrong. Such cases of moral imbecilism and moral monsterism may, however, be ignored for present purposes. We are here concerned primarily with cases where a selective conscientious objector opposes a morally right war for morally wrong reasons, where he believes that what is morally right is in fact morally wrong and where he is nevertheless capable of distinguishing between the two. The question is: What bearing does his morally wrong opposition to the war have on the moral justifiability of exempting him from participating in it?

This question is affected by the distinction drawn by many moral philosophers between "subjective" and "objective" duty. The selective objector sincerely believes, on the basis of certain reasons, that he ought not to fight in some particular war. Now on the subjective conception of duty, a person really ought to do or not do what he believes he ought to do or not do; hence, on this conception, the objector really ought not to fight in the particular war to which he objects. And since a necessary condition of the fulfillment of this "ought not" is that his request for an exemption from military service be granted, it follows that he really ought to be granted the exemption he requests. On the other hand, his opposition to fighting in the war may really be morally wrong, because his reasons may be either factually false or morally wrong or both. But to admit this about his reasons is to admit that what he believes he ought to do is not conclusive as to what he really ought to do. Hence, his belief that he ought not to participate in the war in question may be mistaken, so that it may be wrong to grant him the exemption he requests.

In order to cut across some of these complexities, I shall here consider primarily the sort of situation where a particular war is morally right and a selective objector's reason for not participating in it is morally wrong. This sort of situation has received almost no attention in the literature[18] by comparison with the situations where a selective objector opposes a morally wrong

18. See the brief discussions by Geoffrey C. Hazard, Jr., and John de J. Pemberton, Jr., in Sol Tax, ed., *The Draft* (Chicago: University of Chicago Press, 1967), pp. 292, 316, 326; and by John Courtney Murray and Paul Ramsey in Finn, *op. cit.*, pp. 29-30, 33, 37-38, 56-57.

war for morally right reasons, probably because the latter situations are much more frequent. Nevertheless, the former situation raises important questions which deserve consideration both for their own sakes and because they should help us to understand the general merits of exempting selective conscientious objectors from military service.

As an example of such a situation let us suppose that some selective conscientious objector is an anti-black racist, and that his nation, through one of those developments of which history affords some parallels, is undertaking to fight a war to prevent the enslavement of blacks by a potentially invading racist power. Such cases may seem far-fetched, but an understanding of the issues must take account of such hypothetical cases. Nor are they all that hypothetical: during World War II many British Fascists, for example, became selective conscientious objectors who objected specifically, on grounds of conscience, to fighting against the Axis powers.[19] Certain other objections to this example must also be rejected, such as that no racist could have a conscience or could hold his beliefs in the conscientious way required by the conscription law; or that no moral belief, by definition, could be a racist one; or that a racist couldn't possibly be an objector to military service because racism is necessarily connected with militarism, not with anti-militarism; or that the issue of racists who are selective conscientious objectors applies just as much against racists who are universal conscientious objectors. These contentions must be rejected, because racists may indeed have consciences and be quite conscientious and even "fanatical";[20] racism cannot be excluded from being a moral belief unless we define 'moral' in a way different from the Supreme Court, and if we do, there still remains the problem of the racist's conscience;

19. See Hayes, *op. cit.*, p. 52.
20. See, for example, Hannah Arendt's description of Adolf Eichmann: "as for his conscience, he remembered perfectly well that he would have had a bad conscience only if he had not done what he had been ordered to do—to ship millions of men, women, and children to their death with great zeal and the most meticulous care" (*Eichmann in Jerusalem* (New York: Viking Press, 1963), p. 22).

racists may oppose militarism when they regard it as aiding groups they regard as racially inferior, as for example in the integrated Army of the United States after World War II. As for the contention that universal conscientious objectors may be racists, this important difference must be noted: a universal objector could not logically uphold his opposition to all wars on racist grounds, since some wars have been fought for racist purposes.

The question to be considered, then, is whether a selective conscientious objector who opposes a morally justified war for morally wrong reasons ought to be exempted from participating in the war. What is crucially involved here is the relation between the Conscience Variable and the Reason Variable. One frequently upheld libertarian position is that the Conscience Variable should alone be decisive: if someone conscientiously objects to participating in some war, then he ought to be exempted from participating in it, regardless of the specific content of his reasons for objecting to it, and regardless also of the consequences of granting the objection. His reasons might still be considered, but only as a clue to his conscientiousness, not with regard to their objective rightness or wrongness. On this position, absolute value must be attributed to effective freedom of conscience, including the ability to refrain from doing what one sincerely opposes doing, especially in so serious a matter as military action.

An opposed position on this question focuses on the Reason Variable, and this from two interrelated viewpoints. One viewpoint confines itself to the objector's own giving of reasons. In giving these reasons, the objector's attitude is that of a person who is willing and indeed anxious to engage in a rational dialogue about the objective rightness or wrongness of the war in question. The objector himself thus invokes not only the Conscience Variable but also, more basically, the Reason Variable: he claims that he should be exempted from his legal obligation to perform military service not only because he is conscientiously opposed to performing it but also because his conscientious opposition is based on valid, indeed conclusive, reasons bearing on the moral wrongness of the particular war in which he is legally obligated to fight. He hence makes a claim which purports to be based on the objective merits of the case, and not only on the depth, sincerity, or intensity of his convictions. Now if, as in the libertarian position, one considers only the Conscience Variable in deciding the question of exemption and ignores the Reason Variable, then one ignores the crucial basis of the objector's claim as he himself envisages it. In effect, he is told that although he bases his claim on a certain reason, and although he has engaged, or wishes to engage, in a dialogue with the government on the basis of that reason, the government has no concern with his reason or with participating in this dialogue. In this perspective, the government's exempting the objector from military service is, in an important sense, not an act of respect for him or for his convictions, since it ignores the chief basis for which he here claims to deserve respect, namely, the specific reasoned content of his convictions.

A second viewpoint focuses on the Reason Variable in terms of the objective merits of its specific content as involving a dialogue which seeks to attain the truth about the moral quality of the war and hence of participation in it. Consider again the objector's claim, now formulated as follows: "I ought to be exempted from participating in this war because it has a certain empirical quality (EQ), and whatever has EQ is morally wrong." Let us assume that the "because" here signifies both necessary and sufficient conditions, and let us also suppose, in accordance with my above example, that the "EQ" here in question consists in fighting to prevent the enslavement of black persons. The objector's claim may hence be reformulated as follows: "If I ought to be exempted from participating in this war, then fighting to prevent the enslavement of blacks is morally wrong." Now for the government to exempt this objector would be for it to accept his antecedent but not his consequent. But insofar as the objector's claim is taken seriously in its own terms, his antecedent should not be accepted, since what he holds it to imply is false. For in his claim as formulated, the falsity of the consequent entails the falsity of the antecedent, so that, in terms of the rational debate which the objector invokes when he gives reasons for opposing the particular war as morally wrong, he must be held to lose the debate. Hence, his claim to exemption must, to this extent, be rejected.

What emerges from the considerations thus far is that to make the Conscience Variable decisive is to hold that the racist selective conscientious objector should be exempted from military service, while to make the Reason Variable decisive is to hold the opposite position. It must be kept in mind, however, that "reason" as so far used has been confined primarily to the objector's own grounds for refusing to participate in a war. Now a person's reasons for believing or doing something may not be rational in the sense of rationally justified; they may not be such as would be acquired by a right use of reason, in that they contain either empirically false but corrigible beliefs or morally wrong principles or judgments which are inconsistent, arbitrary, or otherwise irrational. Hence, in order to ascertain what is rationally justified with respect to the selective objector's exemption, we must go beyond the terms set by his own claims, where he has made the rightness of exempting him depend on the judgment that it is wrong to oppose the enslavement of blacks. Even if, within the racist objector's own terms of rational debate, he must be held to have lost the debate because his judgment is wrong, his terms should not necessarily be the determining ones, since they must themselves be evaluated by broader criteria: factual ones of truth and moral ones of equal freedom and well-being.

Let us consider from John Stuart Mill three points which at least partially embody such relevant criteria. First, the moral wrongness of one's beliefs, such as racist beliefs, should not tell at all against one's freedom to express them. Second, however, insofar as one's beliefs are morally wrong, especially in their bearing on the rights and well-being of other persons, one should not have the freedom to act on them; for example, one should not be free to act out one's racist beliefs in such spheres as enslavement, killing, removal of voting rights, discrimination in public accommodations, and so forth. Now the racist conscientious objector of my above example does not merely claim the right to express his beliefs; nor does he, *qua* objector, necessarily claim the right to act out his beliefs in the positive sense of acting to achieve the blacks' enslavement. Rather, he claims the right to refrain from acting toward the achievement of a condition opposed to his beliefs: he opposes participating in a war to help prevent racist oppression. This, then, is Mill's third point: such refraining is unjustified because it shirks a positive duty:

> There are also many positive acts for the benefit of others, which he may rightfully be compelled to perform; such as to give evidence in a court of justice; to bear his fair share in the common defense, or in any other joint work necessary to the interest of the society of which he enjoys the protection; and to perform certain acts of individual beneficence, such as saving a fellow-creature's life, or interposing to protect the defenseless against ill-usage, things which whenever it is obviously a man's duty to do, he may rightfully be made responsible to society for not doing.[21]

If we were to apply Mill's point to the question of the selective objector, we should have to conclude that exempting him from military service is morally unjustified because he would thereby be permitted to refrain from bearing "his fair share in the common defense" or from "interposing to protect the defenseless against ill-usage." It must be noted, however, that in speaking here of "acts of *individual* beneficence," Mill was not dealing with the broader social-institutional context in which the question of the racist selective objector arises. Nor did he here give any independent consideration to either the Conscience Variable or the Action Variable: the fact that some persons object on grounds of conscience to killing for a cause which they believe to be morally wrong.

Consideration of these variables would strongly affect the question of fairness. We saw earlier that this question may be formulated in at least two ways: (a) Is it fair that some qualified persons be exempted from the danger of being killed in war while

---

21. *On Liberty,* Ch. 1 (Everyman's Library ed., p. 74). Later in the same paragraph Mill writes that under certain circumstances which "preclude the enforcement of responsibility, the conscience of the agent himself should step into the vacant judgment seat. . . ." This does not, however, affect the present argument.

others are not? (b) Is it fair that better-educated persons have legally available to them a basis for exemption from military service (through their selective opposition to a particular war) when less well-educated persons cannot take equal advantage of this basis? As with all appeals to fairness, the crucial factor is the criterion of what one takes to be the relevant quality of the persons between whom one is asked to judge fairly. Now if we take this criterion from the Action and Conscience Variables, then the question of fairness would have to be put as follows: Is it fair that some persons be made to violate their consciences in the most drastic way possible—by being required to kill other persons for a cause they deeply believe to be morally wrong—when other persons are not thus made to violate their consciences? To put the question in this way is to reemphasize the principle of freedom of conscience indicated by the Conscience Variable—the same principle as the general policy of exempting universal conscientious objectors is designed to respect.

Such freedom is, indeed, a determinative even if not a conclusive principle of the rightness of social policy. To call it "determinative" is to say that when a question affecting it arises, it should determine what social policy should be; but it is not conclusive in that it may be overridden by other principles. As my above discussions have suggested, considerations of fairness may point in either direction: both toward exempting and not exempting the selective objector. But the policy upheld by consideration of the Conscience Variable is reinforced by further considerations deriving from the Consequence Variable. It would be dangerous to let members of draft boards pass on the moral rightness or wrongness of an objector's reasons for opposing some particular war (as against judging the conscientiousness of his objections), for this would open the door to penalizing other men for unorthodox opinions. In addition, it would do the war effort no good, and might do it harm, to have in the armed forces men who are vehemently in disagreement with its aims on grounds of conscience. Alternative modes of service could be provided which would remove the extremity of potential killing which the Action Variable emphasized.

If exempting the racist objector would prove harmful to carrying out the morally right aims of the sort of war mentioned above, then the exemption would not be morally justified. But if, as seems likely, there would not be such harm, then exempting him is morally justified on grounds of respect for freedom of individual conscience. Note, then, that I am not ascribing absolute value to conscience, since its content may be morally wrong in a very drastic way. But the effective freedom of the depth of feeling and belief which it represents is a value which deserves respect if that respect can be given without endangering policies and institutions which are morally right.

It may be helpful if I now summarize the main conclusions of this essay, although, as I have tried to emphasize, the relation of the Reason Variable to the other three variables involves many complexities. I have here argued for three main conclusions. First, if one supports the universal conscientious objector's exemption from military service, then one does not have adequate grounds for opposing the selective conscientious objector's exemption. Second, where the selective objector's reasons for claiming exemption from military service are morally right, in that the war he opposes is morally wrong, it is morally justified that he and all other persons be exempted from supporting the war. Third, where the selective objector's reasons for claiming exemption from military service are morally wrong, in that the war he opposes is morally right, it is still probably justified that he be given the exemption he seeks, although alternative service should perhaps be required. In connection with all three of these conclusions, but especially the last two, justified resolution of the problem requires consideration not only of the selective objector's conscientious convictions but also of the validity or justification of the reasons on which he bases these convictions.

Two
CIVILIZING THE NATION-STATE

Introduction

In discussions of foreign policy not long ago, the predominant view seemed to be that the domains of morality and of international affairs were so far apart they should not be imagined to overlap. Morality, it was said, concerned an ideal realm; perhaps we could discuss ways of approaching it within the nation-state, or whether it was reflected in domestic law, but in the area of the relations between states, morality was out of place, for foreign policy was and ought to be the servant of national interest. In the classic statement of a leading scholar-architect of American foreign policy, George Kennan, "I see the most serious fault of our past formulation to lie in . . . the carrying over into the affairs of states of the concepts of right and wrong, the assumption that state behavior is a fit subject for moral judgment."* Empirical investigation was thus seen as the only appropriate approach to the study of foreign policy, for nations, it was thought, either do of necessity act only on grounds of self-interest in pursuit of power and its balance, or, if they do not, their leaders are deluded and misguided, bringing about with their moralistic intentions more harm than good.

By now, it is not only a very few critics who decry the immorality of recent American foreign policy, and hence the amorality of many approaches to it. That the behavior of states is a fit subject

---

* George F. Kennan, *American Diplomacy 1900-1950*. (Chicago: Univ. of Chicago Press, 1951) pp. 95-100.

for moral judgment is now widely acknowledged, and yet it is not forgotten that a morality which has no applicability to the factual realities and painful choices confronting statesmen and citizens is an inadequate morality.

In the articles that follow, attempts are made to consider some principles or rules of international behavior which could be both morally acceptable and legally and politically workable. Richard Falk examines whether the recognition of the responsibility of citizens to resist the performance of immoral actions by their governments is more important than the punishment of what could be thought of as international criminals. He considers what the appropriate response may be to American actions in Vietnam, and discusses the advisability of the adoption of an Ecocide Convention. Stanley French and Andres Gutman consider the grounds on which claims for the rights of nations to self-determination should be based.

Finally, Beverly Woodward explores the possibility and possible advisability of a transformation of the existing international anarchy into a rule of law. She takes up the troublesome questions of when and how coercion may be justifiable to bring about and to enforce international law. Considering our concepts of reason, violence, and law, she tries to reconcile the requirements of morality with the need for effective international order, and suggests guidelines for alternative institutions through which reasonable persons may try to bring about a less violent world.

5

Ecocide, Genocide, and the Nuremberg Tradition of Individual Responsibility

RICHARD A. FALK

The issue of ecocide was first raised by Arthur Galston, a biologist, at a Congressional Conference on War and National Responsibility in 1970. In Professor Galston's words:

> After World War II, and as a result of the Nuremberg trials, we justly condemned the willful destruction of an entire people and its culture, calling this crime against humanity *genocide*. It seems to be that the willful and permanent destruction of environment in which a people can live in a manner of their own choosing ought similarly to be considered a crime against humanity, to be designated by the term *ecocide* [Knoll, p. 71].

Would it be beneficial to proceed along these lines and urge the adoption of an Ecocide Convention parallel to the Genocide Convention? (For a draft outline of such a proposal see Falk, 1973.) I would like to argue in this essay in favor of the adoption of an Ecocide Convention on the basis of a reappraisal of the status of genocide as a crime, and the Nuremberg tradition as a corpus of law bearing on individual responsibility.

I

WHAT IS GENOCIDE? HAS THE UNITED STATES GOVERNMENT COMMITTED GENOCIDE IN INDOCHINA?

In the latter stages of the Indochina War there has been an increasing disposition by critics of American involvement to consider the indiscriminateness and magnitude of destruction inflicted

on the peoples of Vietnam, Laos, and Cambodia as "genocidal."
Some more juridically inclined observers have questioned this
usage, contending that some elements of the crime are not
present, either because American policy-makers have not *intended* the extinction of the ethnic components of Indochina or
because genocide presupposes a policy aimed at eliminating an
entire ethnic group. (See H. A. Bedau, the first essay in this volume.)

Louis Pollack, a former Dean of the Yale Law School, writes:

> I don't find it very useful to talk about those alleged offenses as
> genocide. We have nothing that indicates the definition of that of-
> fense has been met. The offenses in Vietnam do not seem to have
> been as eloquent, if I may put it rather grimly, as that. They
> would appear to have been offenses against people who were not
> regarded as human at all, rather than against people whom there
> was an attempt to destroy in whole or in part. I doubt if we have
> crimes of genocide, but undoubtedly we have crimes of murder
> and violations of the rules of war which are treatable by courts
> [Knoll, p. 43].

The decisive criterion for Pollack, apparently, is whether the
agents of the offenses are properly indictable in a duly constituted court for the crime of genocide, and they are not, in his
view, because there has been no systematic effort to eliminate the
Vietnamese people comparable, say, to the Nazi "final solution"
vis-à-vis the Jews. An important interpretative issue is the extent
to which the crime of genocide should be delimited by reference
back to the characteristics of "the final solution," in which event
genocide would normally involve an *international* enterprise designed to eliminate an *entire* ethnic group.

In contrast, Jean-Paul Sartre, on behalf of the Bertrand Russell International War Crimes Tribunal, approaches the identifi-
cation of genocide in a different manner:

> . . . the Americans are ingeniously formulating, without appear-
> ing to do so, a demand the Vietnamese cannot satisfy. They do
> offer an alternative: Declare you are beaten or we will bomb you

back to the stone age. But the fact remains that the second term of this alternative is genocide. They have said: "genocide, yes, but conditional genocide." Is this juridically valid? Is it ever conceivable? . . . the 1948 Convention leaves no such loopholes: an act of genocide, especially if carried on over a period of several years, is no less genocide for being blackmail. The perpetrator may declare he will stop if the victim gives in; this is still—without any juridical doubt whatsoever—a genocide [Sartre, 72f].

Sartre adds that the tactics of war employed by the United States in South Vietnam—"villages burned, the populace subjected to massive bombing, livestock shot, vegetation destroyed by defoliants, crops ruined by toxic aerosols, and everywhere indiscriminate shooting, murder, rape and looting"—are "genocide in the strictest sense: massive extermination" (Sartre, 73). But Sartre's main contention is that America's war policy is genocidal in the sense that it cannot succeed unless the people of the country as a whole are threatened with destruction; allegedly the United States waged war on this basis. Hence, genocide occurs even in the absence of a conscious design to eliminate the people of Vietnam; the inherent tendency of military tactics in a large-scale counter-insurgency warfare is to focus destruction on the civilian sector; high-technology cost-effective weaponry tends toward genocide because the people *qua* people (rather than *qua* soldiers) become the principal victims, and such a counter-insurgency cannot expect to succeed against a popular and determined insurgency unless the *threat* of destruction is both indiscriminate and total in character.

The contrast between the views of Pollack and Sartre presents fundamental issues in terms of juridical versus political conceptions of war crimes, as well as differing images of judicial function. It is impossible to resolve these inconsistent inferences as to whether American policies in Indochina amount to genocide by deciding which approach is "correct." Both judgments are essentially correct if appropriate preconditions are specified in relation to legal definition and judicial function. The controversy is important, however, as it goes to the heart of the matter of whether, and in what respects, it is useful to characterize the cumulative effects of American war policy in Indochina as "genocide" and whether the extension of the genocide approach to a related class of war policies identified as "ecocide" would be beneficial.

In my view, the genocide debate has not adequately distinguished between two basic orientations toward crime:

1. *The Indictment Model:* A conception of crime based on the plausibility of indictment and prosecution of individual perpetrators before a duly constituted court of law operating according to due process and adhering to strict rules of evidence.

2. *The Responsibility Model*[1]: A conception of crime based on the community's obligation to repudiate certain forms of governmental behavior and the consequent responsibility of individuals and groups to resist policies involving this behavior.

In my view, allegations of genocide arising out of the Indochina War might not, depending on complicated issues of treaty and fact interpretation, be sustained by impartial assessors in relation to the Indictment Model, but they have been clearly sustained in relation to the Responsibility Model. Professor Bedau develops a strong argument, it seems to me, for rejecting the allegation of genocide by application of the Indictment Model, although I believe a contrary case could also be as persuasively made by reliance on a different but equally plausible construction of the requirement of specific intent as an element of the crime of genocide.[2] The Indictment Model is concerned, as Sartre also seems to be in the Russell proceedings, with the apprehension and punishment of the principal perpetrators of the crime, i.e. with the architects of the policy who are the top government

1. It is worth noticing that the Indictment Model applies only to the direct perpetrators in the field or the policy-makers high up in the chain of civilian and military command, whereas the Responsibility Model applies potentially to all of humanity, i.e. to anyone whose sense of responsibility is activated by crimes of war. Citizens may have a special "patriotic" responsibility in relation to criminal deviance by their own government.

2. In my view, the legislative history of the requirement of specific intent is neither as clear nor as decisive as Professor Bedau suggests. A duly constituted tribunal, even operating under a canon of strict construction, has a reasonable basis for regarding intent requirements as satisfied if they are accepted as true allegations of indiscriminate destruction of Indochina.

rulers. Sartre is partly arguing, in effect, that high American officials ought to be indicted for genocide in a duly constituted tribunal given the findings of fact and law. Such a conception of "crime" purports to be focused upon ideas of punishment, sanction, effectiveness, although it may also influence patterns of intergovernmental communication, providing governments or international institutions with an acceptable basis for protest, condemnation, or censure. However, the main potential of such a private proceeding is to activate popular opposition to the war by condemning its perpetrators as criminals and implicitly appealing to citizens of conscience everywhere to resist by whatever means are at their disposal. Therefore, although the non-governmental tribunal of the Russell proceedings relied upon the symbolism of the Indictment Model, its real mission and accomplishment is better understood by reference to the Responsibility Model. This mission was harmed, according to many observers who were critical of its format, because it distorted the Indictment Model by carrying the *ex parte* character of the World War II trials to a further extreme. Of course, such criticism probably also partially stemmed from the anarchist features of a tribunal convened without any official mandate by private individuals to prosecute government officials and policy, as well as from the radical identity of its participants and the hostility of mainstream political opinion to even raising the war crimes issue in the Indochina context.

The Responsibility Model is directed toward stimulating populist sentiments and encouraging decentralized assumptions of responsibility to oppose criminal behavior. The purpose of characterizing behavior as "genocidal" is to associate a set of war policies with something of exceptional evil that people of good will should discern and oppose. Even Frances FitzGerald, who explains American failures in Indochina in a deliberately low-keyed and detached fashion, makes reference to genocide:

No one in the American government consciously planned a policy of genocide. The American military commanders would have been shocked or angered by such a charge, but in fact their course of action was indistinguishable from it [FitzGerald, p. 373].

It remains somewhat obscure whether a "course of action" that was "indistinguishable" from genocide is indeed an instance of genocide in the technical sense, required to satisfy the Indictment Model. There is no doubt, however, that FitzGerald's usage reflected her awareness of the symbolic potency of genocide as a means of passing decisive moral judgment on American war policies in Indochina.

My main point is that the principal validity of the war crimes notion, given the present international setting, arises from its relevance to the Responsibility Model. Hence, characterizations of American policies in Indochina as "genocidal" are appropriate provided the factual allegations are generally accurate—massive, indiscriminate destruction of civilian populations as a central feature of war strategy designed to defeat a popularly based revolutionary movement. In other words, not everything tragic in war is properly characterized as "genocidal" under the Responsibility Model. For instance, if civilians are victims of a war strategy in which the principal objective is to destroy the military capabilities of the adversary, then it is misleading to regard the war as genocidal. It may also be the case, although it requires detailed inquiry, that the technology and doctrine of modern warfare is *inherently* genocidal in the sense that its inevitable tendency is to inflict disproportionate harm on the civilian sector of the enemy society. The counterinsurgency context of Indochina is one context where the application of high-technology weaponry seems inevitably to produce results that satisfy the tests for genocide appropriate for the Responsibility Model. The main strategic context of nuclear deterrence also seems to rest directly and inevitably on a threat to inflict major harm on the civilian sector of an enemy actor; Daniel Ellsberg declared that "if we are to believe published accounts of contingency plans that have been prepared, for example, for war in central Europe (such as might arise over Berlin), there even exists in locked safes in Washington right now documents that could very aptly be described as plans for escalatory genocide" (Knoll, p. 158).

There is an argument, then, for suggesting that the modern citizen is confronted by a fundamental choice with respect to national security: pacifism or genocide. This blunt formulation of alternative moral positives gives notice of the kind of drastic world order adjustments that will be needed if human society is to dismantle the war system by voluntary rather than traumatic means (Falk, 1971).

II

THE NUREMBERG TRADITION:
INDICTMENT VERSUS RESPONSIBILITY PERSPECTIVES

Most of our thinking about the efforts after World War II to prosecute German and Japanese leaders has flowed from an acceptance of the Indictment Model as the only relevant basis for reflection and appraisal. In actuality, these trials were flawed from the indictment perspective at their inception, combining features of "victors' justice," non-reciprocity, and retroactivity. (Best critique: Minear, 1971). But even more fundamental, perhaps, was a false promise to the future embodied in the Nuremberg precedents. Karl Jaspers appropriately, I think, suspended judgment on the World War II trials until evidence was available as to whether there would occur a shift in the *pattern* of governmental accountability for the resources and conduct of war[3] (Jaspers, p. 59). Examining international history since Nuremberg makes it overwhelmingly clear that the criminality there delimited and punished has not been deterred and that there has been no organized effort to apply the Nuremberg conception of an Indictment Model to manifest perpetrators of indictable offenses. (Davidson) It is, indeed, ironic that each of the governments that joined in the Nuremberg indictment and prosecution has since World War II taken part in one or more major instance of aggressive warfare; United Kingdom and France in the Suez campaign (1956); the Soviet Union in Hungary (1956) and Czechoslovakia (1968); the United States in the Dominican Republic (1965) and Indochina. On none of these occasions did major

---

3. Reliance on the Indictment Model may have been an essential feature in the development of a Responsibility Model. For important confirmation from a man who was convicted at Nuremberg, see Speer.

rival governments purport to condemn the leaders of the alleged "aggressor" governments as war criminals who should be brought before the bar of international justice. In fact, the war crimes issue became intertwined with the propaganda side of Cold War politics. North Korea evidently fabricated claims that it was the victim of germ warfare in the Korean War and North Vietnam early asserted and later avoided its claim of jurisdiction to try and punish captured American pilots as war criminals and as the agents of an aggressor government.

The point here is that there was no serious attention given to the role and relevance of the Indictment Model as an ingredient of world order in the period since Nuremberg. As a consequence, it seems necessary to reappraise the show trials after World War II as largely victor's justice, at least so far as intergovernmental conduct is concerned, and as probably irrelevant to the future.[4] The leaders of minority regimes in southern Africa may be made the target of some future international criminal proceedings. It is quite easy to imagine a future "war crimes" trial against Rhodesian or South African leaders, with or without possession of defendants, under charges of crimes against humanity or genocide.

Despite this failure of the Indictment Model, which however fairly applied would be dependent on a primitive rationale, the Nuremberg tradition has provided a moral and juridical underpinning for American resistance activities during the Indochina War.

Draft and tax resisters were the first to raise the Nuremberg argument as a legal explanation of why they felt obliged to refuse normal citizen obligations. David Mitchell, a 1965 draft resister, was evidently the first American citizen to rely on a Nuremberg defense in the Indochina context. More dramatically, Daniel Ellsberg and Anthony Russo developed a Nuremberg rationale to

4. No one in 1935 could have anticipated the Nuremberg tradition. It is virtually impossible to assess future international developments well enough to conclude whether or not major war crimes trials will take place. A variety of factors in the Indo-Pakistan War of 1971 almost produced a series of major war crimes trials, and may yet do so, once prisoner and population exchanges have been completed.

explain their decision to disclose the Pentagon Papers. In effect, such individuals argue that individuals have a right and a duty to prevent governmental crime in the area of war and peace, and that the legal order should protect an individual from complicity in international crime either by declaring the war illegal or by upholding the selective conscientious objection of the draft resister or taxpayer who reasonably believes in its illegality. Ellsberg as a policymaker earlier in the war was in the additional special position of seeking to terminate prior complicity by taking a reasonable course of action to disassociate himself. As he put his situation before the release of the Pentagon Papers:

> I speak not as a researcher but from experience as a former official of the Defense Department and the State Department in Washington and Vietnam—experience that makes me a possible defendant in a future war crimes trial [Knoll, p. 158].

The point here is that the Responsibility Model was activated in part—in this extreme instance of apostasy by Ellsberg—by an image of the Indictment Model, i.e. the liability that would follow from a diligent fulfillment of Justice Jackson's promise at Nuremberg— ". . . we are not prepared to lay down a rule of criminal conduct against others which we would be unwilling to have invoked against us." I would argue that it would not be desirable to convene, even if practicable, a criminal proceeding against, say, Dean Rusk or Richard Nixon, but that it would be highly beneficial if future officials in governments were to regulate their perceptions and actions *as if* they sought to avoid the status of being, in Ellsberg's words, "a possible defendant." We should understand the word possible as a moral hypothesis, rather than as a weak prediction of indictment. For many of us Ellsberg's initiative revitalized Nuremberg because it spoke to our position as citizen opponents of a war we believed to be illegal, hence criminal, rather than to our position as accomplices (although being tax-paying, benefit-receiving citizens is properly construed as moral and political complicity).

It does not seem to matter whether the real fulcrum of influence on individual behavior is to strengthen the impulse to terminate links of complicity or to encourage responsible action in opposition to governmental crime. In either setting, the Nuremberg tradition, conceived as a Responsibility Model, provides a rationale. Indeed, the generalization of a Nuremberg obligation widens an individual's horizon of relevant concerns beyond national boundaries and creates a basis for transnational solidarity with every victim of governmental crime. In this sense, the Nuremberg obligation could provide an essential base for one side of global populism, stimulating individuals and groups everywhere to build a new world order based on a curtailed and accountable role for government bureaucracies and other corporate actors with wealth and power at their disposal.[5]

Genocide as the most extreme offense of governments against humankind poses the most significant present challenge and creates an opportunity to relate the Nuremberg obligation to an emergent movement of global populism. Frederic Hunter asks the question "Does an international conscience exist?" because of the failure by the international community to react to the slaughter during 1972 of as many as 100,000 Hute people by the Tutsi leadership in Burundi (Hunter, p. 17). Clearly, the answer is a resounding "no" if international conscience is to be associated with governmental response. There is no reason to suppose that even the most progressive of existing governments would, unless motivated by political considerations, act ˉon humanitarian grounds; one of the grim lessons of the Hitler period was the refusal of almost every foreign government to admit Jewish refugees, even when refusals virtually meant signing their death warrant (Morse).

But if we mean by international conscience individuals of good will and non-governmental groups (e.g. War Resisters International, American Friends Service Committee), then there are some hopeful signs. Several countries, most notably Sweden and Can-

---

5. I see a close connection between interposing the Nuremberg obligation between the state and individuals and the movement to insist that corporate managers be accountable to their shareholders for social goals, as well as for profits and losses.

ada, opened their borders to young Americans in the Resistance movement. Groups in Japan, Canada, France, Sweden, as well as the United States are working to secure the release of political prisoners in South Vietnam who are victims of torture and repression. A major grassroots effort has been made in the United States to raise money for medical aid to Indochina, partly conceived in the spirit of reparations. The anti-apartheid movement is reaching down below governments and becoming a grassroots concern for individuals of conscience in all parts of the world.

It seems reasonable to conclude that the existing Indictment Model of war crimes and genocide in existence is a precondition for the Responsibility Model, the latter presupposing actions that satisfy *in a general sense* the requirements of the former.[6] In this way actions of resistance or of transnational solidarity can be thus placed in a wider tradition that has been sanctified by the ritual of the law. Furthermore, the Indictment Model makes it possible to accuse leaders as well as to activate their opponents. Its origins and existence provide a normative framework for communication with leaders that can be evaded, but not easily disowned. In short, the failures of the Indictment Model to reform behavioral patterns of governments is neither surprising, nor a reason to eliminate it. These failures are part of the underlying weakness of international law as a *restraint* system in the area of war and peace. As discussed elsewhere, this failure to *restrain* behavior should not be regarded as a failure of international law; law has multiple functions. International law does provide a framework for *communication* of claims even in relation to warfare. The Nuremberg Principles make a useful contribution to international law conceived of as a *communication system,* facilitating the transmission of authoritative claims and counter-claims in various arenas of intergovernmental discourse.

At the same time, it is not clear that we would desire the In-

6. A parallel step involves populist protests against atmospheric testing, especially protests against 1973 French tests in the Pacific; these protests were also supported by a number of affected governments and by an injunctive order, defied by France, issued by the International Court of Justice.

dictment Model to work more efficiently and literally. To indict would involve punishment of individuals without any prospect of deterrent or rehabilitary effects, and might tend to encourage scapegoating, that is, assigning excessive responsibility for governmental crime to a few top leaders.

III

SHOULD WE EXTEND THE GENOCIDE APPROACH TO ECOCIDE?

In view of the analysis given above it seems generally desirable to work for the authoritative designation of ecocide as a crime and to provide for the apprehension, indictment, and punishment of its principal perpetrators. Such an objective would mainly have an educational value; informing relevant publics and their leaders about the ecocidal features of certain combat strategies. This kind of educational effort might inhibit some forms of behavior, to the extent governments value an appearance or actuality of non-abhorrent behavior.

A movement to adopt an Ecocide Convention generally expresses a revived awareness of man's dependence on nature. The spectre of ecocidal warfare ironically emerges at the same historical moment as it has become apparent that man's present pattern of habitation on the planet threatens to cause ecological collapse. A prohibition on ecocide—as a deliberate strategy of warfare—and the sanctioning of its perpetrators would represent a positive step in the consciousness-raising process that is needed along the entire spectrum of man's activity harmful to environmental quality.

The Genocide Convention was the product of Raphael Lemkin's imagination and energy, his personal obsession with the extermination of Jews by Nazis. (Lemkin) Governments were passive, embarrassed to refrain from endorsement, although reassured to proceed by the unlikelihood of credible enforcement prospects. Similarly, it is unlikely in the extreme that governments will independently carry forward an initiative against ecocide unless embarrassed into an acceptance. It is noteworthy that the United Nations Conference on the Human Environment held in Stockholm in June 1972 kept environmental warfare off its agenda because of American sensitivities, and that Swedish Prime Minister Olaf Palme's reference to American ecocidal policies in Indochina provoked an official American reprimand.

To succeed in adopting an Ecocide Convention that satisfies the Indictment Model laid down by the Genocide Convention requires generating prior pressures by individuals and groups all over the world. That is, ecologically concerned individuals will first have to educate governments and arouse segments of public opinion, although progressive governments and political figures may join such a movement at an early stage. If an Ecocide Convention is adopted, then given the operative code of international behavior there is no reason to be optimistic about either government compliance with it or about efforts at genuine enforcement in the event of non-compliance. However, with efforts to evolve a world order movement with a populist base and responsive to ecological values, it is likely that a protest and resistance movement—as an application of the Responsibility Model— might ensue in the event that a government in the future wages large-scale environmental warfare as a matter of deliberate policy of the sort evidenced in Indochina during the past decade. Thus, one would not expect (or even necessarily desire) the indictment of the perpetrators of ecocide, but only the increase of a strengthened movement of reaction against them.[7] At the same time, the existence of the Ecocide Convention in a form called for by the Indictment Model, provides progressive governments (which are still socialized into the state system and its prerogatives and tolerances), with an acceptable inter-governmental instrument for the communication of opposition and censure claims, and thereby augments the communication system which, as we have argued, is a component of the international legal order.

---

7. Although some prospect of indictment may be important to ground action in defiance of official policy, i.e. the indictability of ecocide provides underpinning for private "enforcement" efforts by way of resistance.

IV

A CONCLUDING NOTE ON THE LINKS BETWEEN
RESPONSIBILITY AND THE INDICTMENT MODEL

This essay has tried to trace the notion of accountability for crimes of war through a sequence of three main stages. First, there was a mobilization of sentiment giving rise to an authoritative Indictment Model during the latter stages of World War II. Secondly, there was an effort to apply the Indictment Model to the defeated leaders of Germany and Japan under a rather exceptional set of circumstances that engendered controversy as to the authoritativeness of these decisions as precedents in international law. Thirdly, there has been the more recent extensions of this Indictment Model phase of the Nuremberg tradition in a series of contexts in which citizens have acted in defiance of official policy, often at great risk and sacrifice, in order to oppose governmental policies reasonably perceived as crimes of war. Underlying this latest phase of the Nuremberg tradition, what we have labelled here as the Responsibility Model, is the conviction that individuals of conscience are the most reliable check upon the war criminality of governments, given the contemporary world political setting. It must be acknowledged, finally, that individual acts of conscience and of resistance may be virtually impossible in a ruthless and efficient totalitarian system.

REFERENCES

Davidson, Eugene, *The Nuremberg Fallacy* (New York: Macmillan, 1973).

Falk, Richard A., "Environmental Warfare and Ecocide," *Bulletin of Peace Proposals,* Vol. 4, pp. 1-18, 1973.

——, *This Endangered Planet: Prospects and Proposals for Human Survival* (New York: Random House, 1971).

FitzGerald, Frances, *Fire in the Lake* (Boston: Little, Brown, 1972).

Hunter, Frederic, "Burundi and the World Conscience," *Christian Science Monitor,* April 11, 1973, p. 17.

Jaspers, Karl, *The Question of German War Guilt* (New York: Dial, 1947).

Knoll, Erwin, and Judith Nies McFadden, eds., *War Crimes and the American Conscience* (New York: Holt, Rinehart and Winston, 1970).

Lemkin, Raphael, "Genocide as a Crime under International Law," *American Journal of International Law,* Vol. 41, pp. 145-71, 1947.

Minear, Richard H., *Victor's Justice: The Tokyo War Crimes Trial* (Princeton: Princeton University Press, 1971).

Morse, Arthur D., *While Six Million Died: A Chronicle of American Apathy* (New York: Random House, 1968).

Sartre, Jean Paul, *On Genocide* (Boston: Beacon Press, 1968).

Speer, Albert, *Inside the Third Reich* (New York: Macmillan, 1970).

6

The Principle of
National Self-determination

STANLEY FRENCH
ANDRES GUTMAN

On the surface it seemed reasonable: let the people decide. It was in fact
ridiculous because the people cannot decide until somebody decides who the
people are.

Sir W. Ivor Jennings

Does every nation have the right to constitute an independent
state and determine its own government? An answer to this question requires an understanding of the three main notions that are
included in the principle of national self-determination: the notion of a nation, the notion of a nation having a right, and the
notion of a nation determining itself.

Attempts to define 'nation' have been singularly unsuccessful.[1]
One of the common uses of 'nation' is such that it is synonymous
with the word 'state'. The word 'state' refers to "those political
bodies which successfully claim the attribute of sovereignty, i.e.
legal independence from any other human organization. . . ."[2]
In this sense, every state forms a nation, and every citizen is a
member of the nation. This is a perfectly acceptable usage. It is
common to refer to states as nations, the relations among states
as international relations, to the debt of a particular state as the
national debt, and so forth. There is an equally common usage
of the word 'nation' where it may be used to refer to populations

1. A. Cobban, *The National State and National Self-determination*. Revised
edition (London: Collins, 1969).
2. B. Akzin, *State and Nation* (London: Hutchinson, 1964), p. 8. See also
F. Hertz, *Nationality in History and Politics* (New York: Humanities Press,
1943), p. 7.

other than states. The individuals who constitute a nation in this sense either are, or are believed to be, associated with one another by social characteristics such as common history, character, and culture. Appeals to the principle of national self-determination have been made with reference to both of the above senses, sometimes indiscriminately. This paper concerns itself primarily with the second sense. It is this second sense of the word 'nation' which is important to the present study, since it is such a group that is sometimes said to have a right to form a sovereign state.[3]

However, 'nation' in this second sense is itself unclear. Nationalists, and also some academics, have regularly ascribed to nations a wide variety of characteristics which have been supposed to give special status to the nation as the broadest community which commands, or ought to command, an individual's allegiance. A survey of the relevant literature will reveal claims that nations are populations bound together by a common language, history, soul, spirit, destiny, race, culture, character, or some combination thereof.[4]

A consideration of the more common claims about nations reveals no one characteristic that could suitably serve as the criterion for nationhood. Apparently, nations do not possess any characteristic in common that serves to distinguish them from other populations. The strongest statement that may be made about a nation is that it is a population that calls itself a nation, and is so called by others. This, however, results in a significant number of borderline cases. Populations such as the *Québécois,* the Ibos, the people of Bangladesh, and the Basques are examples of such borderline cases. Whether or not they are nations has been and will continue to be the subject of debate. Many people refer to these populations as nations, while many others explicitly deny that they are nations. Consequently, they cannot be classified definitely as either nations or "not-nations." There is no definitive

3. See article by Rupert Emerson entitled "Self-Determination," in *American Journal of International Law,* Vol. 65, 1971, pp. 459-75.
4. See, for example, Louis L. Snyder, ed., *The Dynamics of Nationalism: Readings in Its Meaning and Development* (New York: D. Van Nostrand, 1964).

method for ascertaining precisely which populations constitute nations and which do not.

The consequence of this is that the extent of the principle of national self-determination is ambiguous; i.e. we do not know precisely which populations are supposed to have the right to constitute an independent state and determine their own government and which do not. This problem is particularly significant because most appeals for national self-determination have been made on behalf of populations which are, in fact, borderline examples of a nation such as the *Québécois,* the Ibos, the people of Bangladesh, and the Basques.

Nations do not possess any characteristic in common that distinguishes them from other populations. As a consequence, there is no apparent justification for restricting the principle of national self-determination to those populations which are ordinarily called nations. There is no benefit that a nation may enjoy by achieving independence, and managing its own affairs, that may not be enjoyed by (say) an ethnic group, or a part of a nation, the people of a province, or any other population. Given that nations possess no distinctive common characteristics, the principle of national self-determination is gratuitously restricted to those populations that are ordinarily called nations. There is no obvious justification for such a restriction. Whether or not a population is ordinarily called a nation can change in the course of time, and such a change need not reflect any other change. An illustrative example is seen in the case of Pakistan.

> Of the more recently created nations the most striking and extraordinary case is that of Pakistan where a nation which almost no one had foreseen and few could credit in advance as even a possibility came into being virtually overnight through its own assertion (or that of a small number of leaders) that a nation existed that had not been there yesterday morning . . . Yet once the assertion of nationhood was made and accepted as a living reality by the people concerned, the fact that it confounded the theorists was a matter of singularly little relevance.[5]

5. Rupert Emerson, *From Empire to Nation* (Boston: Beacon Press, 1960), p. 92.

On the other hand, if the principle of national self-determination were presented without the restriction to nations, then it would amount to the claim that the people of any province, ethnic group, city, village, or family could establish an independent state where they so desired. In this variation, the principle of national self-determination is a euphemism for a strange brand of anarchy. Any population that considered its government disagreeable, or did not wish to obey a particular law, could establish its independence. In order to avoid this consequence, supporters of the principle of national self-determination must cling to the false assumption that nations can be identified by the use of objective criteria.

In some cases, there appears to be more justification for a population that is not a nation to constitute an independent state and determine its own government than there is for a nation. For example, there is no obvious or important advantage for the Croatians of Yugoslavia to constitute an independent state. If they did establish their independence, it is unlikely that there would be any significant positive consequences such as an increment in individual liberty, economic wealth, or opportunities for self-realization through cultural autonomy. On the other hand, the population of a colony such as Mozambique, which does not constitute a nation, has much more justification for attempting to establish its independence from Portuguese rule. The Africans and Asians of Mozambique are ruled by an autocratic Portuguese elite which rules purely in its own interest. For the majority of the population, the opportunity to constitute an independent state and determine its own government would undoubtedly have positive political and economic consequences. Nevertheless, the principle of national self-determination restricts the right to constitute an independent state to nations.

This problem, to reiterate, is that there is no apparent justification for restricting the principle of national self-determination to those populations which are ordinarily called nations. The next problem is closely related: there is no apparent justification for *extending* the principle of national self-determination to those populations which are ordinarily called nations. Even assuming the possibility of specifying sufficient conditions for nationhood, there is, nevertheless, no persuasive reason for adopting the principle of national self-determination. If, by chance, every nation suddenly had the right to constitute an independent state and determine its own government, there would be no positive consequences that would necessarily follow. Consequently, there is no apparent reason for giving the principle of national self-determination unqualified support. This is a contentious point of view that many would dispute.

John Stuart Mill, for example, maintained an opposing view since he associated the sovereign nation-state with individual liberty.

> Where the sentiment of nationality exists in any force, there is a *prima facie* case for uniting all the members of the nationality under the same government, and a government to themselves apart . . . Free institutions are next to impossible in a country made up of different nationalities.[6]

Mill does not, however, provide any salient reasons to support this position. Where a state embodies more than one nationality, and especially if the nationalities speak different languages, Mill claims that they will be isolated from, and ignorant of, each other.[7] He does not, however, explain how this impedes the existence of free institutions. Moreover, it appears that people of the same nationality but of different social classes and different regions, such as a Toronto stock-broker and a Newfoundland fisherman, are also relatively isolated from, and ignorant of, each other. This does not constitute an obvious or marked impediment to the existence of free institutions in Canada. Mill also claims that the relations between nationalities in a common state will be marked by antipathy and jealousy.[8] This, however, is not necessarily true; and where it is the case, there is no reason why it cannot be extinguished without having each nationality establish

6. J. S. Mill, *Utilitarianism, Liberty, Representative Government* (London: J. M. Dent & Sons, 1910), p. 360f.

7. *Ibid.*, p. 361.

8. *Ibid.*, p. 361.

an independent state. Relatively good relations presently exist among the nationalities of Yugoslavia, in spite of past frictions. Apparently, conflicts and differences among various nationalities can be resolved without isolating them in separate states.

Mill's final reason is that in a multi-national state ". . . the grand and only effectual security in the last resort against the despotism of the government is in that case wanting: the sympathy of the army with the people."[9] Mill's argument is that a natural sympathy will exist between the people and an army when they are both of the same nationality, and that this will prevent the development of a despotic government since any such government can maintain itself only with the army's support. We see no reason to accept Mill's premise that the sympathy of the army with the people is possible only in a single nation-state. Furthermore, there are few, if any, instances in history where the fact that the army is of the same nationality as the people has hindered the rule of a despotic government. In some contemporary South American states, such as Bolivia, where the army and the people are composed of the same nationality, despots maintain their power because they have the support of the army. In Greece, the people and the army are of the same nationality, yet it is the army that governs; and it governs despotically, with precious little sympathy for the people.

Mill also claims that national self-determination is, *ipso facto,* good. He does not support this claim with any utilitarian arguments; rather, he presents it as if it were perfectly obvious and unquestionable.

> One hardly knows what any division of the human race should be free to do if not to determine with which of the various collective bodies of human beings they choose to associate themselves.[10]

Here, Mill appears to be giving support to an unrestricted application of the principle of national self-determination according to which any population could declare its independence when it so desired. The immediate problem with this view is that it is

9. *Ibid.,* p. 361.
10. *Ibid.,* p. 361.

likely to result in conflicting claims. For example, the people of Québec may wish to disassociate themselves from the rest of Canada, but the people of Canada as a whole may wish to preserve the present association intact. Obviously it is impossible for all populations to determine which other populations they will be associated with.

Bertrand Russell sees nothing admirable in "the sentiment of similarity and . . . instinct of belonging to the same group or herd" which, in his estimation, constitutes a nation. Nevertheless, he regards national sentiment as a fact which should be taken into account by political institutions. "There can be no good international system until the boundaries of states coincide as nearly as possible with the boundaries of nations."[11]

Russell does not say, however, what it is that would be good about such an international system. He claims that "government can only be carried on by force and tyranny if its subjects view it with hostile eyes, and they will do so if they feel that it belongs to an alien nation."[12] While this remark seems to be appropriate to colonial situations where a population has no hand in choosing its government or influencing its policies, it does not preclude the possibility of an independent democratic multinational state. In such a state, it cannot be said that the government belongs to an alien nation; rather, the government is likely to be composed of members of all nations within the state. If the citizens came to view the government with hostile eyes, then they would vote it out of power. Thus, there need not be hostility, force, and tyranny.

Woodrow Wilson unquestionably believed that a world community of sovereign and democratic nation-states would have positive consequences. In his estimation, the only governments which had any natural right to rule were those that were democratically elected by an independent nation, and only ruled over the nation that elected them into power.[13] The principle of na-

11. B. Russell, *Political Ideals* (London: Unwin, 1917), p. 77.
12. *Ibid.*, p. 80.
13. "Special Message to Congress: Fourteen Points Speech, January 8, 1918," in *Woodrow Wilson 1856-1924*, edited by Robert I. Vexler (Dobbs Ferry, New York: Oceana, 1969), pp. 88-93.

tional self-determination is an integral part of Wilson's concept of democracy. In addition, Wilson's

> belief in the goodness and the power of world opinion, which might be termed the General Will of humanity, and in its identity with the General Will of every democratic nation, enabled him to hold the view that the self-determination of nations, and national sovereignty, was a possible basis, indeed the only possible basis, of world peace.[14]

There is no obvious reason, however, why two democratic nations would never go to war with one another. It is difficult to point to a clear-cut example of such an occurrence mainly because democratic governments are not found in any abundance in history. Nevertheless, the onus is on the supporters of the principle of national self-determination to show why it will have this, or any other, positive consequence. All three theorists considered here have failed in this regard.

In fact, Wilson's actions were not always in harmony with his theory. The most instructive example of this is Wilson's Mexican involvement. He decided to make South American republics democratic, beginning with Mexico. An election was held, resulting in the selection of General Huerta. Wilson, who was opposed to Huerta, concluded that the election had not been a genuine expression of the will of the people, and thus was led into two military raids on the country.

> Wilson had arrived at that fatal recurring moment in our country's diplomatic benefactions, the moment when it makes sense to start shooting people philanthropically, for their own good . . . The error of Wilson in Mexico, of Nixon in Vietnam, of our whole quest for "self-determination," is clear: we have reversed the order of cause and effect. Free elections are created by free men, not vice versa.[15]

Based on our examination of the concept of nation, we have discovered three problems: (a) the extent of the principle of na-

14. Cobban, *op. cit.*, p. 59.
15. Garry Wills, *Nixon Agonistes* (Boston: Houghton Mifflin, 1969), p. 433 and p. 455.

tional self-determination is ambiguous, (b) there is no justification
for restricting the principle of self-determination to nations only,
and (c) there is no justification for giving the principle of national self-determination unqualified support. Each of these problems suggests that the principle of national self-determination is
not the product of careful reflection, and each provides grounds
for jettisoning the principle.

Nevertheless, the principle of national self-determination is a
significant feature of contemporary politics. Almost every state
has at least one minority that has claimed the right to secede, appealing to the principle of national self-determination. In Canada it is the *Québécois,* in Britain the Welsh, in Spain the
Basques, in France the Bretons, in Nigeria the Ibos, in Belgium
the Flemish, in the United States the South, in the Soviet Union
the Estonians. For this reason alone, it merits consideration.

It may be argued that the principle of national self-determination is an established rule, whether legal or conventional, which
accords the right. That is to say, some may claim that, because the
principle is established legally or by convention, this alone is a
good reason for adopting the rule. We do not find such a reason
persuasive.

A nation within a state may be said to have rights which are
embodied in the constitution of the state that it inhabits. Where
a nation is divided between two states, part of the nation enjoys
the rights (if any) provided by one state, and part enjoys the rights
provided by the other. Nations, however, do not enjoy such rights
because they are nations, but simply because they are inhabitants
or populations of the particular state in question. It is possible to
have a national right stipulated in the constitution of a state. The
constitution of the Soviet Union, for example, stipulates that every
nation may secede when it so desires. It is doubtful that any nation in the Soviet Union could actually exercise this right; but assuming that it could, this would be an example of a national
right. Where a nation constituted an independent state, it may be
suggested that it has certain rights, such as they are, in the international arena. It seems, however, to be more appropriate to call
these rights the rights of the state rather than the rights of the

nation. The state would have the very same rights whether it was composed of one nation or many.

The principle of national self-determination does not appear to fit in anywhere. It is out of place within state legal systems because it is universal, and ascribes a right to all nations regardless of state boundaries or legal systems. Similarly, it is out of place in international law because it is not based on the recognition of the sovereignty of individual states. In fact, it threatens the sovereignty of the existing configuration of states. In spite of this, attempts have been made to accommodate the principle of national self-determination in the international arena; particularly in the United Nations. These attempts, however, have had very limited success. The earlier Dumbarton Oaks version of the Charter of the United Nations included no mention of the principle of national self-determination. At San Francisco, however, the sponsoring governments introduced it as an amendment to existing articles. Article 1, Section 2, states that

> the purposes of the United Nations are: . . . (2) to develop friendly relations among nations based on respect for the principle of equal rights and self-determination of peoples . . .[16]

Article 55 reads as follows:

> With a view to the creation of conditions of stability and well being which are necessary for peaceful and friendly relations among nations based on respect for the principle of equal rights and self-determination of peoples, the United Nations shall promote . . .

The striking feature of these proclamations is that they are vague and in need of interpretation. Furthermore, any interpretation given must be reconcilable with Article 2, Section 7 of the Charter:

> Nothing in the present Charter shall authorize the United Nations to intervene in matters which are essentially within the domestic

16. Hans Morgenthau, *Politics Among Nations,* 2nd ed. (New York: Alfred A. Knopf, 1959), p. 549f.

jurisdiction of any state or shall require Members to submit such matters to settlement under the present Charter . . .

Finally, let us consider the notion of national self-determination. What does it mean to say that a nation determines itself? It would seem that a self-determining nation freely makes choices and initiates actions in accordance with its own preferences. Is such a phenomenon possible, and if so, what does it involve?

Frederick Hertz argues that the phenomenon of national self-determination presupposes that there exists some means of forming and expressing the national will.[17] If a nation does not have the means of expressing its will, or if it does not have a will to express, then it would appear that one has additional grounds for rejecting the principle of national self-determination.

What is a national will? Is it, as Hertz claims, a prerequisite for national self-determination? In the language of traditional philosophy, one would say perhaps that the national will is the faculty by which a nation makes decisions and initiates actions. It is difficult, however, to imagine how the mass of people that constitute a nation, widely differing in opinions and interests, can be said to possess such a faculty.

Nevertheless, the belief in the existence of a national will is commonplace in the history of political thought, and several contemporary political theorists endorse it as a reality. Frederick Hertz describes the national will as the work of a ruling elite, be it a dynasty, a Church, a ruling class, or a party; and it is composed of the common aspirations of the various parties and classes of the nation overriding their antagonisms. Ruling elites have, indeed, claimed legitimacy for their rule on the grounds that they interpret the national will and rule according to it. If Hertz is correct in his claim that this is all that there is to the national will, then it is probably more accurate to say that the national will is that which the ruling elite either believes to be the common aspiration of all segments of the nation, or it is what the ruling elite propagates as the common aspiration of all. Hans Kohn maintains that "the most essential element [of a nation] is

17. Hertz, *op. cit.,* p. 240.

a living and active corporate will."[18] Similarly, a study group of members of the Royal Institute of International Affairs concludes that one of the six features possessed by nations is "a certain degree of common feeling or will."[19] In none of these cases, however, are the authors able to describe the nature of the national will with any degree of clarity or detail.

Somewhat surprisingly, Karl Deutsch, a committed empiricist, makes an attempt to describe the seemingly nebulous and ephemeral notion of national will.

> Will . . . may be described as the set of constraints acquired from the memories of past experiences of the system [in this case, the nation], and applied to the selection and treatment of items in its later intake, recall, or decisions . . . Will . . . is the ability to freeze the setting of a goal, and even the course chosen toward it, once the decision has hardened.[20]

The meaning of this complex and obscure passage is clarified somewhat by an example that Deutsch gives of the forming of the national will:

> Thus governments in wartime may ban all items of information suggesting the wisdom of making peace; or leaders of a nation may ban from its schools all references to the virtues or achievements of its chief foreign rival. Similar results may be obtained by an opposite kind of constraint through the forced intake or recall or forced circulation of selected items supporting the course chosen, in amounts far beyond the usual, so as to drown out all contradictory items.[21]

Thus it becomes clear that the Deutsch conception of national will resembles Hertz's insofar as it is the handiwork of an elite. National will is composed of the preferences and beliefs that an

18. H. Kohn, *The Idea of Nationalism* (New York: Collier, 1944), p. 15.

19. *Nationalism: A Report by a Study Group of Members of the Royal Institute of Internationalism* (New York: Augustus M. Kelley, 1966), p. xx.

20. Karl W. Deutsch, *Nationalism and Social Communication*, 2nd. ed. (Cambridge: M.I.T. Press, 1966), p. 177.

21. *Ibid.*, p. 177f.

elite has formally taught, and otherwise cultivated, by all and
any means at its disposal, into the population.

On the one hand, there are those who claim that national will
is a faculty by which a nation makes decisions and initiates actions. Descriptions of and evidence for the existence of such a
faculty have been lacking or unconvincing. On the other hand,
there are those who describe the national will as something other
than such a faculty. Hertz and Deutsch, for example, claim that
the national will is merely the product of the efforts of an elite.
This would suggest that national self-determination is a chimera
since it cannot be said that under such circumstances it is the nation that expresses its will or determines its own government.
Self-determination presupposes circumstances in which the members of a nation can determine their own government free from
pressure, terror, suggestion, prejudices, and ignorance.[22]

It is clear that 'the national will' is one of those systematically
misleading expressions that bewitches the intelligence of theorists
and laymen alike. It suggests the existence of some identifiable entity or phenomenon. But when we pause to look and see, no such
phenomenon exists. If we try to make sense out of the phrase by
defining it in terms of the beliefs and preferences of certain members of the population, the phrase loses its rhetorical force. The
principle of national self-determination now may be seen as the
claim that a certain more-or-less arbitrarily defined segment of a
population has the right to act on its beliefs and preferences, provided of course that there is a legal system which grants it this
right.

It may be replied that the phenomenon of national self-
determination is a particular kind of collective choice, where 'collective choice' is defined as the aggregation of individual preferences about alternative social actions.[23] Social actions are those
actions which involve the joint participation of many individuals.
On this view, the phenomenon of a nation determining its own

---

22. Hertz, *op. cit.*, p. 245.
23. Kenneth Arrow, "Values and Collective Decision-making," in *Philosophy,
Politics, and Society,* 3rd series, P. Laslett and W. Runciman, eds. (Oxford:
Blackwell, 1967), p. 223.

government is similar to the phenomenon of the local church group determining the date and place of the annual spring picnic. Since other groups can make choices and initiate actions without a will, there appears to be no good reason why a nation cannot do likewise. Both phenomena, however, require some sort of mechanism for registering individual preferences, and the existence of a rule or rules for determining the collective choice based on the distribution of individual preferences. In direct democracy, for example, individual preferences for alternative social actions are registered by counting votes. On the basis of the distribution of preferences, it may be said that a collective choice is made in accordance with a rule such as "the majority preference determines the collective choice."

On this theory, the application of the principle of national self-determination may be thwarted by the absence of a means of registering individual preferences, or by the absence of a rule for translating the aggregate of individual preferences into a collective choice. The first impediment may be overcome since individual preferences can be registered by holding a plebiscite. But how is the appropriate rule for determining the collective choice to be determined? This cannot be determined by the nation, because the nation's choice presupposes the very rule that it would establish. The likely source for such a rule would be the people that have the power to organize and administer the plebiscite in the nation in question. This, however, changes the complexion of the notion of national self-determination.

Since the members of a nation do not have a role in selecting the rule by which their preferences will be translated into the "national choice," the nation's collective choice must be considered with suspicion. If the rule for translating the aggregate of individual preferences into a collective choice happened to be that "individual preferences must be unanimous," then it could be said that the choice made reflected, indeed, the nation's preference. The high improbability that a large population would unanimously agree to any proposal makes national self-determination a practical impossibility.

Any other rule would be problematic. Let us suppose that a

national choice was to be made in accordance with the rule that "the majority preference shall determine the collective choice." If the result of a subsequent plebiscite was that 55 per cent of the population preferred policy A to policy B, and 45 per cent preferred the opposite, it would be misleading to report that the nation as a whole preferred policy A. Nevertheless, the nation would have chosen policy A in accordance with the rule for translating the aggregate of individual preferences into a national choice. With a different rule, such as "two-thirds majority preference determines any collective choice," then the resulting national choice would have been different even though the distribution of individual preferences would have remained unchanged. Clearly, the phenomenon of national self-determination is significantly influenced by this factor which the nation itself does not determine.

Let us now suppose that a particular population has been identified as a nation and that a plebiscite is to be held in order to determine whether or not it wishes to constitute an independent state. In such a case, the authority with the power to decide upon the rule for translating the aggregate of individual preferences into a national choice must make its choice rather arbitrarily. There is no rule which is obviously suitable. If the unanimity rule is used, then one fool or wise man can thwart the realization of the wishes of the great mass. If the majority rule is used, then almost one-half of the nation may be forced into a political arrangement which it does not desire. There is no *a priori* justification for either of these rules, or for any other that may be suggested. The people whose lives are to be affected have no hand in selecting them. The people on the losing side of the choice may very well refuse to abide by the result, claiming not without justification that the winning side has no moral claim to their allegiance. If part of a nation wishes to constitute an independent state and determine its own government, and another part prefers some other political arrangement, there is no apparent justification for demanding or coercing the smaller or weaker part to conform. In other words, there is no justification for extending the principle of national self-determination to nations and, at the same time, denying it to parts of nations or any other segment of mankind. To reiterate a point already made: extending the principle of national self-determination to a disaffected population is not to introduce into the domain of international affairs a means for lawful and peaceful political change. To extend the principle of national self-determination to any disaffected population is to endorse the very antithesis of lawful political change since any population that did not wish to obey a particular law could circumvent it by claiming its independence as a state.

There is nothing in this paper that should be interpreted as a defence of the *status quo*. There is nothing sacred about state boundaries. Furthermore, there may be instances where it is quite justifiable for a population to try to secede from the state of which it is part. For example: it may be argued that autonomy for Québec is necessary because this is the only efficient way to guarantee that the state machinery be used to preserve and develop the (valuable) *Québécois* culture. Such arguments should be considered on their own merits. We have attempted to show that national self-determination cannot be sanctioned by appeal to the *principle* of national self-determination.

7

Reason, Non-violence, and Global Legal Change

BEVERLY WOODWARD

The existing state of international disorder is often referred to as a state of global anarchy. The time-honored human remedy for such a state of affairs is the establishment of the rule of law. Thus the remedy for the existing situation is often held to be the creation of more and better international law along with the creation of the institutions customarily associated with the presence of law, i.e. institutions for making, interpreting, and enforcing law. But there are many who are not enthusiastic about the proposal. They include those national elites who speak piously of "law and order" at home, but are definitely less reverent when it becomes a question of forms of law that might be less supportive of their (self-defined) "interests" than the legal structures that they are so anxious to see upheld. They include the anarchists who insist that the current perversions in human behavior are not due to too little law, but to too much law, pointing out, for example, that it is *governments* that have authorized the great majority of the more brutal and massively destructive acts witnessed in this century. And they include many "ordinary people" who are neither opposed to law in general nor especially privileged by the given arrangements, but who are apprehensive of law formulated at such a great distance from its potential points of application. Even to those not inclined to rail against government wherever it occurs, "world government" or anything similar may seem a rather frightening remedy for what ails humankind.

The final version of this essay was written under the auspices of the Center for International Studies, Princeton University.

Those, therefore, who advocate major change in the global legal arena are likely to find themselves confronted not only with the kinds of justificatory tasks that are almost always imposed on those who advocate any kind of major change,[1] but also with the rather particular task of showing why change in the global arena should involve any special focus on *legal* institutions. Granted that humankind taken as a whole is not doing too well, why should we expect that changes in or the addition of new *legal* structures will make any significant difference in its (or, more precisely, *our*) prospects?

Global legal change, of course, may be seen not as a means to a better world, but as an outcome which will perforce occur if the political changes for which there seems to be such evident need take place. Those agents of change who hold this view tend to see law not primarily as an *instrument* for change, but as a reflection of more "basic" processes which they as agents of change attempt to bend in more progressive directions. This point of view, which has much to be said in its favor, stems from a reaction against the seeming formalism of the "world peace through world law" approach, a formalism that has manifested itself principally in either or both of two ways, i.e. as a naïve belief in the desirability of law *qua* law and/or as a failure to focus on the social and political processes which generally must precede the coming into being of effective law. The sociological point is important and can be expressed in a slightly different way. Where political processes have *not* provided a firm social foundation for new law, that law will often be ineffective, though in varying degrees depending upon the related social circumstances. At the domestic level the history of the civil rights laws, for example, provides a good illustration of the difficulties of implementing laws where an adequate social basis is lacking.[2]

1. In ethics it is assumed that there is a discrepancy between what is and what ought to be, but in politics the assumption often seems to be the contrary.
2. See, for example, the remarks of Marian Wright Edelman, Director of the Washington Research Project, in her talk, "Nonviolent Social Change as a Political Strategy," printed in *Nonviolence in the 70's: A Strategy for Social Change* (a report on a conference of the Institute for Non-Violent Social Change (Atlanta, Georgia: Darby Printing Company, 1972), p. 26). She speaks

The point raised against the pursuit of law *qua* law has a weak and a strong interpretation. The weak interpretation is that law, of course, can be good or bad depending on its substance and the good will of those who enforce it and that it is not enough to pursue law for its own sake. The strong interpretation is in a sense more fundamental, however, since it puts in question the very desirability of any law, whether "good" or "bad," whether conceived as product or as generator of new social relations. It is especially relevant to the questions surrounding the creation of law in the global arena, for some at least would question whether such a thing as "international law" exists at all, and it is in any case evident that the processes which tend to lead to the creation of new law in the domestic arena do not necessarily do so here. Whether it be a case of the political expression of majoritarian

---

of "a total administrative enforcement vacuum" with "everybody working against our interests . . . in there trying to weaken the effect of the law, i.e. making sure that the guidelines are bad or there are loopholes for evasion; or that appropriations aren't provided or are minimal; that the personnel structure for implementation of the law is understaffed or regionalized, i.e. done in a way to weaken enforcement." Consequently, "Black people and poor people often get hurt by laws that were originally intended to help them." Here the will to implement and the will to enforce have been absent in so many quarters as to undermine greatly the effectiveness of the numerous progressive laws that earlier managed to get through Congress. The absence or partial absence of a favorable social basis may, however, be used merely as a convenient excuse for legislative (and executive) inactivity, as when legislators cover their own lack of enthusiasm for measures of social justice by telling us that "you can't legislate morality." In this popularized form the sociological point becomes a bare half-truth. Indeed the reformative effects of law on human behavior and human character are limited, and legislation that strays too far from human capacities or inclinations will be ineffective. It is also true, however, that there is an ongoing dialectic between law and social will and law and social structure, and that law may have reformative effects on both social structure and social attitudes where those who legislate and those who lead seriously desire to foster these possibilities. In brief, those political figures who speak of the impotence of law too often conveniently bracket themselves out as factors in the social processes that condition the effectiveness of law. Edelman, herself, it should be noted, does not advocate giving up on law altogether, but rather that Blacks and the poor should pay more attention to the matter of "administrative monitoring."

views (as in the case of attitudes towards the existence of hunger) or of the imposition of the will of the powerful (as in the case of the multi-national corporations), law is much less likely to play a role or to be in any form present as a source of authorization for new arrangements (should they emerge) than is generally the case in the domestic arena.[3] While in the domestic arena we may expect to get "good" law or "bad" law, but in any case to get new law over time as power relations and social relations change, the matter is much less clear-cut where global political processes are concerned. Thus "legalism" in the international domain is open to particular challenges, for what is being advocated here is not simply law as a remedy in a domain where law is in any case already an everyday fact of life, but *the institution of a legal order* (or at least what some would characterize in this fashion) in a domain where law in the usual sense is largely absent.[4] Those who challenge the desirability of law *qua* law with respect to this domain, then, are very often not just making the point that not all laws are "good," but rather questioning whether there is any desirability at all of creating in the global arena the institutions characteristic of a domestic legal order.

To be sure, there are some who argue that what we have in the global arena is not the absence of law, but the presence of a distinctive type of law. Gidon Gottlieb, for example, maintains that international law "is a paradigm for legal ordering in a decentralized system"[5] (i.e. for ordering in a "horizontal system" with many centers of power) and that as such it should not be ex-

---

3. The example is meant to indicate just how difficult it is for majorities to affect political reality where they are not politically organized. Since the majority of the world's people are undernourished, we may expect they would approve of rather different arrangements than exist for the distribution of food. By contrast power groups like the multinational corporation constantly have a political impact, but their activity also generates relatively few international legal norms.

4. The reasons for the caveat here are explained in the paragraph that follows.

5. Gidon Gottlieb, "The Nature of International Law: Toward a Second Concept of Law" in *The Future of the International Legal Order*, IV, edited by Cyril E. Black and Richard A. Falk (Princeton, N.J.: Princeton University Press, 1972), p. 331.

pected to resemble the kind of law appropriate for the "vertical" power arrangements characteristic of domestic legal systems. But while the points he makes are important for jurisprudential thinking, the practical issues remain. If one changes one's paradigm of legal order, it may be that one can find a full-fledged order in the international arena. Yet at the same time there exists there a high incidence of the kinds of disorder that we ordinarily expect legal systems to prevent or to control.[6] Thus it is quite natural that those who find the violence and other forms of disorder characteristic of international life morally intolerable and/or unacceptably dangerous should speak of the "institution of law" as a possible remedy. For what they see as only weakly present in the international arena are the institutions and established procedures generally associated with enforcing law, especially law aimed at the control and inhibition of the more obvious forms of violence. In a word what they see as the fatal defect of existing international law is the absence of *mechanisms of coercion* resting on secure authority and employing effective power.[7]

However one may come out then in the formal debate about what law "is," the debate between those who seek "law," understood as including certain coercive mechanisms and those who shun it, in good part *because* of the inclusion of such mechanisms, remains. It becomes particularly acute when law at the global level is in question, since the levels of coercion required for effectiveness there appear at first glance particularly high. Some anarchists will argue that *all* governmental coercion is evil or futile, since it will either fail, when applied to a group that does not form a true community, or if it does not fail will create more harmful effects than its action prevents or suppresses. In this

6. The fact that the usual kinds of enforcement procedures are in some countries proving to be ever less effective does not negate the fact that it is ordinarily expected that a legal system will include some sort of effective means of enforcement.

7. The term 'mechanism' is in my view not ideal, since it may seem to imply that coercive procedures always work mechanically. I think that this is not the case, but unfortunately it is difficult to find a more satisfactory expression.

sharp form the point is difficult to sustain, since it is clear that the presence of community is always a relative matter and that it is precisely law that has been a principal means of securing a higher level of harmonious behavior than a reliance on consensus or the presence of "true" community would permit. (I leave aside for the moment the whole question of what is meant when different groups speak of community and the related one concerning the forms that community may take.) Moreover, the conclusion that the price for these successes has always been too high appears to rest on dogmatic assumptions rather than on careful value analysis combined with thorough empirical study. At the global level, however, the assertion acquires some relevance since one may suspect that here community will always exist in such an incomplete and precarious form that the exercise of high levels of coercion will be a continuous necessity bringing with it all the dangers inherent in this kind of exercise of power. Thus where the institution (or strengthening) of global legal order is concerned, it seems appropriate to ask: Are we willing to see established at the global level the *kind* of coercive machinery that a low level of community would appear to necessitate if law is to be effective in inhibiting or arresting the more obvious and gross forms of destructive individual and group activity? In any event this is the question that opponents of "world government" constantly pose (if not in these precise words) in the confident expectation of a negative response and that in fact is responded to in the affirmative by only a few resolute "world government" enthusiasts.

It seems, though, that neither side in this debate is likely to be much at ease with its position, since neither of the alternatives posed is especially satisfactory. The question then is whether there is not some other possibility which is hidden when the argument is couched in these terms. In what follows I shall maintain that there is, that indeed both sides in the above debate are taking essentially similar positions and that both of these positions represent status quo thinking that is unlikely to move us toward a solution or mitigation of the pressing problems which give rise to this disagreement. Further, the strategy of my argument will be based on the conviction that a way forward cannot be found unless we return to a consideration of some basic questions: What anyway is coercion? Is it ever really justifiable and if so, on what grounds? What might limit the need for it? Are the distinctions between different kinds of coercion of serious practical import? Etc. Naturally it will be impossible to answer these questions completely here, but some kind of beginning can at least be attempted.[8]

I

Is the use of coercion ever justified? Where this question is concerned it might seem that the response of the anarchists will be "no" and that of everyone else "of course." This does not advance us very far. In fact, though, the position of the anarchists and other moral "purists" is less simple—or simplistic, if one will. Many anarchists, to be sure, do reject all governmental institutions on the grounds that all government rests on coercion. Or at least this is their apparent line of argument. In fact, though, it often turns out upon further questioning that many such individuals do not think that *all* coercion is objectionable. Forcibly preventing a person from suffering harm or from doing himself harm is often considered morally acceptable (e.g. forcibly removing a child who has crawled out into the middle of a street and does not want to move or stopping a distraught person who is about to jump off a high building).[9] Forcibly interrupting a chain of events or an action that would do others harm may also seem acceptable (anarchists in the United States have in recent times been involved in the destruction of draft board files and in the sabotage of weapons; many an-

8. I am currently at work on a book in which I consider these and related questions.
9. In politics we usually have to do with situations much more complex than these. Also proper conduct toward a child may differ in certain ways from proper conduct toward an adult. But I do not think the examples are politically irrelevant. It need not be merely the expression of a paternalistic outlook to hold that a political community should in some cases take certain sorts of measures to protect persons from self-injury (whether intentional or not). What is arguable regards the sorts of measures and the kinds of cases.

archists would see nothing wrong with directly or indirectly effectively disarming an individual or group about to commit an act of aggression). To say that such actions may be considered acceptable by the anarchist is not to say that they would necessarily be considered *altogether* desirable or that coercion would be considered in itself a good thing or even "value-free." Coercion may be considered in itself undesirable, but nevertheless acceptable in certain sorts of circumstances, thus making it impossible for one to say that one is opposed to the practice of coercion "no matter what."[10]

The possibilities are somewhat similar for those committed to non-violence. The rejection of violence need not entail the rejection of coercion and in actual fact many practitioners of non-violence have been willing to support or to participate in certain sorts of coercive acts. Indeed some of the preferred tactics of non-violent direct actionists have a coercive aspect, e.g. sit-ins, strikes, and boycotts. For this reason those on the receiving end of such actions have sometimes characterized them as "violent" but in a good many cases this has been merely a reflection of the widespread failure to distinguish between violence and force. In reality the rejection of coercion along with violence is characteristic only of a particular minority in the non-violent community, namely, those committed to what has been termed "non-resistance." Guy Hershberger, a Mennonite who has written on this topic, states that the term "as commonly used today describes the faith and life of those who accept the Scriptures as the revealed will of God, and who cannot have any part in warfare because they believe the Bible forbids it, *and who renounce all coercion, even non-violent coercion.*"[11] Even with this group, however, it is not clear that *every* form of coercion has been rejected either in

10. My concern in this paragraph is with those anarchists who believe they do start from such a position of outright rejection. There are, of course, anarchists who from the outset find coercion acceptable as long as it is not practiced by governments. Some of these anarchists have themselves engaged .in extremely coercive activity.

11. Guy F. Hershberger, *War, Peace, and Nonresistance* (Scottdale, Pa.: The Herald Press, 1944), p. 203. Italics added.

theory or in fact. It is hard to believe, for example, that a Mennonite would not use coercive force to save a child from the path of an oncoming car. Perhaps more to the point it is evident that certain acts of non-cooperation by the Mennonites in fact amount to cases of *passive* resistance rather than *non*-resistance. Indeed the Mennonites seem constantly to be trying to find means of "accommodation" that will fall between lending support to state force and actually resisting it (which would run counter to their beliefs concerning what is permitted to the Christian) and not always coming out well in this regard, since a social situation may be structured in such a way that there is no choice other than either cooperation or resistance.[12] In any event it is apparent that it is the coercion of the state as presently practiced that the Mennonites find most objectionable (or at least most repugnant to the Christian way of life) and from which they do their best to separate themselves, though with varying consistency and success.[13]

12. By passive resistance I mean a form of resistance created by the refusal to act in ways specifically desired. If the behavior is not strongly desired, then the refusal will only be experienced as a weak kind of resistance; but if strongly desired, then this kind of action may have great impact. Thus whether or not a particular behavior is construed as an act of resistance and how great an act of resistance it is do not depend entirely on the intentions of the person engaging in that behavior.

13. The ambiguities of Mennonite action can be illustrated by their differing policies with regard to paying taxes and to serving in the military. Military service is refused on principle, but taxes are paid, even though it is recognized some of the money goes for military purposes, because "to refuse to pay taxes would be equivalent to revolution, something a nonresistant Christian could not take part in" (Hershberger, p. 369). While the refusal to pay taxes may be an act of *rebellion* which aims at undermining the authority of the state in general, this is not necessarily the case, since specific taxes may be refused on limited and specific grounds which put in question only limited aspects of the state's exercise of its authority. But even rebellion is not revolution, and the refusal to pay taxes is not *revolutionary* unless it forms part of some much broader based program of belief and action. Another way of putting this is to say that the state can quite well accommodate itself to a certain number of tax refusers just as it can and not infrequently does accommodate itself to a certain number who refuse military service. (In fact it is groups like the Mennonites who have helped to teach the state this lesson

Even though in practice the rejection of violence does not appear to lead necessarily to the rejection of coercion and even though the avoidance of every form of coercion seems in fact even more unlikely an accomplishment than the avoidance of every form of violence, a theoretical problem remains. If violence is defined so as to include in its core meaning the notion of doing harm or injury,[14] then coercion can only be non-violent if it is non-injurious, and some would deny that this can ever be possible. Thus it is necessary to ask whether there is not always a kind of harm done when one "will" replaces another. This is not easy to answer, for it depends on one's understanding of the concept of "will" and of the different ways in which human decisions may come into being. One might hold, for example, that many "willful" acts are not autonomous acts and that the deflection of such acts does not involve a true usurpation. Similarly one might hold (following Kant) that the development of an autonomous will is equivalent to the development of a "reasonable" will and that this is not necessarily furthered by always permitting the free exercise of individual decision. It is possible, therefore, to hold that the long-continued substitution of an "external" source of decision for an "internal" one is always harmful (because preventing the achievement of autonomy) without coming to the conclusion that every particular instance of the replacement of

vis-à-vis military service.) To point out these ambiguities, however, is not to disparage the kind of witness to their religious beliefs and to the cause of peaceful relations that the Mennonites have made.

14. If we think that violence constitutes a problem, it is because of its effects. Therefore, it seems essential that the notion of injury be central to the concept. This also makes it possible to differentiate violence from force and to speak of "nonviolent force." If violence and force are distinguished not on this basis, but on the basis of the legitimacy of the forceful act, then this expression no longer makes sense. Moreover, if one holds that the legitimacy claims of all governments are false (as does Robert Paul Wolff) then one has no way of distinguishing violence from force at all, and all acts of force (or violence) from the use of psychological flattery to assassination are likely to appear equally acceptable or unacceptable (in Wolff's case it seems that all are acceptable as long as a utilitarian justification can be found; cf. his article "On Violence," reprinted in *Revolution and the Rule of Law*, edited by Edward Kent (Englewood Cliffs, N.J.: Prentice-Hall, 1971), p. 6ff.

will by will is necessarily harmful. For this to be true, however, it would have to be the case that on at least some occasions the experience of coercion was a factor leading to greater understanding and to a greater capacity to act in "reasonable" ways on "reasonable" grounds (I am intentionally not defining this term just yet). If subsequent "improved" behavior came about only as a result of fear, then it would be at least arguable that harm had in fact been done.

The question thus becomes an experiential one. Does the experience of coercion ever lead to greater autonomy, i.e. to the development of a more "reasonable" will or does it not? Can the "unbridled will" be "cured" (or partially cured) of its "irrationalities" by a judicious application of coercion, as a follower of Plato might argue, or is this a mere myth perpetrated by authoritarians? Those who believe the former to be the case would not find any necessary contradiction between a commitment to non-violence and a willingness to use or to support coercion in certain sorts of circumstances. For those who hold the latter position there would be such a contradiction and, if themselves committed to non-violence, such individuals might at least in principle reject all coercive activity. (It is also possible, however, that weight might be given to certain utilitarian considerations and that even those attempting to follow a non-violent way might accept the application of some measure of coercion as causing far less significant harm than the harm done by failing to impede or deflect certain sorts of grossly destructive acts and practices.)[15]

The notion that coercion may have beneficial effects for the person and not alone for the person's behavior is, as just indicated, quite often associated with an authoritarian or paternalistic stance, while the notion that coercion is intrinsically harmful is likely to foster not so much an anarchistic as an extremely quietistic stance. The extremes here may be expressed as the pursuit of a politics of domination based on some form of superior

15. Even if non-violence is considered all a matter of degree, one still might wish to make some distinctions between a range of acts that are relatively non-injurious and can accomplish significant good and those that are clearly injurious and of questionable value in their general social consequences.

"wisdom" contrasted with a withdrawal from politics altogether. Logically, of course, the belief that *some* coercion may be justifiable, because ultimately beneficial, need not lead to paternalism.[16] The argument here, after all, does not uphold coercion as a good in itself, but rather as a means to certain ends. If placed on a scale of desirability it is clear that the coerced will that decides well must be placed between the unbridled will that decides badly and the autonomous will (that by definition decides well). Thus it is not coercion that is desirable, but certain results of coercion, i.e. improved human behavior and in some cases at least an improved understanding of moral good. If the achievement of autonomy is a human good of unique significance (as Kant asserted), then its absence must be seen as a defect and the application of coercion as a social necessity without positive value in itself. But to say that coercion has no intrinsic value or even, as some would, that it is a negative social phenomenon is not to say that in itself it necessarily (i.e. inevitably) harms. The evidence for this last proposition is much more dubious.

It may seem strange that I should spend this much time discussing whether any coercion at all is justifiable, and in particular whether any forms of coercive action might appear justifiable to those adhering to philosophical positions that appear *a priori* to leave so little room for this possibility. After all, one might argue, the anarchists, *satyagrahis,* and other purists form a small minority. Everyone else would concede the need for *some* coercion. It is just a question of the quality and degree of coercion that is permissible in any given circumstance.

In my view, however, the arguments of the purists and the concerns of the great majority are not so unrelated, at least not in this instance. First of all the dislike of coercion is quite common

16. For coercion to be exercised non-paternalistically it is necessary that the object(s) of coercion be in a position to exercise counter-coercion of some significant kind and, just as importantly, that there be a continuing non-coercive relationship between the parties as well where each side accepts the possibility of being persuaded on non-coercive grounds (or what are ordinarily considered non-coercive grounds) by the other. (Ideally, therefore, one's relation to a child should become less and less paternalistic—or maternalistic—as the child develops.)

and in many quarters is currently being intensified in reaction to the excesses and stupidities (I use the term advisedly) associated with (1) the administration of existence by bureaucracies and (2) the progressive replacement of politics with government by executive fiat (characteristics common to life in an increasing number of countries). In these circumstances, I would argue, the anarchist in each of us is becoming strengthened (even though often it may be prudent not to make this fact known) and there is a growing temptation to reject all coercive practices out of hand (rather than to think about justifying circumstances, distinctions between different kinds of coercion, etc.). Thus paying some attention to what the anarchist in each of us would think if he or she were thinking *carefully* may be useful. In addition the more scrupulous often make distinctions that the great majority overlook. The distinction between violent and non-violent coercion is a pertinent example and one that may lead to a consideration of action possibilities that would otherwise be neglected. In fact I shall argue that it is this distinction that provides the key to overcoming the impasse: no (or practically no) global enforcement institutions vs. a large and heavily armed world police and/or army (or no "world government" vs. "world government" patterned on the model of national government). But first it is necessary to attend to the following question.

What is coercion?

We may start with a definition offered by Robert B. Miller in an essay entitled "Violence, Force, and Coercion."[17] In his essay the author attempts to define each of the three principal terms in his title. Starting with a tentative definition in each case he criticizes and corrects it until he comes to what he calls his "final account." In the case of the concept of coercion his "final account" reads as follows:

> C$_F$ An act of coercion is any act in which A (a person) intends to bring it about that B (another person) do Y

17. This essay appears in *Violence: Award-Winning Essays in the Council for Philosophical Studies Competition,* edited by Jerome A. Shaffer (New York: David McKay Company, 1971).

(some action), where B is in the process of doing or about to do X (some action), and where X and Y are not identical, by one of the following methods:

1) introducing as a consequence of B not doing Y, P (some action taken by A, either actual or threatened, intended to be undesirable to B) which is intended to change B's mind so that B will decide to do Y, or

2) intentionally injuring, damaging, or destroying B, or

3) the use of force.

(In some cases $Y = -X$, that is, A will be intending to prevent B from doing some action, as opposed to intending to make B do some other *specific* action.)

COERCION: Any action taken by A with the intent to bring it about that B do Y where B is in the process of doing, or about to do X, where X and Y are not identical, by either (1), (2), or (3) above.

Miller comments: "The treatment of coercion in this section is not nearly as thorough as it might be. Nevertheless, it does achieve the intended goal—to clearly distinguish the concept of coercion from the concept of violence. It is easy to see, however, how persons who view violence as always a means, and coercion as only $C_F(2)$, might confuse and conflate the two concepts."[18]
In fact Miller has defined coercion in terms of one end and four possible means, the end being to change behavior, the means the use of threats or sanctions or violence or force. These four means may, of course, overlap. A threat or a sanction may involve violence just as the use of force may involve violence. But since neither *need* involve violence (except perhaps in some very weak sense of the term), Miller has framed his definition to make that point apparent. To threaten a child with no dessert if he does not behave or to remove someone forcibly from a situation of danger

18. *Ibid.*, p. 30.

is no doubt coercive, but quite distinguishable from a situation where one withdraws someone's food altogether (i.e. starves someone) or beats someone to get him to leave a particular spot.

While Miller's definition makes this point clear, it nevertheless is not satisfying in every respect. There are some small imperfections. First, it is worded in such a way as to imply that coercive action can only aim at the present or the immediate future—"an act of coercion is any act in which A . . . intends to bring it about that B . . . do Y . . . *where B is in the process of doing or about to do X*"—though certainly much coercive activity is aimed at the somewhat distant future (even an indefinite future) and furthermore may aim not so much at producing or preventing any specific act as at producing or preventing certain sorts of acts or acts within a certain range of behavior (this point is only partly covered by Miller's remark that Y may equal —X). Second, coercion may be used to maintain behavior as well as to change it, i.e. coercion may be used in cases where it is believed that without coercive action a behavior change will occur and where that change is for some reason considered undesirable. Finally, Miller excludes "positive sanctions," i.e. the injection of a new element which "adds value" or offers to do so, as forms of coercive activity. But there seems to be no good reason for this. Coercion need not necessarily be experienced as something unpleasant, and the fact is that positive sanctions like negative ones inject an element that deviates from a simple reliance on argument alone in the attempt to influence behavior. That is, positive sanctions like negative ones change the consequences of action and as such may render a course of action "substantially more (or less) eligible" than it was prior to their injection.[19] This is especially true when

19. See "Coercion," by Robert Nozick in *Philosophy, Science and Method*, edited by Sidney Morgenbesser, Patrick Suppes, and Morton White. (New York: St. Martin's Press, 1969). Nozick describes coercion as resulting from threats that render certain courses of conduct "substantially less eligible," but I hold that what he calls offers may be coercive as well. I shall go further into this question in the forthcoming book mentioned in note 8. For other arguments against Nozick on this point see Virginia Held, "Coercion and Coercive Offers," in *Coercion* (Nomos XIV), edited by J. Roland Pennock and John W. Chapman (Chicago and New York: Aldine-Atherton, 1972).

positive sanctions are aimed at fulfilling particularly strong needs or desires. An offer of food to a hungry man in exchange for a bit of corrupt behavior, or certain kinds of sexual offers to persons with particular kinds of compulsive desires, may be more coercive than threatening to fine someone if he parks his car in a certain spot.

More importantly, Miller's definition fails to make obvious the distinction between *total coercion* and *partial coercion* and the related one between *direct coercion* and *indirect coercion.* By total coercion I mean coercive action which achieves its goal in such a way that it cannot fail to achieve its goal, i.e. coercive action which under the given circumstances cannot be successfully resisted. (The concept is important even though it will not always be easy or even possible to tell whether action falls within the category.) Direct coercion, i.e. coercion which applies force (whether violent or not) in such a way as to attempt to elicit directly the desired behavior, may or may not be total.[20] By contrast indirect coercion, i.e. coercion in which one or more of the various means is used to get someone to "change his mind" and as a result behave in the desired manner, is of necessity partial, since it always leaves open the possibility of refusal and resistance. To be sure, if a person is presented with an extreme threat, such as the threat of death, he is likely to feel that he has little choice left, but the fact is that an area of choice still remains, even though it has been severely diminished. If, for example, it has been demanded that a person do something shameful, it can be said that the threat has created the necessary but not the sufficient conditions for the performance of the shameful act.

20. Miller defines "force" as involving the attempt to "physically overpower," meaning not necessarily that a person (or persons) A uses his own strength so that a person (or persons) B will be overpowered, but that some means is used, e.g. administration of a drug, so that B will be overpowered (*ibid.*, pp. 33, 21). By this definition to use force is always to aim at total coercion. But this seems too limited a notion of force and the notion of "physically overpowering" is anyway too imprecise, since one may be overpowered in one respect and not in another. It seems to me preferable to define force in terms of an application of energy in some particular direction. Thus the use of force may aim at partial *or* at total coercion and may in fact achieve the one *or* the other.

Another term for total coercion is compulsion. The use of coercive means that are less than compelling may occur for a variety of reasons. It may come about because of a sense of respect
for the autonomous capacities of the objects of coercive action or
because those coercing have a limited interest in obtaining their
object (these limitations may arise in part out of a sense of proportionality; the end may not seem sufficiently important to justify the resort to certain sorts of measures) or because those coercing are themselves under coercive pressures which limit the
means they may employ or because the desired behavior does not
fall in the category of behavior that can be directly compelled.

Consequently it should be clear that the use of partial coercion
is not in every instance an example of behavior that is morally
superior to the use of total coercion (even though leaving others
a margin of freedom in one's dealing with them may be considered *in itself,* i.e. apart from other factors, morally superior to
leaving no such margin). For example, when partial coercion
rather than compulsion is chosen not out of a regard for human
freedom, but out of seeming necessity—"you can lead a horse to
water, but you can't make it drink"—the means employed may be
extremely violent, e.g. threats of death, torture, or mutilation.
Moreover, the freedom that remains under such conditions has a
highly distorted quality. On the other hand, in a situation of danger to someone's life it would ordinarily seem preferable to use
compulsion to ensure saving the life rather than some means less
likely to secure that result. Indeed Miller's definition permits acts
to be called coercive that are not applied *against* someone's will
properly speaking, but where the will is temporarily inoperative
in some sense, e.g. the person is asleep, or where there is no time
for the will to operate with regard to the matter at hand, e.g. a
person about to be hit by a car. The possible existence of such
situations obviously makes possible a further set of differenti-
ations within the range of acts termed acts of compulsion and
makes it not too difficult to justify the use of compulsion in certain kinds of cases.[21] But even in the case of compulsion which

21. These possibilities arise out of Miller's definition because of the vagueness
inherent in the notion of "doing something." Being asleep is in a sense doing
something, in another sense it is not. Similarly I may intend to do one thing

acts *against* someone's will, the use of this form of action may seem more morally justifiable than action that does not compel, as I tried to show with my examples of the recalcitrant child or the distraught adult about to commit suicide.[22]

It should be pointed out, however, that while the application of non-violent total coercion for short periods is generally preferable to violent partially coercive action (some would say always preferable) and while in certain cases it may even be preferable to nonviolent partially coercive action, the use of total coercion ordinarily cannot be protracted indefinitely without leading to violence. This is in part because the complete elimination of autonomy in any particular regard over too long a time tends to be damaging. It is also because those who are the objects of this total coercion will try finally to find some means of escaping it, and these means are likely to be violent. Thus even those totally coercive strategies whose explicit aim is to prevent manifestations of violence, e.g. by forcibly separating potential combatants, can achieve their goal only for a restricted period. If a "movement of the minds" does not occur which makes such complete control unnecessary, the control itself will either be undermined resulting in expressions of direct violence by those whom it was hoped to restrain or else the control will itself turn into a kind of violence. Those involved in non-violent "peace-keeping" actions may in such a situation decide that it is preferable to relinquish some of their own purity (i.e. absoluteness of non-violence in manifest conduct) for the sake of maintaining restraint, if that is still physically possible, but such a choice clearly will not be an easy one.[23]

---

and in fact do that and several other unintended things, e.g. I may intend to cross the street and I may do that and also walk in front of a moving car. Someone may say, "She's about to get herself killed," but clearly that need have nothing to do with what I think I'm doing. Consequently, coercion need not operate against my will in such a case.

22. One may reach this conclusion without believing that suicide should in all cases be impeded. That is a more involved question. Here I speak of the obviously "unconsidered" suicide.

23. In general, peace-keeping actions involve only partial coercion, but the separation of potential or actual combatants or the disarmament of combatants may involve total coercion.

A final point needs to be considered in an analysis of coercion attempting to be more complete than that provided by Miller's admittedly cursory definition. This regards the different kinds and levels of reason that may inform coercive action. It is sometimes assumed that coercion always involves "irrational" pressures. But the facts are more complex. It is clear, of course, that coercive action may have as its aim compelling behavior that in the absence of coercive pressure would be considered either rational *or* irrational, either morally correct *or* morally incorrect. (I differentiate what is "rational" from what is morally correct here, because what is morally correct may be "irrational" by even a mild standard of self-interest. In such a case someone knowing of someone else's extreme moral rectitude might try to coerce that person into a more "rational" course of behavior. In certain cases this might seem a laudable thing to try to do.) In other words coercion may be employed for all kinds of purposes including moral, immoral, and amoral ones, and the behavior it produces may or may not meet various standards of reasonableness.

If reasonableness is viewed simply in terms of self-interest (rather than, say, in terms of moral correctness) then it can be said that most coercive pressure attempts to change the balance of what is "reasonable" by the injection of a new consequence (whether actual or promised) that will make a particular course of behavior seem more (or less) attractive. Because of the frequent appeal to fear in the application of coercive strategies, those coerced often argue that they have been overcome by "irrational" forces. And this may in a sense be true. But it is not altogether and not always true. In many cases those who "give in" to coercive pressures have simply recalculated what is in their self-interest and coolly chosen the course indicated by their calculations.

Nevertheless the distinction between what is reasonable *before* coercion occurs and what appears reasonable *after* it takes place is important. For in many cases it can be argued that the factor added by coercion is itself unreasonable or inappropriate, e.g. the fact that it is reasonable (i.e. "rational," where "rational" is defined in terms of the furtherance of self-interest) for me to sign a loyalty oath to get a job I very much need does not mean that

it is reasonable for the authorities involved to require the oath;
or the fact that it is reasonable for me to give my wallet to a person who sticks a gun in my face does not mean that this is a reasonable price to pay for the right to walk home unmolested.

It need not be the case, though, that the rearrangement of
what is in someone's self-interest involves an inappropriate or unreasonable pressure as in the above examples. For instance, it
might be considered appropriate that there be a law stating that
anyone stealing any item will, if caught, have to return the item
or its monetary equivalent, plus pay a fine that would be calculated in a specified way. (I do not want to go into detail here
about how a fair fine should be calculated.) Certain circumstances
might also be described in which these consequences would not
follow. Such a provision might be considered fair and appropriate (the price to be paid for stealing does not seem disproportionate) and yet have a coercive impact since it would certainly
render stealing a "less eligible" course of conduct than it would
be without this provision. Thus we can imagine cases of coercion
in which the motive appealed to is in a sense reasonable (self-
interest), the conduct aimed at is reasonable (by standards of
moral correctness—though I do not wish to imply by my example
that stealing if considered in context of its occurrence is always
morally incorrect), and the means of applying coercive pressure
is also reasonable. Other combinations of reason and unreason,
of course, can be imagined.[24] It should be remarked, though, that
since self-interested behavior is not the only kind of reasonable
behavior of which human persons are capable, a heavy appeal to
this motive may well be at the expense of other kinds of reason
(as in those cases when moral reason would advise a different
course of conduct from that which the coercing person or group
is trying to compel).[25] In any case an understanding of the various

24. Coercion may be applied so as to appeal to motives other than self-interest
as ordinarily construed. For instance, someone might threaten harm to a person unknown to the person being coerced and he out of a concern for the welfare of the other person might give in to the coercive threat. This might be
called an immoral appeal to a moral motive.

25. It is difficult to think of coercive strategies that could appeal to moral as
opposed to self-interested rationality and do so in a moral fashion. (See note

ways in which reason or unreason may inform a coercive strategy is important for assessing both its justifiability and its likely acceptability. It is my contention, for example, that non-violent forms of coercion always manifest a kind of reason that does not attach to violent coercion. To make this apparent, however, requires a deeper consideration of the concept of "reason."

II

The concept of reason is value-laden. Moreover, different concepts of reason appear appropriate for different spheres of existence and understanding. That kind of reason which has to do with the interhuman (or social) sphere of existence was called "practical reason" by Kant and he attempted to make explicit the basis for judging whether it was functioning well or badly. The formal nature of the criterion he proposed and the difficulty of applying it have been much discussed, and these critiques need not be reviewed here. Yet in two ways Kant expresses a substantive concern. The first is in that formulation of the categorical imperative that states that we should "always treat man whether in our own person or in that of another not merely as a means, but as an end in himself." The second, equally important, involves his concern with "coexistence" or the harmonization of existences. For the requirement of consistency in Kant regards not merely an internal consistency of symbols and the ways in which they are used, but a compatibility between disparate existences. Kant in spite of his denials is concerned with consequences, but they are not the consequences of action into particular contingent historical situations, but rather the hypothetical consequences of action that might aspire to transcend the given social causality. In the given causality there can be no hope of community because it rests too much on self-regarding desires. Kant might therefore be said to have asked "what are the principles on which universal

---

24 *supra*.) The principal way in which an appeal to moral considerations might become an aspect of a coercive strategy is through the use of partial coercion by respected individuals or groups who could combine persuasive moral appeals with their coercive actions. (See pp. 184-187.)

human coexistence depends?" If we know what these are, then it can be said that insofar as we adhere to them, we introduce or rather attempt to introduce a new kind of causality, one which for the first time makes universal human coexistence possible.[26]

It is at least arguable, then, that Kant's approach to practical rationality is not formal at all in its real intent—the concern with the person as an "end in himself" and with universal community being clearly of a substantive nature. Moreover, as is well known, the Kantian approach aims to put a kind of "substantive limits" on action that is notably absent from other currently more widely accepted criteria for judging human conduct. Today two of the most common criteria for justifying particular political acts—and thus in a sense establishing their rationality—are those of instrumental efficacy and of the presence of widespread or majoritarian consent. In both these cases it is not the "action itself," not its initial substantive content, that is examined, but rather something that either precedes or follows the action. By failing to put any intrinsic limits on what is morally permitted, the instrumental and the majoritarian criteria not only fail to hinder, but actually may give strong support to, an extremely violent politics and extremely violent policies.

The violence not only permitted by but seemingly inherent in the instrumentalist perspective, where an end may justify practically any means, is well known and requires little discussion. But the violence that majorities may permit deserves further comment in the present context. It is not only that political majorities may sanction or at least consent to extremely brutal foreign policies (witness the seeming apathy of the American public in face of the air war in Indochina). This is true enough and terrible enough, but not exactly relevant to the concern with a global polity where there will be no *Aussenpolitik*. What is especially significant here is the structural tendency of majoritarianism to uphold certain kinds of internal violence unless there are special safeguards. For inherent in the majoritarian polity is always the

26. How or whether these underlying concerns of Kant's moral philosophy can be harmonized with certain aspects of his legal and political philosophy is a topic I shall not enter into here.

possibility of great violence toward as well as on the part of various minorities within the polity. This difficulty is likely to be aggravated as the size of the polity increases. In a global polity, for example, there will exist not only the problem of establishing what represent majoritarian views,[27] but the problem of adequately protecting the rights and interests of very large and very well-organized minorities along with protecting the community as a whole against the severe damage which minorities are now capable of inflicting. Even within the nation-state, as Gidon Gottlieb has pointed out, there now exist powerful "veto-communities" which can inflict severe disorder and bring the ordinary functioning of society to "a near standstill."[28] In fact it is the very technology that concentrates such great power in the hands of central authorities that creates their vulnerability against seemingly weaker forces. The power of minorities within the world community is, of course, even greater than that of domestic "veto-communities" since these minorities in many cases have a long history of self-conscious, highly organized, and relatively autonomous existence. In any event majoritarian policies that work or seem to work against the interests of 49 per cent of mankind, to take the extreme example, simply will not be accepted and any attempt to impose them is only too likely to meet with a violent response. Indeed this power of minorities within the world community (and there is no nation, of course, that is not a minority here) might well be considered a happy circumstance were it not associated with the capacity to use such extreme means of "self-defense" (as it is likely always to be called, whether justifiably or not).

Implicit in the foregoing is the notion that the presence of violence signals some kind of failure or absence of reason and that a "practical reason" which sanctions or encourages violence is somehow at odds with itself. Consequently models of reason like those just mentioned must be held to fail to satisfy the full criteria of

27. While modern electronics and modern communications techniques can be of some help with this problem, the difficulties are not only technical ones.
28. Gidon Gottlieb, "Is Law Dead?" in *Revolution and the Rule of Law* (see note 14 *supra*), p. 79.

rationality. Similarly the notion that violence may *serve* reason, and the correlated one that reason may therefore properly be used to serve violence, notions currently much in vogue, must be considered as at best very partial truths and as at worst a betrayal of reason and of reason's capacities.[29] But precisely because conclusions of this kind are at such odds with much contemporary thinking, it is worth recalling the grounds for the more traditional opposition of reason and violence. For in fact there is a complex network of interlinkages that give weight to this opposition. Some of the most important of these may be summarized as follows:

(1) First of all, it is often said that the use of violence is a sign of the breakdown of discourse and of the effort at persuasion. While a kind of reason may be used in the process of employing violence, it is not a reason that concerns itself intrinsically with the source of the conflict. It is a kind of technical reason that aims at efficiency in battle and at exploiting the physical and psychological weaknesses of the opponent rather than at finding the just solution to the underlying problem. Thus the use of force is contrasted with such modes of conflict resolution as mediation, conciliation, and arbitration. I use the term 'force' advisedly, however, since the basic contrast here is between coercion and rational persuasion rather than simply between violence and persuasion. It is from this point of view that all *coercion* may be said to involve an element of unreason.

(2) Reason is often held to have a special relation to what is orderly and what is harmonious (formally this is expressed as the requirement that a reasonable argument be consistent, i.e. internally in harmony with itself). Reason discovers the distinctions that make it possible to order our experience. By the discovery and creation of boundaries it puts limits on what we may correctly say. Thus reason, order, boundaries, and limits are all held to be interconnected. Violence, on the other hand, is held to be associated with disorder, turbulence, and the overstepping of

29. Though I believe there are different levels and different kinds of reason, I shall in what follows not put quotation marks around any particular usage of the word.

boundaries. Accordingly, that which is only very intense, such as an argument or storm, may be described as violent simply because it goes beyond certain accustomed bounds.[30] This set of conceptual associations is no longer so widely accepted with respect to the social domain, however, because of the existence of forms of social order which may be called "artificial" and which rest on the hidden or not so hidden threat of violence. Recent uses of the phrase 'law and order' by retrogressive forces have resensitized some to the fact that the linking of that which is rational with that which is orderly can only have a meaningful social application if our notion of order is sufficiently deep. Those kinds of social order in which there exists respect for person and in which persons are treated not just as means but as ends in themselves evidently respect quite different sets of boundaries than those established by many legal systems, which may be internally coherent and capable of suppressing most outwardly disorderly acts, but which legitimate and perpetuate more hidden forms of disorder.

(3) Related to the above is the notion that reason is to be contrasted with that which is arbitrary, while violence always has an element of the arbitrary about it. Reason is a respecter of proportions; in fact its role in part is to reveal the proportions between things. In the political sphere the work of reason is to elucidate the notion of justice, a concept that may also be associated with the notion of proportionality, of rendering to each his due. In this regard, though, the antithesis between reason and violence may not seem altogether convincing. A great deal of rational thought, for example, may be expended on determining what proportions of harm are due to various persons or groups in certain sorts of circumstances. Rules of war, theories of just wars, and theories of punishment all provide examples of this kind of

30. The example comes from an article by Sheldon Wolin, "Violence and the Western Political Tradition," *The American Journal of Orthopsychiatry*, Vol. XXXIII, No. 1, January 1963, p. 16. This is an excellent article, but somewhat marred by the fact that Wolin, though he points out that there is a difference between violence and force, uses the terms 'violence,' 'force,' 'power,' and 'coercion' more or less interchangeably throughout the article.

use of reason. The existence of an element of unreason here will only be apparent if one finds in every infliction of harm something of the arbitrary, something that is not altogether a person's due in spite of what he may have done or the circumstances in which he finds himself.[31] The notion that capital punishment is unacceptable, for example, rests on just this kind of insight.

(4) Reason may be said to be concerned with that which is universal, with that which links and binds together, and with an understanding of the totality, while violence arises out of a partial perspective, wills to remain attached to particularity, and seeks to exclude or to suppress. In this sense violence may invade reason and distort its functioning. The possibilities are numerous: prejudice may masquerade as truth, simplifications may not be labeled as such, euphemisms may be employed freely, unwarranted generalizations from particular cases may parade as cogent argument, single-factor analyses may be proffered as adequate bases for social policy, etc. The temptation to resort to all of these dodges in the support of policies of violence is well known. In the United States official pronouncements in the past decade have provided a particularly painful example. All reasoning, of course, achieves only partial insights and therefore risks to distort. But the aspiration of reason is toward totality and toward the truly universal, and a properly functioning reason will employ its self-critical capacities so as to make allowances for the distortions of which it knows itself to be capable.

Here as in what precedes it can be seen that a theoretical capacity of reason and an aspiration of theoretical reason have been related to the capacities and aspirations of practical reason. This perhaps hearkens back to a Stoic mode of thought; in any case such linkages do not seem to me improper, but a result of rea-

31. Socrates expressed this insight in the *Republic* as follows: "If, then, anyone affirms that it is just to render to each his due and he means by this that injury and harm is what is due to his enemies from the just man and benefits to his friends, he was no truly wise man who said it. For what he meant was not true. For it has been made clear to us that in no case is it just to harm anyone." (*Republic*, 335e. Translation by Paul Shorey in *The Collected Dialogues of Plato*, edited by Edith Hamilton and Huntington Cairns (New York: Pantheon Books, 1961.))

son's own search for that which unifies, i.e. a result of the very
tendency I have been describing. Thus, for example, the respect
of theoretical reason for truth, and the respect of practical reason
for persons, seem to me not unrelated. Gandhi spoke of his activities in the social and political sphere as "experiments with truth."
The phrase is perhaps misleading since one does not experiment
"with" truth, one discovers it or a part of it. But just as one's pursuit of theoretical truth will be hampered if one brackets out oneself as the knower, so one's pursuit of truth in the social realm
will fail if one brackets out the persons, i.e. the subjectivities, of
those who must be included in any new higher form of community. The reality to be attained in the social domain is not something given, "out there," but an unknown potentiality that can
only be realized and discovered by "experiments" in which each
acting subject recognizes that he or she forms part of the crucial
"matter" of the experiment and that just as theoretical truth
places certain limits and requirements on us in its pursuit, so social (or "practical") truth, which must be attained by those kinds
of beings we call persons, also places certain limits and requirements on the mode of its pursuit. If in the social realm we are
still at such a primitive stage in our pursuit of the essential uni-
versalities, it is perhaps because so little attention has been paid
to some of these limits and requirements. Certainly the pursuit of
universality would seem to be in general inconsistent with policies
of exclusion (which in their extreme form include the imposition
of death and banishment) as well as (though in varying degrees)
with attitudes of separatism and exclusiveness.

If, therefore, the presence of at least certain modes of reason is
quite incompatible with the presence of violence, then the use of
violence as an element in the initiation and perpetuation of legal
order can properly be said to reflect an at least partial failure of
rationality. In fact the paradox is widely recognized. Law, on the
one hand, is that which persuades people to act rightly, that
which makes possible harmony, order, and the attainment of
justice, that which links disparate individuals into a common
community. Put simply, the avowed purpose of law is the elimination of violence in its various forms. On the other hand, law

depends on violence. The degree of dependence, of course, varies. Law may merely reflect the outcome of a violent struggle in which might becomes ratified as right; or law may be the outcome of a parliamentary debate in which greater or lesser degrees of higher order rationality (e.g. a concern with fairness) are manifested. Law may attempt to recommend itself on the grounds of its fairness; or law may impose itself by the most brutal methods. Law may proscribe capital punishment; or law may itself rely heavily upon it. Law may provide the guarantee of basic rights for all; or law may perpetuate unwarranted privileges and disabilities. And so forth. In varying degrees law is interlinked both with the practice of overt (or direct) violence and with the imposition of structural (or indirect) violence.[32]

This ambiguity in the significance and the effects of law leads to various kinds of reactions. There are those who absolutize the one or the other dimension becoming on the one hand anarchists of some kind rejecting all forms of communal law, on the other "legalists" seeing in law a good in itself. Then there are those who acknowledge the ambiguities in law and regard them as inevitable. The difficulty with this last position, which is the prevailing one, is that historically it has involved the toleration of such high levels of violence. I speak, of course, not only of the overt violence employed in the enforcement of domestic law, not only of the disharmony and injustice promoted and perpetuated in even the best domestic legal systems, but also of the very partial community embodied in the concept of "national sovereignty" and the extreme violence with which such partial community may be protected. The acceptance of this limitation on law means that law itself, i.e. the existing international legal structure, may become the source of or at least the legitimator of the most terrible forms of destruction.

32. The practice of calling direct violence "personal" violence and then contrasting it with "structural" violence seems to me misleading. The exercise of both kinds of violence involves persons and the practice of direct as well as structural violence may involve social institutions. The basic distinction is between harm done in a direct and obvious way with weapons and harm imposed indirectly by laws and social practices which prevent human needs from being fulfilled.

This appears to bring us full circle. The existing disorder in the world and the extreme dangers it faces can be seen as the result of law or as the result of anarchy. Thus the question reasserts itself: do we need more law or do we need less law? Or perhaps do we need a different kind of law? For if we are inclined to give up on law altogether we should remember that what the law is concerned with is not primarily recalcitrant children or distraught individual adults. Law at present is particularly concerned with the control of major social forces and where these controls are removed or absent, other forms of coercion can be expected to take their place. With regard to unrestrained economic activity, for example, we have seen well enough how such activity may despoil our environment, deplete basic resources on which all are dependent, and reduce certain groups to positions of economic helplessness. As Edward Kent pointed out in his introduction to the collection *Revolution and the Rule of Law:* "Perhaps the nearest approach in practice to political anarchism, classical liberalism and its *laissez-faire* doctrines of economics, failed because it could guarantee neither minimal standards of justice nor the fiction of consent itself. Tyranny of the majority is just as much a prospect with anarchism as under existing systems of legal rule."[33]

It is no secret that unrestrained social and economic forces are at work today on a global scale and their impact as much as that of war itself threatens human survival. From this point of view there can be no substitute for some form of global law. It is also apparent that if this form of law attempts to impose itself by traditional methods, its failure is highly likely. Even with some form of preliminary disarmament, for example, a highly developed capacity to employ violence will remain with certain elements in the world community. To try to overcome *this* violence *with violence* is likely to lead to disasters as massive as those a world authority would ostensibly be trying to prevent. It is one thing to imagine lightly armed police forces dealing with individual armed or unarmed lawbreakers—and even this is not done very successfully in many countries—and it is another to imagine how a

33. Edward Kent, *op cit.,* p. 6.

global armed force might take on a major power. In such a case it can be expected that the global force will simply begin to act like a sovereign state creating a situation of civil war in which the outcome may or may not be "favorable."[34] If the civil war should involve the use of nuclear weapons, obviously it will be hard to consider any outcome especially desirable. From this point of view, then, there is no very great difference between our existing troubles and the threats they entail and those we could expect to be associated with a world state. This appears all the more true when one considers the rather widespread skepticism with which the claims to legitimacy and authority of many existing states are currently greeted. If the propensity to challenge is great in the case of well-established nation-states, what might it be in the case of a fledgling world body?

It seems, therefore, that some different kind of enforcement model is needed, one that will enable us to break through the prevalent patterns of action and response. Moreover, certain short-range "inefficiencies" may have to be accepted for the sake of better long-term prospects. While alternative enforcement structures may not succeed in preventing the worst—unfortunately matters have come to a point where there appears to be *no* means of guaranteeing that—they would have the advantage of initiating something fundamentally different rather than perpetuating what I have elsewhere called "the violence system" by merely adding new but essentially similar elements to it. In this regard the present military weakness of the United Nations can be considered an advantage since the need for disarmament is not present and since this absence of military strength creates an opening or space in which other forms of power may come to be developed. In itself, of course, a lack of armament does not create power. This is only a negative form of non-violence and in many cases a non-violence that has not been intentionally chosen. By contrast non-violence

34. In an article on UN peace-keeping actions Guido Brunner shows that this is just what has taken place in certain UN operations. See Guido Brunner, "Die Friedenssicherungsaktionen der Vereinten Nationen in Korea, Suez, im Kongo, in Zypern und im Gaza-Streifen," in *Friedensforschung*, hrsg. von Ekkehart Krippendorf (Köln and Berlin: Kiepenheuer & Witsch, 1968).

as a positive political force requires conscious choice, conscious organization, and a commitment to consistent practice.

The attempt to replace violent with non-violent power faces different obstacles in different social domains. Further, the kinds of institutional and organizational forms required to carry forward the struggle to institute this kind of power and to protect its achievements differ in varying social environments. Formally there is a particular affinity of non-violent concepts and ideals for global concepts and ideals—both are intrinsically concerned with the highest and most all-embracing form of community. But practically it is in the global domain that non-violence seems to have the slimmest chances. The magnitude of violence here is so great, the reality of violence so overwhelming, that it has a paralyzing effect on nearly all of us.

The overcoming of this kind of paralysis requires particular kinds of thought and praxis, the two having coordinate roles to play. Part of the role of reflection is the imaginative construction of models based on principles other than those that inform the given reality. The implementation of such models requires the help of further kinds of reflection as well as the commitment to action. In what follows I shall limit myself to the first task in its connection with the enforcement problem. That is, I shall attempt to outline the guidelines that might inform the actions of alternative enforcement institutions. At the same time I shall hope indirectly to aid the implementation process by showing the special appropriateness of the kind of model I propose for the resolution of the dilemmas just outlined.

III

An ideal coercive procedure can be briefly described. An ideal coercive procedure is one that (1) is non-injurious to those to whom it is applied; (2) is used to uphold a statute or measure that is fair and that supports or furthers just social relations; and (3) is applied by persons who have proven themselves worthy of trust and who maintain parallel non-coercive relations with the individuals and groups who are the objects of coercion. Most coercive practice strays far from this ideal. In part this is because of the interest in expediency and also, of course, because human beings are imperfect in the best of circumstances. But in part it is because the ideal is often not recognized as such. Expedience *is* the ideal, i.e. some kind of short-term efficiency. The purpose of coercion, it is believed, is to coerce. A concern with non-injury or egalitarian relations or service to the objects or potential objects of coercion are frills or luxuries (or even impediments to effectiveness).

But another perspective is possible. From this point of view coercion is only one part of a larger social process. From this point of view the goal of coercion is not just to succeed in the given instance, but to make itself progressively less necessary. Traditionally this has occurred through the substitution of authority for coercion. There is a catch to this, however. Authority that comes to be viewed as having no valid basis, that comes to be called "irrational," must once again resort to coercion. Therefore, if one cares about the long run, it is not just any kind of authority that should be striven for, but rational authority.

Insofar as the ideal coercive procedure just outlined conforms to ideal standards of rationality, its application can be expected to help further the creation of such rational authority. That it does adhere in important ways to such standards should be in part immediately evident, but it may be helpful to note explicitly some of these connections. The ideal proposed involves a concern with the measure being enforced, the mode of enforcement, and the person of the enforcer (or enforcers). The measure I have said should be fair, i.e. it should manifest a concern with proportions and with what is due, and it should support or further social justice, i.e. it should aim at a certain kind of order. The mode of enforcement should aspire to be non-injurious, i.e. should respect certain boundaries (such as the prohibition against killing, but not only that) and should strive especially to avoid those forms of injury that are inconsistent with the development of all-inclusive community (e.g. banishment and death). Finally, the person of the enforcer should be trustworthy, i.e. he should have shown himself to be a respecter of rationality and of the potential rationality (understood in its full sense) of the human person. Moreover, he should rely on persuasion to the extent permitted by a balancing of rational considerations and should engage in parallel cooperative community-building projects along with his coercive activities. (It is quite important, however, that these be truly cooperative projects, not imposed ones.)

The concern to leave room for persuasion and for autonomous decision will be advanced if partial rather than total coercion is generally employed. From my earlier discussion it should be evident that partial coercion leaves room for the operation of rationality in a way that total coercion does not (how much room will depend on the particular coercive means employed). Threats and sanctions may be accompanied by higher order arguments as well in the attempt to elicit a desired behavior and even when they are not, the object(s) of coercion may exercise such higher order rationality himself in deciding which of his options to choose. Furthermore, as already mentioned, the experience of total coercion is more likely to provoke violence than the experience of partial coercion, *unless* this partial coercion itself relies on threats of violence.[35] It should be noted, moreover, that the kinds of behavior one would be trying to elicit through global law would very often not be those kinds of behavior that can be totally forced or even directly forced. Of necessity there will have to be a heavy reliance on indirect and partial methods. A virtue can be made of this necessity, however, if there is a conscious decision to accompany these forms of coercion with persuasive non-coercive efforts. In some United Nations peace-keeping actions this has been the case and the same persons involved in "policing" actions have carried on parallel efforts at mediation and conciliation.[36] But the insertion of higher order rationality which the employment of partial

35. My discussion of alternative enforcement procedures is intentionally rather abstract here, as I intend elsewhere to consider the more concrete aspects of the problem. It is worth noting, however, that both imprisonment and capital punishment involve total coercion, although imprisonment is not in every respect totally coercive.

36. For illustrations see the pamphlet by Geoffrey Carnall, *To Keep the Peace: The United Nations Peace Force,* published by *Peace News,* 5 Caledonian Road, London, N.1, 1965.

coercion permits is likely to be obscured or not even to take place if other forms of unreason are present. Therefore, it is highly desirable that the measures on whose behalf partial coercion is being used be seen as fair and that the coercive methods used be relatively non-injurious.[37]

To speak of relative non-injury, however, is to acknowledge that perfectly non-violent coercion is difficult to achieve and that some measure of harm may result from the practices employed.[38] Thus another criterion of rationality would be the proportionality of the harm inflicted to that of the harm prevented. I would nevertheless argue that there should be some absolute limits here. This proportionality criterion is the very one, of course, that is used to justify the "just war." But violent war is just what the global authority or authorities ought not to engage in, even when it cannot be prevented on the part of others. Here it seems to me that significant conclusions can be drawn from Guido Brunner's discussion of the UN action in the Congo, though he fails to draw these conclusions himself. He points out that some of the authority that the UN had won in the Suez action was lost as a result of its activities in the Congo. He explains: "Der Hauptgrund dafür ist, dass die Organisation, wenn sie einmal in einen Konflikt von der Dimension des Kongokonfliktes gerät, keine andere Wahl hat, als sich wie ein souveräner Staat zu verhalten und durch den Einsatz all ihr zur Verfügung stehenden Mittel, einschliesslich der militärischen, ihrer politischen Auffassung zum Sieg zu verhelfen. Diese Art des Vorgehens führt selbst dann, wenn die Friedenswahrung als letztes Ziel des Einsatzes der Vereinten Nationen erkennbar bleibt, zu einer Einbusse an dem moralischen Ansehen

37. It is important to note also that the use of partial coercion permits the operation of "counter-rationality" on the part of the person being coerced, i.e. permits the one being coerced to present a set of higher order arguments opposed to those of the coercer and perhaps even to persuade the coercer of error on his part.

38. It must be recognized also that the notion of non-injury is not an independent concept, but related to one's concept of human personality and of the essential needs of human persons. Non-violent forces may deprive a wealthy person of half his wealth, e.g. through a boycott. He will *feel* injured, but they will believe they have been non-violent.

der Weltorganisation."[39] Nothing seems wrong in this assessment except Brunner's assertion that the UN has "no other choice" in such a case. This is always the argument when violence is resorted to, and here it seems rather less compelling than in some other instances. When one cannot prevent violence except through the use of violence, then clearly one cannot prevent violence. But one can act in a way that makes future violence less likely. This, I think, involves setting some absolute limits. If the UN had "no other choice" in the Congo, it was in good part because so little had been done previously to create experienced and respected non-violent forces. This was the result not only of the conflict among the superpowers in the UN which prevented *any* permanent peace-keeping forces from being created, but also of a failure on the part of most to think of the "peace-keeping" problem outside of a conventional framework. Even to switch from the military conception to the police conception of a "security force" is to remain within conventional, and not necessarily appropriate, categories.

Drawing the line at killing may seem both too weak and too strong a measure if one's aim is a major reconstruction of transnational political relations. Too weak because there are after all many other ways of injuring human beings that may be adopted if this one is given up and too strong because it may seem quite impossible that enforcement procedures can be sufficiently effective if the resort to lethal weapons is renounced. The first objection is partially correct. Non-violence cannot be achieved by the adherence to any particular set of rules or any particular explicit limits and, if a more general orientation toward non-violence is not present, coercive forces will find new ways to inflict injury. But the point of insisting on the need for such a general orienta-

---

39. *Op. cit.*, p. 463. The English translation is: "The main reason for this is that the organization, once it gets into a conflict of the dimensions of the Congo conflict, has no other choice than to behave like a sovereign state and to help its own political perspective to victory by using all available means, including military ones. This manner of proceeding then results in damage to the moral authority of the world organization insofar as the principal aim of the activity of the United Nations remains the preservation of peace."

tion toward the ideal is not in order to dispense with all "absolutes," but to ensure that such "absolutes" do not make up the whole content of the commitment to the ideal. The alternative to drawing lines is the situation that actually prevails. Many armed forces today think that they are "peace forces," but constantly engage in acts that are intrinsically acts of war. Because perfect non-violence appears impossible, it is often concluded that there is no point in setting any standards at all and that in fact any sort of act may be justified as really fostering peace. Given the distorted social causality with which we have to deal, there is some truth in the latter insight. Any act, no matter how awful, *may* serve the cause of peace (if only by making men more fearful of war). On the other hand every act of war contributes to maintaining the institution of war and puts off till another day the experimentation with other ways of confronting the violence problem. The generalization of what appears to be utilitarian behavior is merely a prolongation of the condition that utilitarian conduct pretends to remedy.

It seems, therefore, that in this area as in other areas of human life, any major reconstruction of behavior and relationships requires setting some limits and at the same time recognizing that these limits (or rules) only partially embody the ideal. While non-killing is not the only absolute to be recommended in the development of a new model of coercive activity, it is a particularly significant one. It is significant because the line between life and death is especially significant and it is significant because the infliction of death is, as already pointed out, especially inconsistent with an essential political ideal, namely, the achievement of universal community. Furthermore, looking at the matter empirically, it is evident that killing is central to the existing world-wide violence system and that its delegitimation and renunciation would entail major institutional change. An insistence on non-killing in other words need not result simply from an abstract ethical decision, but may stem as well from an analysis of the given global historical and institutional context.

It would be a serious mistake, though, if the prohibition on killing were thought to apply only to direct killing, i.e. to the kind of killing that is done with guns. Economic measures can just as effectively destroy human life and may be even more difficult to resist. The interdependence of the contemporary economy, moreover, is likely to make economic manipulation a preferred form of coercive action in the future. From the point of view of this essay, of course, economic coercion is of especial interest because of its potentiality for being neither violent nor total, but the more sinister possibilities must be recognized as well. If the concern to eliminate direct violence is not also accompanied by a concern to eliminate structural (or indirect) violence in the construction of new enforcement institutions, then the destruction now permitted by laissez-faire economic practices could achieve the status of authorized public policy. (In fact economic measures are already used by national governments in highly questionable ways.) This possibility is all the more to be taken into account and warded off in view of the general tendency of governments to reject responsibility for the indirect results of their actions.

But can we "do without" killing? Clearly the world could do with a good deal less. But this is not quite the question. The question is whether public authority can do with less killing, whether it can maintain itself if it does not resort to lethal measures. One can solve this definitionally by saying that by definition authority is not present where it has become necessary to resort to violence. But this is too easy a way out. Certainly there is a widespread belief that established authority can manifest its power effectively only if violence is met with violence, even that authority is dishonored if it does not use every means possible to assert and defend itself. There are elements in these beliefs that fall outside what is arguable, other aspects of the matter that would take me beyond the limits of this essay. Still there is a basic point to be made. All such attitudes involve the assumption that the legitimation of certain violence is the only way to meet the violence problem. Yet if we look at the historical record it seems that the authorization of certain violence as a way of curtailing other violence has had a rather questionable effectiveness in reducing violence in the world as a whole. It is really impossible to say what might have been had there been concerted and consistent attempts to de-

velop non-violent political power and non-violent political traditions, i.e. what might have been had those of our forebears who
were committed to non-violence not given up on the affairs of this
world so early and accepted the designation of their attitudes as
"apolitical" or even "antipolitical." In the absence of such traditions what we have seen is more the replacement of one form of
violence by another, e.g. feudal violence by nation-state violence,
unregulated violence by organized violence, than a general lowering of violence levels. In fact the arguments about legitimacy have
always had a mixed reception. Often enough the victims of violence have found these arguments unconvincing and their effect
has been merely to stimulate counterviolence, a tendency that
grows stronger in the present age.[40]

The only alternative to this approach is the one recommended
here, i.e. an effort in the direction of a general delegitimation of
violence. This appears to be the only way in which the vicious cy-
cle of violence in which all are entrapped might be broken. To
be sure, this effort too may fail. Where so much blood, treasure,
and "honor" have been invested, it is exceedingly difficult to institute new ways. But while the work of delegitimation is hard
and demanding, there is much evidence that it is the approach
that best answers to our general condition.[41]

40. This point was illustrated by Howard Zinn writing about "Munich" and
its aftermath: "Would that raid [the retaliatory raid by the Israelis] 'show
them' (the language of the mafia and the Pentagon, of criminal gangs and
officialdom all over the world)? Clearly, the only result will be more retaliation.
The same dispatch quoted a Palestinian guerrilla officer after the air attack:
'We will do the same thing to them one day.' The violent acts of outlaws, of
revolutionaries, of governments are all mutually reinforcing, and never 'show'
anyone anything. Aren't the unprecedented increases in private crime and
governmental crime we see in our time endlessly reciprocal?" (*The Real Paper*,
Sept. 20, 1972, p. 9).
41. We are so used to "doing with" killing that a renunciation of this practice is bound to seem to many like "doing nothing." Goeffrey Carnall says
that Lord Mountbatten described Gandhi as "the one-man boundary force
who kept the peace while a 50,000-strong force was swamped by riots," and
that General Sir Francis Tuker "estimated the Mahatma's powers at the equivalent of two battalions." But much more experience with this form of power
will be required before it is really understood and trust in it begins to grow.

The pursuit of higher order rationality in coercion may be rejected not on practical grounds of effectiveness, but on more theoretical grounds. Some will argue, for example, that reason itself is coercive and that its alliance with force can only make a free existence all the more difficult to attain. This argument tends to identify reason with a particular form of reason, that manifested in logic and mathematics; and even here there may be more "liberty of thought" possible than is generally recognized, as those who have done work in the foundations of mathematics know. In any case once one leaves the domain of the very abstract, the possibilities of multiple viewpoints increase considerably. The role of judgment in choosing or modifying premises, interpreting data, and, where social questions are concerned, in applying moral standards is well known. The autonomous will, therefore, is not simply the will that adheres to the self-evident. The autonomous will is the will that has accepted the responsibility to make the carefully weighed choice. That is why coercion can never be *fully* rational. One reasoning faculty cannot simply replace another. When one faculty of reason takes over for another, something irreplaceable is always lost.

On another level it remains true that reason seeks certainty and final insight. Even here, though, reason can be regarded as some sort of internal dictator only if reason is held to be an alien force. But to say that reason seeks is to say that the human person seeks, i.e. the human person seeks truth (sometimes anyway) and in the process becomes more truly human. Thus Spinoza held that a person is most free when his understanding is greatest. However, while the individual may find resting points in his pursuit of understanding, resting points where he uses terms like 'obvious', 'certain', and 'true', from the point of view of human collectivities, i.e. from a political perspective, every insight attained must be regarded as partial, as a step in a process in which each human

---

Moreover, it is unfortunate, though perhaps inevitable, that the history of non-violence as a positive form of social power has been so marked by a few charismatic individuals. This may have led many to see the effective practice of non-violence as more dependent than it really is on the special capacities of a few unique individuals.

person has a potential further contribution to make. To refuse to employ violence, therefore, is to refuse to short-circuit the process in which collective reason is fulfilled.

The model of coercion I have presented is meant to resemble in its dynamics this two-sided character of reason, a force that both seeks and rests, struggles with partial truth and attains moments of certainty. If it is the moment of certainty that permits coercion, it is the moment of doubt that counsels non-violence. Similarly the movement that characterizes the internal process of reasoning (and the multiple voices that are heard in internal argument) would be paralleled by a social system in which coercion could be exercised from numerous directions rather than being regarded in at least some of its forms as the sole prerogative of special institutions, i.e. of governmental ones. The elimination of violence from coercion would in fact significantly modify the whole distinction between that which is governmental and that which is non-governmental. Weber, it will be remembered, *defined* the state in terms of its claim to have a monopoly on the legitimate use of violence.[42] But if a general delegitimation of violence occurs, then this specific defining characteristic will be lost. Thus the range of associations considered political might be greatly expanded and with it the sources of legitimate coercive political activity.[43]

Such a prospect may seem to leave the way open for a form of social chaos with no clear-cut hierarchies and no clear-cut distinction between the "authorized" and the "unauthorized." I am not at all convinced, however, that this is the case. What is revealed rather is the need to rethink the whole issue of legitimacy apart from certain traditional claims. It is quite possible, moreover, that in a framework where violence is largely absent the nature

42. Cf. Max Weber, *Politics as a Vocation* (Philadelphia: Fortress Press, 1965), p. 2. The typical world government advocate simply wants this claim to be assumed by global authorities as opposed to the existing nation-state authorities.

43. Weber believed that the state had to be defined in terms of its means since "there is scarcely any task that some political association has not taken in hand" (*ibid.*, p. 1).

of rational authority will be more clearly manifest. Finally, in the context of a discussion about global authority and institutions it is appropriate to note that the drive toward larger forms of community and the recognition of the claims of the more inclusive community has been a recurrent factor in the historical process, though one manifesting itself in distorted forms. We may hope that in the present circumstances the weight of those distortions will not merely have the effect of pushing people back into privatism and the comfort of smaller groups, but that the claims of the most encompassing community, that of humankind, will be recognized.[44]

The alternative to an equalization of coercive capacities based on the generalization of the habits and institutions associated with non-violence is a system of authority having at its disposal a well-developed capacity for repression. Abstractly the order made possible by such imposed hierarchy may seem reassuring. In fact many "revolutionaries" prefer such models in practice whatever they may uphold in theory. But here content is all. When an official decision is the one that we would have made, then we will hope that there are means of its being enforced. But when such a decision offends strongly our notions of justice, then we will hope to have recourse against it. In both cases it will be reasonable to hope that the destructive impact of the measures taken can be minimized. Moreover, there is nothing inconsistent in this two-sided orientation to legal authority. Certainly it does not preclude our giving more weight to decisions made according to certain kinds of processes than others. We need not like or agree with that which has the status of law to acquiesce in it or to follow it. We tacitly consent to many laws on the basis of the way in which they have come into being and because the creation of alternatives is in the best of circumstances difficult.

IV

The model of coercion presented here is intended to provide a few hints about the possible contours of one element, i.e. the en-

44. We are currently suffering from crises both of intensive community and of extensive community. In my view the solutions at the two levels are interdependent.

forcement element, in a legal order that would differ markedly from those legal systems with which we are most familiar. The conscious decision to follow such guidelines in behalf of the "global interest" would, of course, be revolutionary. As indicated earlier the existing lack of military might in the United Nations is by no means the result of such a decision. In fact as long as the United Nations relies on existing national governmental structures to enforce and carry out its decisions, its enforcement machinery will remain an integral part of the existing violence system. Even in those instances where the enforcement measures are relatively non-violent, e.g. where certain economic rather than military measures are used, the very nature of the actors employing these measures will preclude their being perceived as genuinely non-violent. Thus it is essential to recognize that the application of the guidelines advocated here will require the reliance on and even the creation of *other kinds* of actors in the global arena.

Such considerations bring us to the implementation problem and to issues I have said I shall not take up here. I think, however, that implementation is unlikely to get under way, and implementation strategies are unlikely to be given serious widespread attention as long as the need, indeed the necessity, for a reliance on non-violent approaches has not become apparent. It is this argument that I have attempted to outline here.

Whether humankind is capable of meeting the challenge of creating legal institutions that are at once more inclusive and less oppressive remains, of course, to be seen. In any event the unique problems connected with the institution of law at the global level should, I think, be seen as an opportunity rather than as an occasion for retreat and despair. For they bring to light in a forceful way the inadequacies of our current concepts of law and our current legal institutions. Indeed nothing should be so obvious as the fact that the generalization of these failings to the global level is an occurrence that is rightly resisted.

Our interdependence, however, does not diminish. Temporarily secret negotiations and old-fashioned bargains struck by those who for the moment hold enormous power may prevent the worst catastrophes (though at a high price for many who are the pawns in this game), but there is nothing that is secure or reliable, certainly nothing very just, in this manner of proceeding. It has been argued that little human progress is made from individual to individual, since each new human being must so to speak start from scratch, but that our institutions can embody in a more permanent way the progress of human insight. This is a partial truth, but an important one. If we care about our collective human future, then we must care enough to attempt to set in motion the beginnings of new traditions and new political forms in which there can be a firmer trust than in the models which we have inherited.

Three
TOWARD CONCEPTUAL ORDER

Introduction

Reflecting on the state of their discipline some political scientists have lamented the lack of an acceptable general theory of international affairs or international relations. The four articles that follow all bear on the possibility of overcoming this lack. In the article on imperialism it is observed that many Marxists (but of course not only they) were skeptical of the chances of a general theory of imperialism. Similar doubts may be raised here not on the popular grounds that general theories of international affairs may be hard to find but on the more deviant ones that there may be no such general theories to discover. To be sure students of international affairs may use laws and theories for explanatory purposes, but why need they seek a special theory they can call their own?

Still, a political scientist venturing to discover and confirm such a theory may gain much. What kind of theory, it may be asked? To some, part of the answer is obvious: Theories here should

   (a) be continuous with those in the natural sciences and
   (b) be tested by the same criteria that are used to test theories in the natural sciences.

Nielsen argues against those who attempt to rebut (b) and who note that the subject matter of the political scientist is subjective and hence differs essentially from the subject matter of the natural sciences; the latter argument at best holds against (a), and (a) is not as it stands very illuminating.

Amplifying (b), many add that theories of international affairs when scientific should

    (c) be descriptive and non-normative and be reducible to theo-
        ries about the behavior of individuals.
Or perhaps more generally
    (d) all statements about groups and nations, when clear, are re-
        ducible to statements about the behavior of individuals of
        which the groups are composed.

As French argues, there are difficulties not only with (d) but with
its more plausible version that requires reduction to statements
about rule-governed actions of group members. Those who deny
(d) and its variants may of course admit that there are conceptual
links involved and argue perhaps that statements about groups
are partially reducible to statements about individuals. But what
predicates applicable to individuals are admissible as the basic
ones? The recommendation in (c) that they be descriptive is no
more illuminating than its kin that they should be observable
ones. Still waiving such objections one may ask with Margolis
whether 'is at war' and allied predicates are simply descriptive
ones. And surely the student of international affairs needs such
predicates.

    Statements about the aim of a discipline are best supported in
light of the outcome of inquiry whether philosophical or scientific. When one attempts to deal with imperialism, responsibility,
war, etc., philosophical and scientific issues naturally intertwine.
The papers that follow may without category mistake be classified
as papers both in political science and philosophy.

8

Imperialism:
Some Preliminary Distinctions*

SIDNEY MORGENBESSER

I

Lately we have all anguished, frequently in protest, about imperialism and its horrors. But protest without theory is blind, and hence we have all been thinking of the varied and confusing and surprisingly widespread theses that purport to describe and explain the behavior of the United States—but not only the United States—in Vietnam, and not only in Vietnam, by reference to imperialism. These theories both convince and confuse, and—to invert in part the early Russell on mathematics—we may say that though we are convinced of the truth of such theories, we are never quite sure that we know what they are about.

First, a word about the history of the term and its sorrows. As such terms go, 'imperialism' is a relatively recent one. It was coined in France in the nineteenth century and introduced into English by critics of Louis Napoleon, who accused him of attempting to revive the policy of his uncle. By an "imperialist" regime these critics meant one in which a great deal of power is held by the central authority, with a corresponding decline of liberty. Despite its recent appearance, the term has as rich and varied a history as some older and more entrenched ones, such as 'revolu-

* This paper is based on an informal talk given before a meeting of the New York Group of the Society for Philosophy and Public Affairs on February 10, 1973. As the title indicates, there is need for refinement and amplification, but I shall not apologize lest I give the impression that I think I have something very profound to say. I want to thank Joann Haimson, Virginia Held, and Tom Nagel for being good friends and critics.

tion.' According to its most reputable historians,[1] the term has changed its meaning at least twelve times; according to others it has lost all meaning. It has been denounced as a useless term, an imperialistic one, a nuisance one, a term to be avoided by scholars (philosophers were not mentioned), a mere term of abuse. Political scientist Hans Morgenthau has recently stated, "The arbitrary use of the term for political purposes has become so widespread, that today *imperialism* and *imperialistic* are indiscriminately applied to any foreign policy, regardless of its actual character, to which the user happens to be opposed."[2]

Similar prima facie reasonable but nevertheless exaggerated views and suggestions were voiced at the end of the nineteenth century.[3] In 1893, when a new government was formed in Hawaii, some Americans suggested that it be recognized by the United States, and the area annexed. President Cleveland was asked to act on the matter, and in his reply to the Congress he denounced American intervention in Hawaii, and insisted that it would be immoral for America to recognize this new government, which

1. See *Economic Imperialism,* edited by Kenneth E. Boulding and Tapan Mukerjee (Ann Arbor: University of Michigan Press, 1972), Introduction by Kenneth Boulding, and "The Concept of Economic Imperialism" by Richard Koebner. Also see Michael Harrington, "Imperialism in the Middle East" in *Israel, Arabs and the Middle East,* edited by Irving Howe and Carl Gershman (New York: Bantam Books, 1972); Conor Cruise O'Brien, "Contemporary Forms of Imperialism" in *Readings in U.S. Imperialism,* edited by K. T. Fann and Donald C. Hodges (Boston: Extending Horizons Books, 1971). See in particular Richard Koebner and Helmut Dan Schmidt, *Imperialism: The Story and Significance of a Political Word, 1840-1960* (London: Cambridge University Press, 1964); A. P. Thornton, *Doctrines of Imperialism* (New York: John Wiley and Sons, 1965); and E. M. Winslow, *The Pattern of Imperialism: A Study in the Theories of Power* (New York: Columbia University Press, 1948).

2. Hans J. Morgenthau, *Politics Among Nations,* 3rd ed. (New York: Knopf, 1960), p. 45.

3. "Imperialism! Hang the word! It buzzes in my noodle
Like bumble-bees in clover time. The talk on't's mostly twaddle;
Yet one would like to fix the thing, as farmer nail up vermin;
Lots o' big words collapse, like blobs, if their sense you once determine."
Quoted from *Punch,* November 23, 1878, in Koebner and Schmidt, *Imperialism.*

he claimed was imposed on Hawaii by American forces. Cleveland was opposed by many who approved of American expansion, but certainly it would not do for critics of Cleveland to denounce *his* action as "imperialistic."

Cleveland's response is an amazing one. There are passages—such as the following—that might have been written by radical critics of present American foreign policy.

> The lawful government of Hawaii was overthrown . . . by a process every step of which, it may safely be asserted, is directly traceable to and dependent for its success upon the agency of the United States acting through its diplomatic and naval representatives.
>
> But for the notorious predilections of the United States minister for annexation, the Committee of Safety, which should be called the committee of annexation, would never have existed.
>
> But for the landing of United States forces upon false pretexts respecting the danger to life and property the Committee would never have exposed themselves to the pains and penalties of treason by undertaking the subversion of the Queen's government.[4]

It is a sign of our times that we find some of his statements amazing instead of platitudinous:

> I suppose that right and justice should determine the path to be followed in treating this subject. If national honesty is to be disregarded and a desire for territorial extension, or dissatisfaction with a form of government not our own, ought to regulate our conduct, I have entirely misapprehended the mission and character of our Government and the behavior which the conscience of our people demands of their public servants.[5]

Neither is it the case that 'imperialism' and 'imperialistic' are necessarily terms of abuse—or "mere terms of abuse," whatever that may mean. There were many in the nineteenth century

4. Cleveland's address may be found in *Documents of Modern History, the Diplomacy of World Power: The United States, 1889-1920*, Arthur S. Link and William M. Leary, Jr., editors (New York: St. Martin's Press, 1970), pp. 9-15.
5. *Ibid.*

who approved of imperialistic policy, and were not using that term deviantly, not even by reference to our own usage. But waiving nineteenth-century cases, we might appeal to some current ones. In a recent work, a number of the Latin American statesmen quoted have come to the conclusion that imperialism is the best form of development for their underdeveloped countries. "De la Torre of Peru proclaims that 'imperialism is necessary for Latin American development', and Ibarra of Ecuador, comes to a similar conclusion: 'Ecuador has no native capital, only foreign investments will bring in such capital which is needed to develop the country.' "[6]

It may be suggested also that many who use the term as one of reproach do so because they disapprove (if they do not abominate), the many late-nineteenth-century paradigm cases of colonialism. They treat the actions of England in China, the actions of the United States in the Philippines, and the actions of all the great powers in Africa, not only as paradigm cases, but as *the* paradigm cases. Many apply the term 'imperialism' to these paradigm cases, and to others believed to resemble them. Note the emphasis on belief. Thus, if one believes that the export of surplus capital characterizes these cases, he or she will define imperialism by reference to this factor; whereas one who does not share this belief will not, of course, allow that proposed definition.

The foregoing considerations relate to the motivation, if not to the point, of the recent theses about so-called U.S. imperialism to which I have already alluded. For their authors often invoke the term 'imperialistic' because they believe present-day American foreign policy resembles the late-nineteenth-century imperialistic behavior whose blameworthiness they take for granted. Not too long ago, certainly prior to U.S. involvement in Vietnam, everyone and his ghost writer seemed to believe that American foreign policy was motivated by a disinterested desire to pursue liberal ideals—albeit, according to the realist, perhaps imprudently at times; today, everyone and his editor seem to be saying

6. J. P. Morray, "The United States and Latin America," in *Latin America, Reform or Revolution,* edited by James Petras and Maurice Zeitlin (Greenwich, Conn.: Fawcett Publication, 1968), p. 106.

that we are imperialistic and, in a way, have been imperialistic all along. To some, all this merely bespeaks our fall from innocence; and some, I am sure, will insist that we have fallen into confusion and are using 'imperialism' simply as a term of reproach—although, as I have indicated, there is certainly more to it than that.

In any event, the popularity of this thesis of U.S. imperialism presents a problem to the radical.[7] A few years ago the radical or revisionist thesis that the United States is an imperialistic nation was a challenging one; today it seems banal, an echo of a commonplace. If the radical is to get a hearing on these issues, perhaps he should drop 'imperialism', and use 'predatory democracy', as suggested by Barrington Moore.[8] But of course the radical—at least the Marxist radical—would resist, for he thinks that he has some good reason for using the term 'imperialism', that he can build a moral case against the United States, if not against all capitalist countries, since he has a theory that such countries must be imperialistic, in his sense.

Below I shall remind you of some well-known criticisms of certain versions—if not the standard version—of that theory. Here I want to suggest that the moral case just referred to may not be a strong one. Observe first that the moral case most radical Marxists make against capitalist society does not require them to show that such a society is or must be imperialistic. Note further, the case that many of these radicals make is weakened if they cannot

7. I am using 'radical', and 'Marxist radical' rather loosely. The picture is this: By 'radical' I mean one who believes that American society is unjust (because, say, of unjust distribution of political and economic power); and that the injustices cannot be removed without fundamental structural changes. (This is admittedly vague.) For our purposes now, we view the Marxist as believing that American society is self-defeating (or self-contradictory), raising problems it cannot solve; and that he can confirm this by appeal to some version of a Marxist theory. The Marxist need not (although actually most do) condemn our society as unjust. Needless to say, not all radicals are Marxists.

There are obviously analogous differences in reaction to imperialism, and I shall try to elucidate them.

8. Barrington Moore, Jr., *Reflections on the Causes of Human Misery* (Boston: Beacon Press, 1970), esp. chap. 5.

show that the type of society they envisage, and whose establishment they support, is itself free of the seeds of imperialism. Of
course their case is weakened even more if it depends upon the
acceptability of a theory about the interconnection between capitalism and imperialism, and then that theory turns out to be debatable. The radical, of course, would appeal to his theory not for
moral reasons alone, but for methodological reasons as well. He
is convinced that there is no point in trying to develop a general
theory of imperialism, and that moreover there is good reason to
believe that we can construct a restricted general theory that will
explain the late-nineteenth-century cases to which I have alluded.
Hence his insistence that the nineteenth-century cases are the
paradigm cases, which in turn supports his view that imperialism
is a stage of monopoly capitalism, or a stage of exploitation of
backward areas by advanced capitalist nations.[9]

I do not follow the radical in this, and not only because I am

9. For a typical Marxist approach, see Howard Sherman, *Radical Political
Economy* (New York: Basic Books, 1972).

"Has there always been imperialism? Certainly, there has been colonial
occupation and plunder since the days of the ancient Egyptians and Persians.
The phenomena of modern imperialism, however, are quite new and different.
The radical, Marxist definition of 'imperialism' emphasizes that the internal
environment of modern imperialism is monopoly capitalism, which only became predominant in Western Europe and the United States in the 1880's and
1890's—so imperialism in the modern sense dates from that period. Furthermore, we emphasize that modern imperialism utilizes not only plunder and
unequal trading, but especially vast amounts of international investment."
(P. 148)

"The Soviet Union cannot be considered imperialist in the capitalist sense,
since it has no private enterprises making profits from exploitation of other
countries. The public firms engaged in foreign trade may still make some
extra profits out of unequal treaties imposed on East European countries, but
these are small amounts in terms of aggregate Soviet incentive to imperialism—while no Soviet individual makes private profit from foreign trade. On the
contrary, like any occupying power, Soviet costs of keeping Eastern Europe in
control to any extent are probably much higher than their current extra
profits from unequal foreign trade. Since the benefits are not concentrated
in a small group, as in the large capitalist firms, it is hard to attribute Soviet
control of East Europe to economic imperialism." (P. 318)

It is not clear whether Sherman is trying to define 'modern imperialism', or
'economic imperialism', or 'imperialism' in the modern sense.

dubious of his theory. One may be dubious about the chances of a general theory of imperialism,[10] as I am, and still concede that theory *A* will explain some instances of imperialism, and theory *B* will explain some other instances, without insisting that only instances explained by theory *A* or instances explained by theory *B* are the paradigm cases of imperialism. There may, for example, be one kind of theory or of explanation required to explain

---

10. The most interesting attempt to construct a general theory of imperialism is that of Schumpeter, who defines imperialism as an objectless disposition on the part of a state to unlimited forcible expansion. This definition has been used by others to support the alternative definition: that imperialism is a quest for world conquest, and a quest for world conquest for its own sake. I do not think his definition appropriate; thus, the United States, when it was imperialistic in the Philippines, was not out for world conquest. On the other hand, his ingenious theory does not actually require that definition, for he himself applies it to cases that do not fit that definition. The more relevant criticism of his theory of imperialism under capitalist situations is, I think, as follows:

Schumpeter believes that imperialism is not necessary for capitalism, and may even be detrimental to it; that, further, the quest for imperialism is due to the pressure of many groups and interests that play an important role in pre-capitalist societies and a less important role in capitalistic societies. And it is because of the fact that such capitalistic societies are losing power, and yet still have status, that they pursue imperialism in order to afford them a role to play. What Schumpeter overlooks in all this is that although imperialism may not be in point of fact useful for capitalism, it may be *believed* to be useful for capitalism, by various capitalist statesmen and capitalists themselves; and to that extent there may be a connection between capitalism and imperialism. There is a converse point that we shall raise in discussing contemporary Marxists who talk about the commitment of current American statesmen to the belief that capitalism is necessary for imperialism.

Schumpeter's theory is a contrary to Lenin's. They both may be wrong: imperialism may be useful for, and neither necessary for nor harmful to, capitalism. Recently some have argued that the Army's influence in the United States may be taken as evidence for a Schumpeter-like thesis. But I do not believe that the U.S. Army is an atavistic institution; its role as an instigator of the Vietnam War has been overemphasized, especially by Bosch. See Joseph Schumpeter, *Social Class. Imperialism* (New York: Meridian Books, 1955; originally published by Augustus M. Kelly Inc., New York, 1951); the discussion of Schumpeter in R. J. Barnet, *Roots of War* (New York: Atheneum, 1972), and Juan Bosch, *Pentagonism. A Substitute for Imperialism* (New York: Grove Press, 1968).

Teapot Dome, and another kind of theory or of explanation needed to explain Watergate; and yet we may or we may not take both of these as paradigm cases of corruption. The Marxist approach, if correct, requires only that we distinguish between types of imperialism, as Durkheim did between types of suicide.

Note, for whatever it is worth, Lenin had no qualms on this matter, for despite his doubts about the advisability of a quest for a general theory of imperialism, he did not deny that there were many pre-capitalist stages of imperialism, Roman and other. And I note in passing that because of our guilt toward the East, we Westerners have frequently talked as though imperialism were exclusively a Western aberration. Statesmen of the East are not that self-abasing. Prince Sihanouk is reported to have said "When we speak of imperialism, we know what we are talking about; we practiced it too long."[11] I must note also that despite my disagreement with some radical theses, I share their main point: that American foreign policy has in recent years often been aggressive, coercive, predatory, and, if you will, imperialistic.[12]

II

In an article by Richard Koebner, Lord Cromer is quoted as stating that, "in a sense it may be said that imperialism is as old as the world," and Koebner adds, "This is the first of many disquisitions in which the concept meant neither more nor less than the phenomenon of empire building throughout history."[13] The conceptual and linguistic links between 'imperialism' and 'empire' are there, but they are not so strong and intimate as the

11. Quoted by Jean Lacouture in *The Demigods* (New York: Knopf, 1970), p. 202.

12. In support of these assertions, see the discussion of Noam Chomsky's analyses in the article by Kai Nielsen in this volume. For additional information see Barrington Moore, Jr., *Reflections on the Causes of Human Misery*, chap. 5 and 6; R. J. Barnet, *Roots of War;* and Michael Hudson, *Super-Imperialism* (New York: Holt, Rinehart and Winston, 1968), especially chap. 6.

13. Richard Koebner, "The Concept of Economic Imperialism" in *Economic Imperialism,* edited by K. Boulding and T. Mukerjee, p. 63.

quotation from Lord Cromer and Koebner's comment upon it suggest or imply. Note first that we may apply 'imperialistic' to a country or more properly to an act of that country even though that act does not express the intention of the country to acquire an empire, or have the result of helping to build one. Such I think was the case when it was said—and correctly, in my opinion —that the United States was acting imperialistically in Mexico at the time of Wilson. Secondly, during a certain period a nation may be an empire or acting as one, without being in any obvious sense imperialistic. The term 'empire' is often employed merely for historical reasons: e.g., when the thirteen ex-colonies became unified the result was called an empire, as was Germany after 1870. It would not do, however, to decide that we were imperialistic in 1790, simply because we were an empire.

More generally: If S is an empire composed of previously independent states, none of which dominates the others, one is not entitled to call S or any one of the states within S imperialistic.

Koebner's proposal allows that S is trying to build an empire, or develop one, though S is not a state; and this is all to the good. We might want to say that princes, emperors, or people not organized as states are building or have empires. The Congo, for instance, was a personal colony of King Leopold's. And S might be a corporation rather than a state, and act imperialistically without being or trying to develop an empire. At all accounts, the suggestion or implication of the quotations with which we began, that S is imperialistic at time t if and only if S is an empire at t, or S tries to acquire or has formed the intention of acquiring an empire, is not warranted as it stands.

Still, the suggestion requires not rejection but emendation; for this, we may consider some restrictions suggested by Lichtheim:

> It so happens that the term 'imperialism' describes a particular kind of reality, even though it is not the kind that can be statistically weighed and measured. What it denotes is a relationship: specifically, the relationship of a ruling or controlling power to those under its dominion. Empire is a state of affairs even when the imperial power is not formally constituted as such.[14]

14. George Lichtheim, *Imperialism* (New York: Praeger, 1971), p. 4.

Once again, we have a proposal which, though congenial, requires minor but we hope not trivial emendations. Note first that it would not do to use 'is imperial' and 'is imperialistic' interchangeably, as does Lichtheim. Portugal, although imperialistic during the twentieth century, has not been imperial. The attribution of 'imperial' to a nation suggests that the nation is a major power, or a power that plays a dominant role in world affairs. Some would argue, and perhaps not without reason, that although the United States has been "imperial" after World War II, it has not been "imperialistic."

Note secondly that Lichtheim attempts a definition. I suggest, rather, that we restrict ourselves to a family of sufficient conditions, and think of S as "imperialistic" if, but not only if, (a) S is the center of an empire, where S is the center of an empire if there are separate areas, or regions, or states U that are ruled by S (in the degenerate case this may be a small and impoverished one), and S is not ready to abandon its dominion, but at best is prepared to promise eventual liberation when, as the saying goes, the colonized are ready for self-government; (b) S uses or is disposed to use force or coercion up to military force and coercion to assure that the dominion continues, or at any rate S has not renounced a policy of coercion either for the acquisition or maintenance of its dominion, although to be sure it may have acquired some of its areas without using coercion; (c) S will not continue its dominion unless S believes that the benefits to it from this dominion outweigh the losses. Some would add (d) the liberties, rights, and political powers of the citizens or inhabitants of the dependent areas are less than those of S. I am not sure about the necessity of (d), and it might be entailed by (a). I think it more acceptable to add (d_1) the dependent community does not have the ultimate authority about its rights and its privileges, or the ultimate authority about the rights and privileges of its citizens; if it has autonomy it has autonomy only in the areas allowed by S.[15]

15. For a definition of 'colony' and types of colonial rule, see J. L. Brierly, *The Law of Nations*, 6th ed. (Oxford: Clarendon Press, 1963), pp. 173-81; Wilfred Cartey and Martin Kilson, *The African Reader. Colonial Africa*

Notice that (a) is really a determinable part of a sufficient condition. At least three more determinants are worthy of note: U might be a non-contiguous (most often overseas), culturally distant[16] area acquired by S as a colony; U might be an area or state proximate to S and annexed by it; U might be settled by mi-

---

(New York: Random House, 1970). See the alternative approach in Herbert Lüthy, "Colonization and the Making of Mankind," in *Imperialism and Colonialism*, edited by G. Nadel and P. Curtis (New York: Macmillan, 1964).

Condition (c) may obtain even if the monetary costs outweigh the monetary benefits. The entire discussion by Adam Smith in *The Wealth of Nations* is valuable. See pages 523-625 of the Modern Library Edition, or pages 144-240 of the Arlington House edition.

"To propose that Great Britain should voluntarily give up all authority over her colonies, and leave them to elect their own magistrates, to enact their own laws, and to make peace and war as they might think proper, would be to propose such a measure as never was, and never will be adopted, by any nation in the world. No nation ever voluntarily gave up the dominion of any province, how troublesome soever it might be to govern it, and how small soever the revenue which it afforded might be in proportion to the expense which it occasioned. Such sacrifices, though they might frequently be agreeable to the interest, are always mortifying to the pride of every nation, and what is perhaps of still greater consequence, they are always contrary to the private interest of the governing part of it, who would thereby be deprived of the disposal of many places of trust and profit, of many opportunities of acquiring wealth and distinction, which the possession of the most turbulent, and, to the great body of the people, the most unprofitable province seldom fails to afford. The most visionary enthusiast would scarce be capable of proposing such a measure, with any serious hopes at least of its ever being adopted. If it was adopted, however, Great Britain would not only be immediately freed from the whole annual expense of the peace establishment of the colonies, but might settle with them such a treaty of commerce as would effectually secure to her a free trade, more advantageous to the great body of the people, though less to the merchants, than the monopoly which she at present enjoys."—From Adam Smith, *The Wealth of Nations*, Vol. II (New Rochelle, N.Y.: Arlington House) p. 211.

16. On cultural distance and cultural change, see H. A. C. Cairns, *The Clash of Race* (New York: Praeger, 1965); V. G. Kiernan, *The Lords of Human Kind* (Boston: Little, Brown, 1969); G. Balandier, "The Colonial Situation: A Theoretical Approach" and F. S. West, "The Study of Colonial History," both in *Social Change: The Colonial Situation*, edited by Immanuel Wallerstein (New York: Wiley, 1969).

grants from S.[17] Cases of both annexation and colonization have frequently been denounced on moral grounds, involving, as they usually do, foreign rule and domination, rule without the assent of the governed, and hence violations of the rights or claims to national self-determination.[18]

17. 'Settlement' was often, of course, a polite word for 'conquest.' For, as the following quotations show, the British Foreign Office often had to defend the rights of the "aborigines" and oppose the settler. " 'It cannot be too strongly impressed upon every European within your government that the lives of the natives must be considered as equally valuable and entitled to the same protection as those of any European settlers,' a governor of western Australia was told. Coloured men were to become assimilated to the Europeans by the diffusion of 'civilisation' (including Christianity) as well as by integration into an economy inevitably dominated by Europeans." From Donald Southgate, *The Passing of the Whigs 1832-1886* (New York: St. Martin's Press, 1962), p. 173.

"An increase in national wealth and power would be inadequate compensation for the injury flowing from the injustice of the act and the calamity to the numerous and inoffensive people who had a recognised title to the soil and to sovereignty. 'It is impossible that the Government should forget that the original aggression was our own,' wrote Russell to the Governor of New South Wales." (Ibid., p. 169)

18. Of course the discussion about the rights of national self-determination of colonized groups became intense only after colonial nationalist movements, often inspired by European ideologies, became popular. But even if we say as J. S. Mill did that "barbaric nations" only have a right to *become* nations, we must add that such people always had a right to be treated as a people, they could demand—or someone "civilized" could demand for them—that their chances of becoming viable nations with pride in their cultures should not be minimized by imperialism.

Mill's strange-sounding words are as follows:

"To suppose that the same international customs, and the same rules of international morality, can obtain between one civilized nation and another, and between civilized nations and barbarians, is a grave error, and one which no statesman can fall into, however it may be with those, who from a safe and unresponsible position, criticise statesmen. Among many reasons why the same rules cannot be applicable to situations so different, the two following are among the most important. In the first place, the rules of ordinary international morality imply reciprocity. But barbarians will not reciprocate. They cannot be depended on for observing any rules. Their minds are not capable of so great an effort, nor their will sufficiently under the influence of distant motives. In the next place, nations which are still barbarous have not got beyond the period during which it is likely to be for their benefit that they

Colonization gives rise to other problems and considerations: the colonized, or at least their culture, may often be treated as inferior; the colonizers have economic advantages as they establish economic enclaves; the economy of the colonized may be hurt. China's president, Mao Tse-tung, once remarked to a delegation of nationalists from a still French Algeria, "The bond that unites

---

should be conquered and held in subjection by foreigners. Independence and nationality, so essential to the due growth and development of a people further advanced in improvement, are generally impediments to theirs. The sacred duties which civilized nations owe to the independence and nationality of each other are not binding towards those to whom nationality and independence are either a certain evil, or, at best, a questionable good. The Romans were not the most clean-handed of conquerors; yet would it have been better for Gaul and Spain, Numidia and Dacia, never to have formed part of the Roman Empire? To characterize any conduct whatever towards a barbarous people as a violation of the law of nations, only shows that he who so speaks has never considered the subject. A violation of great principles of morality it may easily be; but barbarians have no rights as a *nation*, except a right to such treatment as may, at the earliest possible period, fit them for becoming one. The only moral laws for the relation between a civilized and a barbarous government are the universal rules of morality between man and man."—From John Stuart Mill, *Dissertations and Discussions: Political, Philosophical, and Historical*, Vol. III (New York: Henry Holt, 1874), pp. 252-53.

On the issue of national self-determination, see John Plamenatz, *On Alien Rule and Self-Government* (London: Longmans, 1960), and Rupert Emerson, "The New Higher Law of Anti-Colonialism," in *The Relevance of International Law*, edited by Karl Deutsch and Stanley Hoffmann (New York: Doubleday/Anchor, 1971), pp. 203-31. Compare Hannah Arendt, *The Origins of Totalitarianism* (New York: Harcourt, Brace, 1951), pp. 126-27:

"In contrast to the economic structure, the political structure cannot be expanded indefinitely, because it is not based upon the productivity of man, which is, indeed, unlimited. Of all forms of government and organizations of people, the nation-state is least suited for unlimited growth because the genuine consent at its base cannot be stretched indefinitely, and is only rarely, and with difficulty, won from conquered peoples. No nation-state could with a clear conscience ever try to conquer foreign peoples, since such a conscience comes only from the conviction of the conquering nation that it is imposing a superior law upon barbarians. The nation, however, conceived of its law as an outgrowth of a unique national substance which was not valid beyond its own people and the boundaries of its own territory.

"Wherever the nation-state appeared as conqueror, it aroused national consciousness and desire for sovereignty among the conquered people."

us, is that we have both been humiliated."[19] For many, this is the bond of the victims of either colonialism or imperialism.[20]

Notice that when we say that U has been colonized by S we are not asserting simply that S has acquired U as a colony, and let it go at that. When an area U is colonized by S, there are citizens of S who settle there, some as representatives of the state, some as homesteaders or colonizers, and these latter especially acquire

---

19. Quoted in A. P. Thornton, *Doctrines of Imperialism*, p. 7.

20. Recently many have suggested that the arrogance toward the colonized was a compensation-phenomenon; the colonizer felt inferior because he did not make it at home. Consider, however, the following from the biography of a non-failure at home.

"In the summer of 1857 the Indian Mutiny had broken out. Miss Nightingale longed to leave her desk and go out to the troops, but Sidney Herbert prevented her. 'I may tell you in confidence,' she wrote to Dr. Pattinson Walker in 1865, 'that in 1857, that dreadful year for India, I offered to go out to India in the same way as to the Crimea. But Sidney Herbert . . . put a stop to it. He said that I had undertaken this work, caused him to undertake it and that I must stay and help him.' She consoled herself with the reflection that by her work for the army in England she was saving more lives than by going to India. 'What are the murders committed by these miserable Bengalese compared to the murders committed by the insouciance of educated cultivated Englishmen?' she wrote to Sidney Herbert in September, 1857."—From Cecil-Blanche Woodham-Smith, *Florence Nightingale* (New York: Avon Books), p. 221 (originally published by McGraw-Hill, 1951).

And David S. Landes writes:

"More than anything, more even than the enormous material costs of imperialism, it was the imposition of inferior social and moral status that shaped the reaction of the Egyptian to the European. Actually, the one implies the other: material exploitation is difficult if not impossible without the sanction of a double set of values and a corresponding double code of behaviour; if they were not there to begin with, the exploiter would have to create them. The fact remains, however, that in the many-sided impact of imperialism, it is the injury to self-respect that hurts most. It is the resentment aroused by spiritual humiliation that gives rise to an irrational response to rational exploitation. The apparently unreasonable, and certainly unprofitable, resistance of many of the world's underdeveloped countries today to Western business enterprise makes sense only in this context."—From *Bankers and Pashas* (New York: Harper Torchbooks), p. 323 (originally published by Harvard University Press, 1958).

Notice, however, that there is no rule about ruling. The Romans, as the saying goes, captured the Greeks and were captured by them.

disproportionate political and economic power. Colonization is therefore unjust not only because of the bond of colonization, a bond which to many is evidence of the arrogance of the colonizer; it also either gives rise to or accentuates an unfair distribution of income and political power in U. Some may argue that this distribution is not really unjust, since there could be no equally beneficial alternative, let us say, to the least advantaged; but I seriously doubt that this can be demonstrated in any case. Colonization is perhaps subject to another criticism: it may very well increase the disparity of wealth between nations, perhaps unjustly. And these criticisms retain their force even if we grant that European imperialistic activity has brought some benefits, perhaps even important ones, to the areas it colonized, and admit with Marx and others that the European imperialists on occasion replaced unjust governments or even empires.

Since it is apparent that colonialism gives rise to special moral problems, it might be helpful to distinguish among colonization, the acquisition of distant areas as a result of settlement, and annexation or aggrandizement. First let us consider these three as types of imperialism or imperial domination, and then classify colonization as the paradigm type of imperialism. And it would be even more appropriate to do so if it developed that three kinds of theories or three kinds of explanations are needed to account for them. There is, however, no canonical way of dealing with these matters. Even Marxists, who are often terminologically fastidious in using these terms, have not been very consistent here.[21] They generally argue that colonialism or the economic domination of backward areas is the distinguishing mark of imperialism, they admit that Hitler was imperialistic even though Nazism did not involve colonialism; Hitler thought colonialism a mistake. And of course many who define imperialism as the policy or the quest for world domination regard Hitler's behavior as *the* para-

---

21. I find Dobb helpful but not convincing here. See Maurice Dobb, *Studies in the Development of Capitalism* (London: Routledge and Kegan Paul, 1951), pp. 372-81. See also the valuable discussion by Oscar Lange in his review of Paul M. Sweezy's *The Theory of Capitalist Development* (1942) in *Journal of Philosophy,* Vol. 40, no. 14 (July 1943), pp. 378-84, esp. p. 380.

digm case of imperialism. From one perspective Hitler's policy may be considered a paradigm case of ultra-aggrandizing imperialism, but not one of imperialism *simpliciter.* When Bismarck and other European statesmen sought colonies, they were not seeking world domination, and indeed often, perhaps paradoxically, sought colonies, especially in Africa in order to stabilize the power relations between states. I add that many have seen Hitler as a perfect instance of Schumpeter's version of imperialism, "the objectless disposition on the part of a state to unlimited forcible expansion."[22] That seems to me a good definition of military barbarism.

We might mention a converse point and in the process repay our debt to Lord Cromer and to Koebner. If a state S builds an empire even though originally by force or coercion, and if all the incorporated states are treated equally under a common law, and none wants to leave the empire, I shall say that S has been engaged in "empirialism." Some historians might maintain that Rome engaged first in imperialism and then in empirialism—but we need not decide the issue here. The distinction might be relevant for discussion of cases of annexation. Perhaps it is the case that hawkish Israelis are opting for an aggrandizing empirialist policy.[23]

22. Joseph Schumpeter, *Social Class. Imperialism,* p. 51; see also p. 64.
23. Some authors distinguish between two types of imperialism—the imperialism of the colony-acquisition (Greek) type, and the imperialism motivated by idealism and striving for world empire (Roman type). And some authors insist that the term 'imperialism' should not be used in the second way at all. Thus, according to some the Roman Empire was not really imperialistic, since it attempted to afford all people the equal protection of common citizenship and of a rational law. The Roman Empire, at least in principle, was committed to the end of imperialism in the first sense—that is, committed to abolish the dominion of one state over another. It will be obvious that I tend to consider imperialism of the colonizing type in this section, imperialism of the second type below; but there are differences in approach which will be easily noticed, I hope.

There are other important variations which deserve brief attention here. In the nineteenth century many in England defended what they called "true imperialism"—that is, the policy of trying to establish close ties between a mother-country and countries settled by English subjects. They were opposed to colonizing alien cultures and acquiring alien colonies. I label this "associa-

It is widely believed that the United States was not imperialistic until the end of the nineteenth century—until, as it is usually put, it attempted colonization and acquisition of territories overseas. But even those who insist that the United States was not imperialistic until that period do not deny that the nation often acted imperialistically in areas it was not interested in colonizing. Above, as against Koebner, I called attention to Wilson's actions, and I must now deal with those and comparable instances. There is no major problem, for I believe that such cases may be handled by a minor extension of the sufficient conditions thus far introduced—that is, by weakening some of the conditions, and applying 'imperialistic' either to acts of a certain type or to a nation disposed to perform acts of these types.

Notice that if U is colonized by S, U has lost its sovereignty. By extension we may say that S has acted imperialistically in U if S violates or diminishes the sovereignty of U, if S is a powerful country and U is not, if S undertakes the action with little presumed risk to itself and in order to have U adopt a policy believed by S to be beneficial to S itself, or to some of its members or interest groups. Instances abound: sending in the Marines, establishing extraterritorial rights, interfering with or rigging elections. Strictly speaking, we should distinguish between aggrandizing and other types of imperialistic acts. I hope I need not press this point. Let's not multiply distinctions beyond possibility!

The extension is obviously a relatively minor one; some would probably claim that it is too minor. They would revise condition (a) slightly and not focus attention upon (c) and (d); they would argue that a country S is imperialistic if, or perhaps only if, it expands its area of domination—by conquest or violence if necessary, and by other means (e.g., by purchase) if possible. And many who argue this way conclude that the United States has been imperialistic since its inception, since it has been continuously

---

tive imperialism." There were also variations in colonial policies. France tried to *assimilate* into French culture the elites among her colonial subjects. As is well known, the assimilative policy has strong political consequences today.

adding to its dominion, pursuing repeatedly by conquest a policy of expansion, first westward and then overseas. This is misleading; there are good grounds for the widely adopted thesis that this was not an imperialistic nation until the late 1890's. The grounds I have already alluded to—namely, that those who were included in the new area did assent to their inclusion, and were not given fewer rights than the ordinary citizen. The real case for American imperialism is based not on the expansion, but on our treatment of the Indian, and perhaps the Negro. Even here—although I hesitate to say this—we were not necessarily imperialistic toward the Indians. More accurately, we were not colonizing them but rather were behaving in a predatory manner toward them.

There are of course certain kinds of behavior that are worse than imperialistic behavior. Obviously, Hitler was not colonizing the Jews, yet what he did was unspeakably worse; so that when I assert that we were not imperialistic toward the Indian, I am not suggesting that we were behaving toward the Indian better than the English behaved toward the peoples of India and Africa. Again, some may argue that though we did not colonize the Negro, but rather enslaved him, slavery is a form of internal colonization; but to my lights enslavement is obviously worse than colonization. At all accounts it would be stretching language needlessly to say that if A coerces B for A's benefit, then A colonizes B. And it is not the case that all coercive acts and policies of imperialistic nations need be labeled "imperialistic." We may have been imperialistic vis-à-vis Vietnam; yet some of our acts there are, I think, better labeled "barbaric."

Needless to say, there is room for dispute; I have thus far only suggested some conditions sufficient for the application of 'imperialistic.' Perhaps, then, the United States acted quasi-imperialistically toward Spain and Mexico: it expanded at their expense, and certainly with violence and not with their consent. It did not act imperialistically toward the settlers in the West; it acted imperialistically in its treatment of the Philippine people, and perhaps repeatedly barbarically toward the Indians and others. Thus, e.g., the Philippine rebels who fought originally with the consent and encouragement of Admiral Dewey for their freedom from

Spain, and then were slaughtered when they fought for their freedom from the Americans. And though, as I have suggested, it is misleading simply to say that we were an imperialistic nation from the beginning, and false to say that all our foreign policies were imperialistic, it is nevertheless true that neither our actions after 1890 nor our actions in Vietnam were our first acts of infamy.

I have reminded you of the moral case against imperialism. Needless to say in the nineteenth century there were many who saw the issues differently. There were many who defended, if not each one of our actions in the Philippines, at least our over-all policy there. There were many in the nineteenth century who thought that imperialistic activities of the sort I have described were justified in general, since they were indispensable to the viability of their state, or indispensable if their state was to play a leading role in the world of nations, or important for their nation's economy. The moral limitations of these positions are, I hope, obvious, for such positions overlook the effects of imperialism on those colonized. Still, not all those who defended imperialism defended the type of policies thus far considered. Many defended a version of what may be called benign or beneficial imperialism—namely, that a state should rule over backward regions only if such rule is beneficial to the citizens or inhabitants of those regions and not coercive. And believing as they did—that rule by advanced states was necessary not only to increase the welfare of "backward areas" but also (to use current lingo anachronistically) to satisfy the basic needs of the inhabitants of these areas—they pressed for colonization.

It would, I think, be unfair to classify the attitudes and beliefs of the benign imperialist as paternalistic and arrogant and expressive of an insensitivity to the values of non-white cultures. Benign imperialism is compatible with an appreciation of the cultures of African and Asian peoples, and many African natives appreciated the work of some of the benign imperialists, especially of the missionaries, who were often obviously persons of good will and dedication yet engaging in what may be called imperialism-inducing behavior. That is to say, their activities, though not necessarily sanctioned by their home governments, increased the likelihood of imperialism, as their activities in certain regions led to their states' becoming increasingly interested in those regions, and later to imperialistic policies in those regions.

As I shall argue below, many Americans want their country to be a beneficial imperial power. Those who argue thus face some problems that were also faced by the defenders of benign imperialism. Let us therefore stay a brief while if not with the benign imperialist, then with some of his conceptual burdens.

Note that when missionaries called upon their states to act beneficially they were not necessarily hopelessly naïve. Many of them realized that most modern states are not beneficial ones and that statesmen, even those believing that they would act only beneficially, would soon enough sanction or have to sanction imperialistic policies that were not beneficial. Still, the missionaries had some reason to believe that there was no necessity in this, and that their state was potentially beneficial. Note that many Marxists at the end of the nineteenth century also believed in beneficial imperialism, but thought it realizable only by socialist states of the future. They thought that under capitalist conditions beneficial imperialism was doomed to absurdity or impotence. The option, even admissible as a possibility, would never in practice be accepted; because of class interests it would always have to give way to a non-beneficial policy.

The beliefs of the Marxists and missionaries are difficult to analyze and cannot be criticized without review of, among other things, complicated theories about modern nations and states. But they are understandable, and call attention to an important distinction that perhaps we all tacitly make. Before Hitler it was believed that modern states were not disposed to genocide, and further it was believed that modern states were not possibly genocidal, that either they had ruled out that option, or would rule it out if it were ever suggested. Cleveland's address could be interpreted to mean not only that the United States was not disposed to imperialistic action, but also that as a nation we had ruled it out as an option.

It may therefore be incumbent upon us to add to our lexicon such phrases as 'is possibly imperialistic at t,' and 'is potentially imperialistic at t.' But I am not sure what I can say in a systematic way about possible and potential imperialism. The reasons certain options are accessible to a given state or institution, are not ruled out either as absurd or impermissible or silly, are not always apparent. To be sure, often enough there is no mystery. I think we all know or at least believe we know why the option of dividing the world between states and princes is not now accessible to the Pope. I am not quite sure we know why the option of sending in the Marines to the Dominican Republic to "save it" from an ostensible threat of Communist takeover was accessible to President Johnson, and the option of sending in the Marines to collect a debt was not accessible—at least it was not in my perhaps naïve opinion. We often do not know why one type of imperialistic option is accessible at t when another one has vanished. And of course projections about accessible options are hazardous, and may be made with assurance only by those who believe that all options are accessible to major power-seeking states that apparently have no shame. Still, many are surprised and/or shocked that the Nixon Administration allowed itself such options as the Christmas bombing of Hanoi, and the Watergate activities.

There is another point here that deserves attention. Once a very horrible option is chosen, the less horrible ones are seen in a new light, they are not quite that bad. When Leopold acted the way he did in the Congo, the behavior of the other imperialists seemed quite decent by contrast; and after all, we are not so bad as Hitler and Stalin. Once a very horrible option is acted upon and becomes a matter of policy, critics of apparently less horrible policies often fall into a trap. They try to prove that appearances are deceptive, and they have often weakened their case by leaving themselves open to counterattack. This may very well have happened when some critics of the Vietnam War tried to prove that we were really genocidal there. But of course each case must be argued on its merits; there is no point issuing the general notice that others may have fallen into traps.

Taking options as given, viewing them as explained or easily explainable, we may attempt to explain why a given option is acted upon by reference to the interests, wants, utilities—to be fashionable—of citizens or, more particularly, of relevant powerful interest groups, and the beliefs and utilities of statesmen. Presuming these latter to be honest, we may view their utilities as expressing state interests, and then use whatever laws or lawful statements we have available.

Assume now that we had laws to the effect that S acts imperialistically if and only if S has certain interests, or acts imperialistically if and only if it has certain desires, or acts imperialistically if and only if it is committed to a specific ideology. Then we could propose identifying imperialism with any of these factors, and hold that 'imperialism' means the same as 'commitment to expansion for its own sake,' or 'the desire for economic domination of the world,' or 'belief in the white man's burden.' But I doubt that we know any such laws, and hence my pedestrian attempts at specification of sufficient conditions, attempts that I cannot justify by appeal to theory.

What we do have is information that supports the claim that certain types of activities, or interests, or beliefs, of a nation are imperialism-inducing. And we may—perhaps with an abuse of language—apply 'imperialistic' to these particular activities, interests, and beliefs alone. Thus it is not literally true that heavy investments by corporations in a backward area are imperialistic, but still we can understand those who insist that they are. Why quibble, and say that heavy investments by corporations in under-developed areas are merely imperialism-inducing? Why quibble especially when it is claimed that the results of corporate investment (using this last as a code word for diverse types of economic activities and interests) in economically underdeveloped countries resemble some of the results of colonization?

Above I indicated that many claimed—and with good reason, I thought—that colonization results in an unjust distribution of political and economic power in the colonized areas, and accentuates an already unjust distribution of income and wealth between states. Here it is important to add, that many claim that the relevant heavy investments have similar results, although not in colonized areas; still we may, some say, use the term 'neo-colonized' for them. Though the latter bundle of theses has often been contested, I shall not question them but rather observe that they show only that colonization and certain types of heavy investment are both unjust. The justification for labeling the latter type of investment "imperialistic" and not only unjust depends upon the acceptance of either of two claims: (1) that corporations are imperialistic,[25] manipulative of governments, and so on; or

25. I have been concerned with political or state imperialism. Many who speak of economic imperialism do not mean simply state imperialism induced by economic interests. Perhaps we can understand them to be referring to imperialistic relations between corporations and weak states, or between policies and weak states.

Thus, assume that we treat all overseas-investing corporations of a given state S as an entity C. Then we may say that C is imperialistic in U if (but not only if)

1. U is a weak state, C is economically powerful.
2. C pursues policies K that are not beneficial for U.
3. U is coerced into accepting policies K.
4. Policies K accentuate unjust distributions of economic and political power in U, and between U and S.
5. C would not opt for K unless the benefits to C outweigh the costs to C, as perceived by C.
6. C dominates the modern sector of the economy of U. Citizens of U have inferior jobs in the industries or companies financed and/or owned by C.

K may also be considered imperialistic.

We may also talk about the imperialism of a given economic policy (not imposed by corporations or by states) if such policy is imposed on a weak state and is not beneficial to it. There is much interesting discussion of free-trade policy from this perspective in *Unequal Exchange. A Study in the Imperialism of Free Trade,* by Arghiri Emmanuel (New York: Modern Review, 1972).

I do not know how useful these suggestions will be. It is not often plausible to treat all corporations as a unit; further, even weak nations can play off corporations from the same nation against one another, and even more so, corporations from different nations. Observe also that when the state S offers grants-in-aid to U, these grants and the policies or corporations may combine to be beneficial to U. Far too often radical critics write as though economically backward countries have simply been pillaged by strong states. Taiwan and Korea, e.g., have grown economically as a result of American policy.

Frequently discussions of the skewed international distribution of economic power and wealth concentrate attention upon the power and wealth of inter-

(2) that they are imperialism-inducing—that is, that they induce imperialistic action by the state. Since I am here primarily concerned with state imperialism, only the second need concern us. I have already cited and not challenged that thesis. Now I do so —or rather I challenge some of its uses and interpretations.

Two men may be irritable but have become irritated by different kinds of things, and one of them may lose his irritability temporarily. He has heard that his girl-friend has left him, or he is temporarily under sedation.

Similarly certain types of activities, interests, and beliefs may be imperialism-inducing for one person or state and not for another, and may induce imperialism for one state or person at one time and not another.[26] Thus, the desire to increase trade will not be imperialism-inducing if leaders of a country have ruled out imperialism as a policy for increasing trade, and the desire to be the leading scientific nation in the world may become imperialism-inducing if conditions between nations change. And of course if we distinguish between types of imperialistic option the issue is even clearer. As we have already noted, debt-defaulting on the part of South American states induced military imperialistic ven-

---

national corporations. Russia and China must, however, be considered too, as in the following quotation.

"James Ridgeway has recently calculated ownership patterns of the earth's mineral resources. He predicts that the mineral resources of the earth will soon be under the control of four centers of power: the predominantly American multinational corporations, the predominantly European multinational corporations, the Soviet state enterprise, and the Chinese state enterprise. If the attempt of a few hundred corporate managers in multinational private and state enterprises to determine how and where the resources of the whole earth shall be developed is successful, these members of the new international managerial class will for practical purposes be the first world conquerors in history." (R. J. Barnet, *Roots of War*, p. 237)

See Walter Elkan, *An Introduction to Development Economics* (Baltimore: Penguin Books, 1973), for a balanced view of some of these issues, and compare to the more conservative views of Charles Perrow, *The Radical Attack on Business. A Critical Analysis* (New York: Harcourt, Brace, Jovanovich, 1972), chap. 3; and Charles P. Kindleberger, *Power and Money* (New York: Basic Books, 1970), chap. 5.

26. Virginia Held's comments have been very helpful here.

tures on our part not too long ago, but does not do so at present. If we return to economic interests we may recall that in the great nineteenth-century debate on imperialism a large number of people who were anti-imperialistic and opposed to acquisition of the Philippines—Carl Schurz and Andrew Carnegie among others—did want the United States to have an increasing share of the world market.

Recently some critics and historians of imperialism, influenced by what I take to be a skewed reading of a seminal article by Gallagher and Robinson[27] have argued that Great Britain in the mid-nineteenth century adopted a free-trade policy, or a policy of informal empire, when the government held that that policy would allow the nation economic domination, and later adopted a colony-acquiring policy when that policy was believed necessary to retain her relative economic power and her position. Free trade and informal empire, and colonization and formal empire, are then considered by some as alternative methods to accomplish the same ends, and are both identified as forms of imperialism—one the imperialism of free trade and one the standard form of imperialism. But since these critics have not argued that the free-trade policy was coercive—although to be sure free-trade policies may very well be—and some of them have even noted that England's policy was not coercive,[28] their phrase 'imperialism of free trade' seems to me to be misleading.

Consider a man who wants money and has been a crook for a long time; if he suddenly decides to go straight, and gets an honest job, we won't say, Well look, this man hasn't really changed —now that he's working he's an informal crook. Obviously, there are different ways of getting the same results—namely, money. Similarly, we should not say that there are two forms of imperialism, the imperialism of free trade and the regular kind. We are,

27. John Gallagher and Ronald Robinson, "The Imperialism of Free-Trade," reprinted in *Great Britain and the Colonies, 1815-1865*, edited by A. G. L. Shaw (London: Methuen, 1970).

28. See the discussion in Bernard Semmel, *Imperialism and Social Reform, English Social-Imperial Thought 1895-1914* (New York: Doubleday/Anchor, 1968), pp. 134-36 (first published by Allen & Unwin, London, 1960).

however, likely to say—and correctly—about a crook who takes a job, Look here, he is still crooked, if we *think* that he hasn't really changed and, if he finds the job too boring or secure, would easily go back to his old ways.

We might similarly say about a nation that it is still imperialistic, although it has stopped colonizing, if we believe the country still has the disposition to colonize again, or more generally to be imperialistic again in another sense of that term. But it does not follow that a nation eager to expand its share in the world-market and believing that it can do so by free trade or by following an open-door policy automatically has the disposition to become a colonizer or an imperialist. It is better, I think, on the basis of the specific information provided, to say of the free traders in England in the nineteenth century that even though not imperialistic, or disposed to demand imperialistic policies of their government, they had the disposition to become imperialists. As Marx noted, "If the free traders cannot understand how one nation can grow rich at the expense of another we need not wonder, since these same gentlemen also refuse to understand how within one country one class can enrich itself at the expense of another."[29]

Perhaps, then, those who argue that certain economic interests or activities are imperialistic intend to claim that states which prize such activities and interests are actual or potential imperialists, that the options of acting imperialistically in order to safeguard these interests are accessible to such states. As I have already stated, I am not in a position to say anything systematic about potential imperialism and hence cannot claim reasons to dissent from the thesis just introduced. An imperialist option is accessible to a state if the state does not rule it out or would not rule it out if ————. But I do not know how to fill in the blank.

With more information about specific states we may be in a position to be more informative. Thus if we know or have reason to believe that a state is not averse to the use of coercive and aggressive means up to the use of military ones, that it is a pow-

29. Karl Marx, *The Poverty of Philosophy* (Moscow: Foreign Language Publication House, n.d.), p. 223.

erful state and prizes certain economic interests, then we risk
little if we claim that these interests are imperialism-inducing in
or for that state.

Some have argued that the American policy toward underdeveloped countries is a form of neo-colonialism[30] or neo-imperialism
because that policy is motivated by a desire to assure access to
markets and raw materials. I suggest that they also mean to add
that America is not averse to using coercive means to increase
the probability of satisfying these purposes. Here then we have
guides for inquiry: if the United States has used coercive and
aggressive and even military means, then it may very well have
used them to accomplish economic ends; if it deems it necessary
or even convenient, the United States will use coercive and even
military means to accomplish these ends.

These guides or theses are reasonable and are of course compatible with a variety of subsidiary ones.[31] The United States has

30. The terms 'neo-imperialism', 'neo-colonialism', and 'client-state' are used
in many ways. Consider the following conditions:

  I. S is a major state. U is not . . . , U is economically weak.
 II. Citizens of S have access to the markets and materials of U and domi-
     nate the modern sector of U.
III. U is a military ally of S; U depends upon S for military aid.
 IV. U receives grants-in-aid and loans from S, and depends upon them for
     needed projects.
  V. U has been coerced by S into accepting conditions I or II.
 VI. U had been a colony of S; U-citizens have been assimilated into the cul-
     ture of S.

  I suggest that

if I, III, IV obtain, then U is a client state of S;

if I, II, III, IV obtain, then U is a neo-imperial state of S;

if I, II, III, IV, V obtain, then U is a neo-colonized state of S;

if I, II, III, VI obtain, then U is a neo-colonial state of S;

if I, II, III, IV, V, VI obtain, then U is neo-colonized and neo-imperialized
by S.

  See the interesting article by Martin Bronfenbrenner, "Burdens and Benefits
of Empire," in *Economic Imperialism*, edited by K. Boulding and T. Mukerjee,
esp. pp. 296-97.

31. For a review of some of these issues see Michael Hudson, *Super-Imperialism*; Robert W. Tucker, *The Radical Left and American Foreign Policy*
(Baltimore: John Hopkins University Press, 1971); Noam Chomsky, Hans

on occasion not acted to satisfy economic interests; it has often been coercive and imperialistic for other reasons; it has often not acted coercively or imperialistically to accomplish economic ends. The United States was not imperialistic when it adopted the Marshall plan, even though the Marshall plan was not a disinterested one, and was undertaken at least in part to help the recovery of Europe, which was deemed necessary for our economy and for our export trade. Can we advance beyond the reasonable or perhaps too reasonable and timid theses just introduced? Many recent critics of American policy think they can. They believe that the ends of imperialism and its *necessity,* not its mere possibility or probability, were made evident by Lenin. So let us turn to a consideration of his views. Though they have frequently been discussed, they have also, on some issues at least, been misinterpreted and abused.

III

I warn that I shall use the discussion of Lenin's thesis[32] as a con-

Morgenthau, and others, *Symposium on the National Interest and the Pentagon Papers, Partisan Review* (Summer 1972), pp. 336-75; G. S. Jones, "The History of U.S. Imperialism," in *Ideology in Social Science,* edited by Robin Blackburn (New York: Pantheon Books, 1972), pp. 207-38; and Peter Dale Scott, *The War Conspiracy* (New York: Bobbs-Merrill, 1970).

32. For this section I am deeply indebted to Professor Alexander Erlich, from whose manuscript of an article on Imperialism I have learned so very much.

For Hobson's thesis see J. A. Hobson, *Imperialism. A Study.* (Ann Arbor, Univ. of Michigan Press, 1965, originally published 1902). I note also the following references from which I have profited: "The New Imperialism: The Hobson-Lenin Thesis Revisited" by D. K. Fieldhouse, in *Imperialism and Colonialism,* edited by George H. Nadel and Perry Curtis (New York: Macmillan, 1964); "Economic Imperialism Revisited" by Mark Blaugh, in *Economic Imperialism,* edited by Kenneth Boulding and Tapan Mukerjee; "Reflection on Imperialism and the Scramble for Africa" by L. H. Gann and Peter Dunigan in *Colonialism in Africa, 1870-1960* (Cambridge University Press, 1969); "The Problem of Effective Demand with Tugan Baranovski and Rosa Luxembourg," chap. 13 in Michael Kalecki, ed., *Selected Essays on the Dynamics of the Capitalist Economy* (Cambridge University Press, 1971); *An Essay on Marxian Economics* by Joan Robinson (New York: St. Martin's Press, 1966), esp. chap. 5.

venient opportunity to consider a family of what I take to be relevant theses, and will often seem to resemble the medieval theo-
logian. More often than not I shall be trying to say that Lenin is
not saying this or that.

In our discussion up to this point we have assumed that for
capitalist states imperialism is one option among many. Lenin,
as hinted above, challenged that assumption; for him, imperialism is not an option for capitalist states, but a necessity. Note,
however, that Lenin, and before him Hobson, did not say that S
is imperialistic if and only if S is an advanced capitalist state. Nor
did he say without qualification that imperialism is simply a late
or last stage of monopoly capitalism. Repeated attempts to discredit Lenin and Hobson on the grounds that capitalism and imperialism do not go hand in hand are, I think, beside the point.
Lenin explicitly recognized Roman imperialism and acknowledged that there were motives other than the ones he specified
for imperialistic behavior, even for capitalist states. As he explicitly said, he was restricting his attention to some of the important
economic aspects of imperialism. We might add that Lenin knew
his Marx, and that Marx did not believe that the British conquest
and continued domination of India and Ireland were induced by
the needs of capitalism.[33]

Some of the criticisms in the text apply also to the approaches of Baran and
Sweezy. See, however, "Notes on the Theory of Imperialism" by Paul A. Baran
and Paul M. Sweezy, in *Economic Imperialism*, edited by Boulding and
Mukerjee; *Advocates of Colonialism* by Z. Chernyak (Moscow: Progress Pub-
lishers, 1968); and "Monopoly Capitalism and Neo-Marxism" by Raymond
Lubitz, in *Capitalism Today*, edited by Daniel Bell and Irving Kristol (New
York: New American Library, 1970), pp. 189-92.

33. "The late Russian war may fairly be charged to the Indian account, since
the fear and dread of Russia, which led to that war, grew entirely out of
jealousy as to her designs on India. Add to this the career of endless conquest
and perpetual aggression in which the English are involved by the possession
of India, and it may well be doubted whether, on the whole, this dominion
does not threaten to cost quite as much as it can ever be expected to come to."
—From Karl Marx, "British Incomes in India," in K. Marx and F. Engels, *On
Colonialism. Articles from the New York Tribune and Other Writings* (New
York: International Publishers, 1972), pp. 171-72.

But is Lenin not contradicting himself when he says that imperialism is the last, or a late, stage of monopoly capitalism, and then includes Rome among the cases of imperialism? Strictly speaking, Yes, but there is no problem. Lenin may be interpreted as either offering a comparative definition or attempting to specify the distinguishing mark of modern imperialism. Assume that $F_1 \ldots _n$ play a causal role in all imperialistic contexts, that they are invariant inducers of imperialism, that E^0 plays a causal role in and only in Roman contexts, and that E^1 plays a causal role in and only in modern ones. Then when we attempt to compare Roman and modern imperialism we may appeal to E^1 as the distinguishing mark of modern imperialism. Hence Lenin's statement that imperialism—that is, modern imperialism—is the last stage of monopoly capitalism—that is, that the needs, interests, and problems of monopolies are uniquely the inducers of modern imperialism. But of course not the only ones.

Remember that Lenin, in commenting on Kautsky, said: "Imperialism is a striving for annexation—that is what the *political* part of Kautsky's definition amounts to. It is correct but very incomplete, for politically imperialism is, in general, a striving toward violence and reaction."[34] There may be some misunderstanding produced by Lenin's thesis that monopolistic capitalist states must be imperialistic. But of course there shouldn't be. I may predict safely enough that a man will eat because he has to eat, allowing of course that he will eat for other reasons as well.

Marxists, or certain Marxists, write as though they must deny the facts of life, and cannot admit that some imperialists wanted imperialism for the sake of glory, others to have their state keep up with other states, others in order for their state to have expendable soldiers, and others to satisfy the cries of the missionaries. Far too often Marxists write as though the imperialist must be a capitalist who thinks only of income and profit. But there is no need for a Marxist to assume that, at least if he is merely trying to establish a Lenin-like thesis that capitalism leads to imperialism.

34. V. I. Lenin, *Imperialism, the Highest Stage of Capitalism: A Popular Outline* (New York: International Publishers, 1939), p. 91.

Of course it may be claimed that as capitalism develops, non-economic motives and non-economic interest groups and institutions play a decreasing causal role within capitalist states. But not all do; patriotism and nationalism have not declined. Moreover, as capitalism develops, new motivating factors may appear, especially when non-capitalist states develop as well. The commitment to the capitalist ideology may then motivate more strongly, and become imperialism-inducing. Once one tried to make the world safe for Christianity; then for democracy; why not for capitalism? I add that Marxists frequently underestimate the role that, in Senator Fulbright's phrase, the arrogance of power plays in the game of nations.

All this is compatible with Lenin's thesis. And that is as it should be. It is a commonplace that Marx and Engels believed that the economic factor was not the sole causal one but only the ultimate causal one. To be sure, that message is mysterious, but we need not attempt to unravel the mysteries here.

Recall my warning about and justification of negative Leninism. It was not without cause. Now we must contrast Lenin's approach with one widely accepted today. According to Lenin, imperialism was necessary because of the deficiencies of the capitalist system. Today many authors claim that the United States is imperialistic because its leaders, or those who decide its foreign policy, believe imperialism necessary for the stability and growth of the American economy. Perhaps so, but the evidence for that thesis is not evidence of support for a Leninist theory. Further, the difference for policy purposes is not of minor significance. If leaders believe that imperialism is necessary, when in point of fact it is not, then demands for policy changes that are not demands for change in the system are, if not sensible, at least admissible. There is also a difference in our approach to explanations of American action. Leaders may be muddled in their assessment of the importance or indispensability of a specific act or specific undertaking. The thesis that Vietnam was a quagmire or a muddle is compatible with the thesis that the leaders of the country thought imperialism necessary.

It is only fair to add that there are many who argue that American statesmen must be imperialistic for economic reasons and who do not argue thus in order to support Lenin's thesis, of which they may be dubious. Why then should they think that the American state (that is, any typical or representative administration of that state) must be coercive for economic reasons? Above we granted that since the American state has not ruled out the option of acting aggressively and coercively in order to satisfy varied economic interests, it is potentially imperialistic. But still there may be no need for coercion. For as the assertions of South American statesmen quoted in the introductory section indicate, economically non-developed countries may welcome American investment (using that phrase as the code term introduced above for varied American economic activities and interests).

Still the issue is not settled. It will be argued that since invitations from economically underdeveloped countries will be extended only by capitalist states and would not be forthcoming from Communist or revolutionary ones, then the American state will have to be coercive openly or covertly against revolutionary groups and movements, and will have to be so because American statesmen believe that trade with economically underdeveloped areas and the accessibility of raw materials from such countries is indispensable for the stability if not for the growth of the American economy. But this argument overlooks three factors: (1) there are at least some American statesmen who do not believe that trade with such areas is that important (recall that the bulk of American investments is in highly developed countries), and their views may ultimately prevail; (2) recent developments show that trade with capitalist countries may turn out to be necessary for socialist states; (3) the beliefs of American statesmen may change if evidence is produced that such trade and investment are not indispensable. Lenin's thesis or a variant of it may be relevant after all. So let us return to it.

For Lenin as for us, imperialism involved coercion; for him it involved war as well—and war between major states. In this he differed from some other Marxist writers, e.g., Kautsky, who is sometimes interpreted as holding that imperialism is a matter of choice, while Lenin thought imperialism necessary. But this is, I think, a slightly misleading way of putting the issue. What Lenin emphasized, as opposed to Kautsky, was not simply that individual countries will be imperialistic, but that imperialistic wars will be necessary. One can, I think, interpret Kautsky as admitting that imperialism is necessary, but as denying that rivalry between various capitalist groups or states is, and as maintaining that various capitalistic groups or states might, as it were, combine in partnership and together as a group dominate (as he put it) backward agricultural areas. So one could reconstruct the argument between Kautsky and Lenin, not as over the necessity of imperialism, but as over the necessity of imperialistic wars. Lenin claimed, I think, that because of unequal development and the necessity to compete, capitalist states will necessarily have to fight it out and ultimately go to war. Hence, there is reason to believe that current developments are not in accord with Lenin's prediction. To be sure, many writers have tried to show that the interests of imperialistic countries are not compatible and may often be in a state of rivalry with each other. Once again, perhaps so; but once again, evidence for this thesis is not evidence for Lenin's. I do not think that we anticipate war between England, France, and Japan, because of the economic competition. The hegemony of the United States, as an imperial state, is not support for Lenin's theory; but of course the rivalry indicates the limitations of Kautsky's approach as well.

Incidentally, it is not clear—at least to me—why Lenin took for granted the continuation of the nation-state under capitalism. If the proletariat had no fatherland, why should the capitalist class? The capitalist class, of course, might not challenge the state so long as it is not in its interest to do so; but Lenin held that imperialistic wars did not safeguard the interests of the capitalist class as a whole. Needless to say, a specific war might be undertaken to satisfy the interests of a specific national capitalist class, but of course only at the expense of another such class. A Marxist theory about the importance of the role of class should not degenerate into an interest-group theory.

There are thus some aspects of the current situation which are not in accord with the whole of Lenin's imperialism thesis. Still, we have not dealt with the more limited and perhaps most often discussed thesis that capitalism must lead to imperialism. Lenin's thesis is based upon the Marxist view that a closed capitalist economy is self-defeating. Since I believe that the objections to that thesis are well known, I allude only to some of the more important ones. Lenin argued for the law of the decline of the rate of profit, a decline due to the rise in the organic composition of capital. To compensate, capitalists will invest in economically backward areas where production is not capital-intensive, and wage rates are low. On this point it has been noted that Marxist theory does not entail such a law. Lenin also argued that capitalist economies evolve and then arrive at a stultifying monopolistic stage; monopolies will restrict output, the share of the wage bill will decline; and monopolies will have to dump goods overseas in order to keep prices high. Here it has been argued, by Schumpeter and others, that monopolies, because of their power, may very well be innovative.

Again, Lenin argued that, by reason of the impoverished state of the masses, which is in turn due to the fact that wages are held down as mechanization proceeds, the capitalist cannot find profitable investment opportunities. On this score many writers have argued that the data do not suggest a Marxist theory of the long-run behavior of the capitalist economic system, but rather a Keynesian business-cycle theory to the effect that there may be, or even likely will be, a short-run inadequacy of private investment but that this can be overcome by public investment.

Given these considerations, many have argued that Lenin has not shown that capitalism necessarily leads to imperialism, and further have argued for the stronger thesis that imperialism is not necessary for capitalism. This may very well be the case, but those who argue in this manner assume—and perhaps dogmatically—that we now have or know the true theory of capitalism and can rely on it. It seems more reasonable to conclude that we cannot on the basis of current knowledge claim that imperialism is necessary for capitalism. Strictly speaking, moreover, Lenin's argument even if correct only shows that under conditions of monopoly, capitalists who want to continue to play the game must be able to invest in underdeveloped areas. Of course he assumed that they would continue to play the game, for he thought that they had no other game to play. And of course he assumed that the state would be coercive to ensure that they could continue to play.

Granted that public investment can enable capitalists to play their game, what game are they playing? Or more particularly, what game is the American state playing? Since 1950 the U.S. Government has spent over a trillion dollars on the military. Why? Many have argued in the words of Michael Rieff,[35] "that this output is required in an advanced capitalist economy that both suffers from the problem of inadequate private demands and plays a leading role in the preservation and the expansion of the international capitalist system." Many radicals are now stressing this or kindred theses.

Note that investment in the military is not needed to solve the problem of inadequate private demand. After all, Germany and Japan have progressed economically without heavy investment in the military. Recall, too, that it is at least debatable whether American interests in underdeveloped countries must induce imperialism. And so we are left with the not surprising hypothesis that the imperial role of America has induced military outlays that may themselves be imperialism-inducing. It seems necessary, therefore, to consider the notion of an imperial state and to discuss some of the problems, especially the normative ones, such a state gives rise to. Not surprisingly, the discussion will lead us to consider approaches to imperialism we have thus far neglected.

IV

In a recent interview[36] Walter Lippmann criticized the American state for being in a romantic period of imperialism and took it to be the historical role of President Nixon to usher in a new epoch.

35. Michael Rieff, "Does the U.S. Economy Require Military Spending?" in *The Second Crisis of Economic Theory,* edited by John Kenneth Galbraith (Morristown, N.J.: General Learning Press, 1972), p. 296.
36. Interview reprinted in *New Republic* (April 14, 1973), pp. 16-21: "An Interview with Walter Lippmann," by Ronald Steel.

I am not sure whether Mr. Lippmann allows for non-romantic imperialism and hence am unsure also about his use of "imperialism," but I am morally certain that he does not believe that we have been engaged in colonization or neo-colonialism or expansion for the sake of the economic domination of foreign territories or areas. So here we have another use of the term 'imperialistic behavior' and another sufficient condition for its application.

Recall that when we spoke of Lichtheim, I distinguished between the terms 'imperialistic' and 'empirialistic'. Now I'll simply use the predicate 'is imperial'. I shall say that a country S is imperial in a region if (1) that country is the dominant one in the region; (2) it assumes that it is entitled to certain spheres of influence in that region; (3) it is prepared to offer economic and military benefits to countries in that region; and (4) it assumes that the minor or weaker countries in that region cannot enter into alliances with its potential enemies. Many writers such as Lippmann seem to have assumed that the United States as a major country is entitled to be a regional imperial one, that it is expected to have Mexico, the Caribbean countries, and possibly even Canada within its sphere of influence, and is entitled to ask such countries not to enter into alliances with potential enemies of this nation, or perhaps is entitled to forbid them to do so. Lippmann apparently believes that the United States had the right to invade the Dominican Republic if the Dominicans actually were close to becoming a Communist country that would form an alliance with Russia. The major objection he had, or could have had, was that there was no good reason to believe that that was the case, and that we rushed in without sufficient evidence or provocation. But what he is opposed to—and many would agree with him—is the attempt by imperial powers (in the trivial sense of major powers) to be not merely regional imperial powers but to undertake a more global role.

Before I describe that role I should indicate three things: First, in my belief no good reason can be given for the position that a major nation is entitled to be a regional imperial nation in the sense thus far specified. Why, for example, is the United States entitled to prevent Mexico from entering into alliances with Russia? It might of course be very unwise for Mexico to do so; in the event of war, Mexico would certainly suffer. But the claim that the United States has a right to this because its security would be diminished if Mexico had an alliance with Russia is weak. If one were to generalize this, one might say that in the nineteenth century France had a right to have Germany not armed, because the arming of Germany diminished her security. And of course we might say that Mexico has the right to have the United States not armed if there is some reason to believe that the United States might actually want to invade Mexico.

Second, in many discussions of regional powers it is assumed that a given country is primarily an association of citizens, and that a foreign policy must be undertaken for the benefit and security of those citizens. This assumption is not tenable. It seems dubious if not perverse, when we discuss a tariff—which is, after all, part of foreign policy—to consider only whether it is beneficial to our citizens and to ignore altogether its effects on the citizens of other countries. It is to the credit of the much maligned liberal economists that they were concerned to show that free trade was beneficial all around. Even charity only begins at home but is not supposed to end there.

Third, one might make a case that we are obligated to engage in what many would consider altruistic behavior if we approach the problems under consideration by appeal to the notion of the original position as developed by Rawls. When one is in the position described, one does not know where one is going to find oneself: it may be in any number of places in any number of societies. Hence one should ask, What would I want done if I were to find myself in the least advantaged position in the least advantaged society?

If that question is an appropriate one, the answer may require that when we consider a policy, we must consider its possible effects not only on those who are least advantaged in our society but also on the least advantaged in the least advantaged society. I doubt that many of us would go quite that far; some might insist that the members of one society owe certain obligations to their fellow members first, since with their common interests and common burdens they deserve special consideration from each other. At any rate we can hardly assert that foreign policy is simply a matter of satisfying national interests, much less satisfying only security interests, and that foreign aid and grants to underdeveloped countries are at best a matter of charity.

There are many who insist that the United States as a powerful state has moral responsibilities and should play a global role. The previous remarks are intended to support that claim and to challenge both the view that we should only be a regional imperial power and the increasingly popular view that we should go isolationist. Now of course there are many alternatives to the regional-imperial position or the isolationist one. But of these alternatives I shall consider only one, that of being an ideologically imperial power, which I think is the role that the United States has frequently claimed to be playing.

I shall say that a nation is an ideologically imperial power if (1) it is militarily and economically the dominant power of all those who are willing to abide by a certain ideology; (2) it is willing to assume the major military burdens for this particular group; (3) it is willing to provide benefits for those who agree to abide by this ideology. If these conditions alone hold, the nation may be a beneficial ideologically imperial power. But if condition (4) is present—i.e., the country is prepared to coerce those who do not accept the ideology, then you have an imperialistic and coercive ideologically imperial power. And many, I think, have insisted that this country has been an ideologically coercive and hence imperialistic country. But let us assume that a nation agrees to and attempts to use force and coercion only against nations that are aggressive and violate the laws of nations. I think, in this purview, that the United States can be described as claiming to play the role of a beneficial defensive ideologically imperial power. The role could prove as burdensome as its description.

Note first that a beneficial imperial power need not be an altruistic one. While such a power claims that its policies would benefit others, it may well seek and accept only policies that benefit both itself and nations that share its ideology. Needless to say, such policies may be difficult to find. Note further that a beneficial power need not be a just one. Justice may demand that it try not only to benefit others, but also to correct for an unjust distribution of wealth between nations. A beneficial imperial power may therefore face many problems. But before we consider them, a comment on the conceptual connection between "power" and "empire" is in order. Beneficial powers have frequently been described as aspiring to set up empires, and many who (to my mind rightly) believe that the United States has been coercive, think it essential to posit that the United States has been an empire and has been imperialistic because it has tried to defend its empire. On this point, however, I tend to agree with Lichtheim:

> When one speaks of imperialism one may be tempted to look for formally constituted empires held together by military force. In this sense, the two great political alliances which have confronted each other since American and Russian troops first met on the Elbe in 1945 are "empires" controlled respectively from Washington and Moscow; but this usage, albeit hallowed by tradition, is so vague and sociologically empty as to be meaningless for analytical purposes. If there is an American empire confronting a Soviet Empire, we may as well resign ourselves to the impossibility of saying anything concrete about imperialism in the meaning that term acquired, for liberals and socialists alike, during the first half of the present century.[37]

But I only *tend* to agree—that is to say, I doubt that there are true law-like sentences in which the term 'empire' appears essentially even when the term 'empire' is used in his sense. Moreover, I doubt that there are acceptable moral generalizations to the effect that all empires are bad or that in all cases the world would be better off if an empire disintegrated. According to many, the world was a better place when Rome was dominant, the Persian empire was not coercive, and Alexander's quest for world empire did not aim at the annihilation of other cultures. And even Marx, while acknowledging the vileness of British motives, and lament-

37. George Lichtheim, *Imperialism,* p. 153.

ing the coercion and the price in blood, pointed out the beneficial results of British rule in India.[38]

Earlier I used the term 'imperialism' in contradistinction to
'empirialism' in order to call attention to some of the moral
problems that certain modern versions of empire-building and

38. Thus he wrote,

"We must not forget that these idyllic village communities, inoffensive
though they may appear, had always been the solid foundation of Oriental
despotism, that they restrained the human mind within the smallest possible
compass, making it the unresisting tool of superstition, enslaving it beneath
traditional rules, depriving it of all grandeur and historical energies . . .

"We must not forget that this undignified, stagnatory, vegetative life, that
this passive sort of existence evoked on the other part, in contradistinction,
wild, aimless, unbounded forces of destruction . . . We must not forget that
these little communities were contaminated by distinctions of caste and by
slavery, that they subjugated man to external circumstances . . .

"India, then, could not escape the fate of being conquered, and the whole
of her past history, if it be anything, is the history of the successive conquests
she has undergone . . . The question, therefore, is not whether the English
had a right to conquer India, but whether we are to prefer India conquered
by the Turk, by the Persian, by the Russian, to India conquered by the Briton
. . . The British were the first conquerors superior, and therefore, inaccessible
to Hindoo civilisation. They destroyed it by breaking up the native communities, by uprooting the native industry, and by levelling all that was great and
elevated in the native society . . . The work of regeneration . . . has begun."
From Karl Marx, "The British Rule in India" and "The Future Results of
British Rule in India" in *On Colonialism*, by Karl Marx and Frederick Engels,
pp. 40-41 and 81-82.
And, farther along,

"Modern industry, resulting from the railway-system, will dissolve the he-
reditary divisions of labour, upon which rest the Indian castes, those decisive
impediments to Indian progress and Indian power.

"All the English bourgeoisie may be forced to do will neither emancipate
nor materially mend the social condition of the mass of the people, depending
not only on the development of the productive powers, but on their appro-
priation by the people. But what they will not fail to do is to lay down the
material premises for both. Has the bourgeoisie ever done more? Has it ever
affected a progress without dragging individuals and peoples through blood
and dirt, through misery and degradation?

"The Indians will not reap the fruits of the new elements of society scattered
among them by the British bourgeoisie, till in Great Britain itself the now
ruling classes shall have been supplanted by the industrial proletariat, or till
the Hindus themselves shall have grown strong enough to throw off the English yoke altogether." (*Ibid.*, p. 85)

of colonization give rise to. I add that there is nothing in Lich-theim's approach to rule out our contention that the United States and the U.S.S.R. are empires. True, he has stated that the relation of ruling can obtain even if the relation is not formally recognized as one of ruling. But he would, I suppose, deny that we are an empire, for it is not the case that we informally rule over our allies—that is, it is not the case that we can control our allies. We may be able to annihilate Canada; it does not follow that we can control that country. Admittedly, the case is different with weaker states, but then the domination of weaker states is not proof that the dominating country has an empire.

To return to the difficulties beneficial imperialism may en-counter. It has often been argued by realists that ideologically imperial powers (in my use of the term) will necessarily be in-volved in self-defeating behavior. They have to try to be major powers not merely in areas near home but also in areas far re-moved from their shores; and, it is said, even the United States with all its wealth cannot be expected to play the role of an im-perial power successfully in areas remote from its shores. The ar-gument does not seem convincing. It is true that although the United States after World War II was an ideologically imperial power, American policy was dominated at least in part by the at-tempt to avoid conflict between major capitalist states, to avoid conflicts of interest between Germany on the one hand and France and England on the other, to avoid conflicts of interest between America and Japan, for such conflicts had led to World War II. And I think it plausible to say that at least some Ameri-can leaders tried to arrange for Japan to be the regional imperial power in the Far East—although, to be sure, only a regional quasi-imperial power, since Japan was not allowed to militarize, and was not in a position to offer military benefits to weaker countries in that region. It is therefore not the case that an ideo-logical world power need be a regional imperial power on a world scale.

Some will object that one difficulty avoided is merely replaced by its offspring. Thus, in order to be prepared to play the domi-nant military role, the nation will have to invest heavily in the military; and, as many economists have pointed out, the result may be that the growth rate of the economy may be diminished and various other economic difficulties, such as in foreign exchange, introduced. But this argument against ideological imperialism is not decisive, for all it shows is that the major imperial power may itself have to assume some burdens, and may have to pay a price for being the imperial power that it is. Moreover, it might be to the advantage of the imperial power to play this role, as it is, for example, if the chances of war are diminished when only the United States and not also Japan and Germany can be major nuclear powers.

Let us note in passing that even many radicals are not convinced that the United States should unilaterally disarm, since they are apprehensive about the mischief Russia might do and are also eager not to have Germany and Japan militarized. And the McGovern budget (which was acceptable to many radicals) was not, after all, a request for bows and arrows. Even followers of McGovern, it may be said, were concerned to show that the United States may become a beneficial imperial power, while dropping its role as a coercive imperial power whose foreign policy is dominated by the military and the Executive Branch. Perhaps now in the 1970's the McGovern options—not to mention more radical ones—are no more potent than were the options of the benign imperialists of a century ago.[39]

Still, no matter what our faults may have been, we have avoided

39. The relation of the issues reviewed in this paragraph to some classical theories of imperialism are of interest, especially that to Hobson's theory. According to Hobson there was a need for imperialistic investments abroad only on condition that the problem of insufficient demand was not solved by a more just distribution of income-at-home. Imperialism is therefore only conditionally necessary, and for Hobson had the unjust result of increasing the income of the rentier to whose euthanasia he looked forward before Keynes. Today many believe that the amount of investment in the military cannot be justified by reference to military needs alone and that the amount can be fully explained only by reference to their desired unjust consequences. The degree of military expenditure was conditionally necessary, on condition that no money was earmarked for a more just distribution of power and income-at-home.

It is not as the Marxist claims—that capitalism required unjust imperialism; imperial demands could be used to unjustly ensure state capitalism at home. On these issues the works of Seymour Melman are of great importance; see especially *Pentagon Capitalism* (New York: McGraw-Hill, 1970).

imperialism—or so it is claimed by those American statesmen who have insisted that we were not an imperialistic nation—at least not since World War I—since we did not seek colonies and did not seek to add territory to our domain. But these statesmen have not been consistent, for they repeatedly argue that the U.S.S.R. has been imperialistic in Eastern Europe, and in the 1950's they argued that it was imperialistic in China and in Vietnam. (And yet these statesmen did not believe that Russia was eager to have China as a colony, or was seeking to annex East Germany.) I suggest that these statesmen were concerned to show that Russia was engaged in what may be called neo-aggrandizement, that Russia was trying to have nearby areas that were not simply within its sphere of influence, but within its sphere of domination, a sphere in which it could ensure, and impose if necessary, its own form of government and civil society. And of course Russia returned the compliment, and insisted that the United States wanted neo-colonization.

There is perhaps some point to this distinction between neo-colonialism and neo-aggrandizement if Russia claims that the United States wants spheres of domination not only in areas proximate to its borders but far away as well. There is also some warrant for the label 'neo-colonialism' if its application calls attention to the fact that it was frequently undertaken to satisfy some American economic interest. But the label is misleading if in our opinion it means that the American economy necessitates such expansion, as indicated in the discussion of Lenin. It may be more appropriate to consider both neo-aggrandizement and neo-colonialism as forms of neo-empirialism.

Of course we were not only anti-colonialists in theory but were also concerned to defend freedom and to help various nations to grow economically. But that ideology, which was the most plausible of all the ideologies[40] defended by U.S. spokesmen after World

40. On these issues I am indebted to the articles: "Counter-Revolutionary America" by Robert L. Heilbroner and "Introduction: American Power in the Twentieth Century" by Michael Harrington in *A Dissenter's Guide to Foreign Policy,* edited by Irving Howe (New York: Doubleday/Anchor, 1968); and "American Intervention and the Cold War" by John Schrecker and Michael Walzer in *Radical Papers,* edited by Irving Howe (New York: Doubleday/Anchor, 1966).

War II, was triply defective. It assumed that we knew how to ensure the economic growth of nations. It tacitly identified freedom and capitalism. It maintained that justice demanded certain liberties, but that to develop a just society its members may voluntarily give up some liberties; or that at any rate liberty is not always required as prior to social welfare for a just society. There was an arrogance in all this: the United States assumed that its community was the model that all right-thinking nations had to follow.

With the decline of the Cold War, with the relative decline of American economic power, with the increasing evidence that we cannot have the guns the Pentagon wants and a just distribution of butter, with the increasing economic strength of Japan and the European community, many of the issues I have discussed may well be dated. But not all of them. The reduction of tension between the United States and China, for example, has often been at the expense of others, e.g., in Bangladesh. The European nations, especially France, still want to retain certain areas, especially in Africa, within their sphere of influence if not domination. And the Japanese businessman is becoming known as the "ugly Japanese" as he roams about carving out areas on economic terms beneficial to himself. The U.S.S.R. and the United States seem ready to co-operate not to ensure a just solution to various problems, but to bring about a solution of benefit to themselves and their client states. And despite all the talk about a world attack on poverty, the European imperial powers convene not in order to attack world poverty, but to lend a hand when one of their states experiences a difficulty with its foreign exchange.

I presume that the United States is still *a* dominant imperial power, if not *the* dominant imperial power. And it needs an ideology. Perhaps one could recommend that it adopt the simple one of seeking justice. In practice, of course, no power will deny that it is seeking justice; but in practice, too, whenever justice and self-interest do not coincide, self-interest seems to win out. Perhaps the only thing we can expect is for societies to seek justice in their own domain and to treat each other in accordance

with the law of nations. But at this moment no one knows how
to ensure justice, economic growth, and the needs of military
security in *one* country, much less universally. And perhaps the
ultimate absurdity of all this is, as Beverly Woodward has
claimed, that we are still committed to the system of world violence. It may be added that when members of a society do not
perceive it to be wrong that a few can economically dominate the
many in their society, they will not perceive as wrong that some
imperial nations can dominate other nations. Perhaps therein lie
certain attitudinal connections between capitalism and imperialism.—But, of course, not only here. The attitudinal connections
also develop, as we have learned to our regret, under conditions
of state socialism.

Power corrupts, but not only the powerful. In a powerful state,
the powerless, who often have very little else, assign, or can be
induced to assign, a high utility to their state's remaining powerful, or even becoming Number One. Hence the phenomenon of
a people's imperialism, of which Renner, and after him Schumpeter,[41] spoke: of imperialism to which a whole population is devoted but which is not to the social or economic advantage of any
class of that society.

41. For discussion and references see Bernard Semmel, *Imperialism and Social
Reform,* pp. 2, 228f.

9
War and Ideology

JOSEPH MARGOLIS

The most striking and obvious feature of war is the general destruction of human lives on the part of people who do not know their victims personally, who profess to be opposed to wanton killing, and who nevertheless firmly believe themselves justified in the name of principles not directly construed in terms of mere personal advantage. Still, for all the confidence so often exhibited in actual wars—even where, to the eye of an unengaged observer, the alleged principles or the application of given principles to a case in question seem preposterous—it is extremely difficult to say what a war is. Clearly, not all killing is thought to be unjustified; not all killing, justified or not, is an act of war; and not all acts of war are acts of killing.

In a well-known discussion, Richard Wasserstrom offers the following plausible analysis of war: first, it "is something that takes place between countries, nation-states, rather than lesser groups of individuals"; second (on Wasserstrom's view, possibly "the most essential and distinctive" characteristic), "wars almost surely involve the use of a variety of forms of violence under a claim of right"—perhaps, as a minimally necessary condition, they involve the use of specialized functionaries, a soldiery *prepared to kill* the soldiers of the opposing army"; third, wars are either "a circumscribed, clearly definable instrument of foreign policy" or "some indeterminate, indefinable, and unlimited fight or struggle between countries."[1] Wasserstrom's proposed analysis

1. Richard Wasserstrom, "On the Morality of War," *Stanford Law Review,* XXI (1969), 1627-56.

quite naturally allows for some accommodation of borderline cases, for example, civil wars and the sort of private wars that have taken place in China; but it disallows such secondary or metaphorical wars as those against poverty and disease.

The trouble is that it is, however plausible, a conventional view and, consequently, it fails to find a proper and indisputable place for unconventional but increasingly important instances of war. For example, there is every reason to think that the kind of war the radical Arab guerrilla groups are waging against the Is-raelis—not, be it noted, the deliberate and public engagements of countries like Egypt and Syria—cannot be specified in terms of the foreign policy of nation-states or suitable surrogates but only in terms of the convictions of an ethnically and religiously cohesive population and in terms, somewhat less comprehensively, of geographical unity of some sort. Again, there is every reason to believe that radical black groups in the United States—particu-larly those closely associated with the Black Muslim movement or those inspired by Frantz Fanon—have supposed themselves to be in an incipient state of war against the Establishment and have contemplated continuous, violent guerrilla activities as either use-ful to their cause or unavoidable; such activity has been muted, for instance by various attacks on the headquarters of the Black Panthers and by the general stiffening of the forces of public law and order in the country, but the conception of war involved could not be subsumed under Wasserstrom's formula. Also, the Marxist view of class warfare, historically developed in opposition to admitting the legitimacy of wars between states and only lat-terly skewed in the interests of so-called wars of national libera-tion, cannot be adequately characterized in terms of wars between states or even of merely civil wars; in this connection, the French Revolution, the Russian Revolution, the Chinese Revolution— even the American Revolution, which could not actually be called a class war—cannot be subsumed simply under the formula given. Finally, if one admits allegedly criminal organizations of such sweep as the Mafia or the Cosa Nostra, it is easy to see that a sustained and articulated war may be claimed to obtain in a con-text in which national boundaries, though strategically relevant, do not serve to define the very form of the war at hand. The charge that cases of these sorts are either secondary or metaphorical seems to be either tendentious or naïve; and the claim that they are subsumable as instances of wars between states, possibly with minor adjustments in our conception, is simply mistaken. It is not helpful, it may be noticed, to disqualify violent revolution as a true form of war, since there is no reason to think that revolution must be confined within a "country" or a "nation-state," or that it will fail to exhibit armies prepared to kill "under a claim of right," or that opposing sides will not seek allies and military supplies among other powers. The same holds for other seemingly marginal forms of warfare, for instance, ethnic and racial warfare. Of course, if contests of power are, say, primarily economic and characteristically lack any form of sustained violence and killing by partisan forces of some sort, we may, in such cases, reasonably withhold the ascription of war; although, bearing in mind a larger issue, there can be no doubt that the outbreak of relevant forms of violence is noticeably continuous with certain political and economic struggles typically said to obtain under conditions of peace.

The reason the quarrel is important is that one of the most desperately pressing questions of the day asks whether and when war may be morally justified; and an answer presupposes that the phenomenon of war may be conceptually segregated in a fair-minded way. But, of course, *if,* say, the Arab guerrilla killing of the Israeli athletes at the 1972 Olympics was a bona fide act of war, then—now that the guerrillas are out of Germany and will not be extradited—the complication of local jurisdiction (in terms of which they would have been tried for murder) need not affect our reflections on the legitimacy of what they did; but, on the other hand, if we adhere to the conventional view of war—say, Wasserstrom's—then there is no possibility even of attempting to justify their act *as an act of war*. Since, presumably, that is their own serious view of the matter, it seems tendentious to disallow the possibility in order merely to remain consistent with Wasserstrom's formula. Of course, it is reasonably clear that the guerrillas' action could not be justified as an instance of conventional warfare: that is important in itself, but it does not bear on the ulterior issue.

All the vexed questions about the justification of war and the justification of killing in war depend on how we manage this definitional issue. For instance, it is stalwartly maintained by Elizabeth Anscombe, speaking of war (and of murder) in the context of Catholic conviction though not as a sectarian, that "the deliberate choice of inflicting death in a struggle is the right only of ruling authorities and their subordinates."[2] There are constraints regarding innocence that Miss Anscombe holds qualify the precept given, but they need not concern us for the moment. Verbal quibbles, conceivably, might allow us to claim, consistently with Miss Anscombe's thesis, that an unjust authority is a contradiction in terms and that such putative authorities do not actually *rule*. The debatable, even chaotic possibilities of such a reading are perfectly obvious. But even so, for the counterinstances proposed, there is no way to specify a "ruling authority" that would be recognized as such within the framework of conventional warfare. In fact, in genuinely revolutionary or ethnic wars, for example, the very concept of a ruling authority must itself be somewhat metaphorical; and yet, it would be widely maintained that the inflicting of death in such circumstances was justified.

The point is that it may well be that the very effort to define war, with a view to distinguishing it from merely organized killing or even organized murder or banditry or the like, is itself nothing but a strategy sought by potential parties to wars of a certain form, who understand that the security, the orderliness, the predictability of their own favored form of conflict is jeopardized by admitting the radical variety of war itself, its changeability with regard to fundamentals, and the prospect that the old order of things may be challenged or even eclipsed by an emerging order. These possibilities were certainly felt with the advent, say, of Marxist criticism and, more particularly, with the rise of palpable forces committed to the concept of class war-

2. G. E. M. Anscombe, "War and Murder," in Walter Stein (ed.), *Nuclear Weapons: A Catholic Response* (New York: Sheed and Ward, 1961).

fare. Again, it is entirely possible—in America, for instance—that the polarization of the races may shape an extreme and compelling ideology of prolonged racial war, the palpability of which will be confirmed by the regular appearance of pitched battles in the cities or at least sustained guerrilla activity and all that that entails.

There is only one effective basis for avoiding the conclusion suggested above, namely, that, in some sense, the moral norms essential to human nature can be discerned *and* that political life of every possible sort, including the forms of war, may be judged in terms of those norms. The first consideration bears on the prospects of providing independent cognitive grounds for normative constraints on human behavior in general;[3] the second, the prospect of applying such distinctions in some straightforward way specifically to the conduct of war. The first is *not* as such the issue of relativism: it is not a question of the likelihood of convergence among competing ideologies or moral doctrines; it is only a question of whether any given set of putative moral constraints can be shown to be defensible on relevant cognitive grounds. The second obliges us to consider more closely the conceptual peculiarities of war itself—particularly, the features of entities said to engage in war.

Certainly, realistically, given the problems of war itself in just the terms here specified, it is inconceivable that the parties to armed conflict—that characterize their own engagement as a just war—would be able to agree with Miss Anscombe's substantive judgments about just and unjust wars, though they might (each from his own partisan vantage) appear to agree that "there [is] such a thing as the common good of mankind" and that we can discern "an objectively unjust proceeding" (presumably in most of the important disputed cases). Also, it is undoubtedly by reason of such a belief that Miss Anscombe is prepared to rely on the "right of ruling authorities," even when those authorities are themselves parties to a dispute or war. The only other conceivable basis for avoiding the conclusion proposed rests on the

---

3. Cf. Joseph Margolis, *Values and Conduct* (New York and Oxford: Oxford University Press and Clarendon Press, 1971).

belief that warring parties somehow come to agree—perhaps by way of a common tradition—about the very rules of the game of war to which they intend to subscribe. This is surely the officers' view in Erich von Stroheim's *Grand Illusion,* possibly even in a muddled way the view of Clausewitz. But it is unworkable precisely where the competing forms of war already mentioned are in play. What violates the rules of war of comradely professional European armies of World War I vintage may well be entirely admissible in the context of contemporary racial and ethnic war; or, at any rate, it will not be easily disqualified on the basis of anything like a formal or traditional agreement. There is nothing like a Geneva Convention for modern guerrilla warfare, and yet such warfare is not at all "indeterminate, indefinable, and unlimited" fighting between countries, as Wasserstrom supposes.

One of the favorite issues that the genteel discussion of war has insisted on concerns the treatment of innocent parties. Miss Anscombe, registering the prevailing view, says that it is murderous to attack innocent people. The difficulty with this pronouncement is not that it is open to telling counterinstances but that it is vacuously true.[4] She also says that "innocence is a legal notion,"[5] but if it is, then apart from an appeal to a higher law—the law of nations (which is unhelpful in the sense already supplied) or the law of nature or the divine law (which are argumentative, as already suggested)—the very idea of an innocent party will be controlled by the overriding conception of (internally) justifying a given war. For example, in a racial or ethnic war, or even in a more conventional war between states, that is expected to run for generations, there is no clear sense in which, say, bearing children (the future warriors of the enemy power) can be irresistibly discounted as itself the activity of non-combatants. And what is true of women and children in this regard is true, *a fortiori,* of factory workers, Red Cross personnel, priests, and the like. The constraints on attacking this or that fraction of

4. Cf. also, John Ford, "The Morality of Obliteration Bombing," *Theological Studies,* (1944), 261-309.
5. *Loc. cit.*

an enemy population depends at least on the clarity with which a distinctly professionalized army may be specified: talk about the people's militia, treat every infant as a budding soldier, organize the farmers as the nation's fighting force, and you will have blurred the very basis on which the older distinction between combatant and non-combatant was drawn. That the United States, for instance, has had, because of its traditions, difficulty enlisting public support for bombing the North Vietnamese countryside at will is a concession to culture lag, not to the persistence of an independently and indisputably defensible doctrine. At any rate, in the face of novel and emergent forms of war and in the face of the apparently sincere rejection of constraints that were thought, in more conventional wars, to have been properly binding on the behavior of combatants, it is difficult to see that the old constraints can be merely *assumed* to be morally binding. What is the reason for thinking that newer views about what is admissible in newer wars and newer kinds of war ought to conform to what, in an earlier time, was taken for granted?

But the point about innocence and the demarcation of combatants forces us to pay attention to a much more profound difficulty in all the human talk about confining war within moral boundaries. Wasserstrom was in a way right in linking war to the foreign policy of national states—not right in what he explicitly says but, so to say, right about the kind of linkage between war and human societies. For, war need not be an instrument of *foreign* policy; it needs only to be construed as an instrument of *external* policy. And, it need not be an instrument of *national states;* it needs only to be construed as an instrument of *collective entities.* The war, for instance, between the Palestinian guerrillas and the Kingdom of Jordan—that ended so disastrously for the guerrillas—cannot possibly be viewed as concerned with foreign relations: it was concerned, however, with the external relations between two collective bodies—Jordan as a conventional national state and the guerrillas as a distinct people within the geographical boundaries of that state. The concept of foreign relations does not provide for the distinction of relevant entities where no conventional geographical divisions can be supplied.

Now, here, we must be as hard-headed as we can be. On an economical view of what there is in the world, collective entities —states, nations, corporations, clans, socioeconomic classes, societies—do not exist as such; only individual human beings exist, whose beliefs, behavior, objectives, and the like may be directed to the alleged interests of such collective entities. Only human beings, as biological entities, exist and have interests; but, given their development and training as competent agents of this or that cultural sort, they learn to divide their efforts spontaneously between their own personal interests and the doctrinally projected "interests" of purely fictitious (but not for that reason unimportant) entities. Nations, so to say, "have interests" because aggregates of interested human beings actually interpret their *own* behavior as serving the national interest. The reason this is crucial to the issue of war is quite straightforward: war as a form of organized conflict is an instrument of external policy on the part of a collective entity. But, of course, if the enemy in a given war *is itself a collective entity,* then the demarcation between combatants and non-combatants, that is, between distinct aggregates of individuals, cannot but be a distinction of a secondary sort. War is not fought against individual men but against collective entities, though only individuals actually fight. That is, the conception that we are engaged in war entails that we are in some sense agents of an ideologically specified collective entity, whose "interests" and "activities" are of principal concern and are ranged against other externally specified collective entities. In the case of civil war, in the case in which the competing ideology of the rebels would construe relations properly internal to the life of some "legitimate" entity as merely external relations between distinct powers, we have what may be termed a logically degenerate instance of war.

Of course, the thesis is arguable and needs to be defended. But we may, at least for the moment, notice that *if* it can be sustained convincingly, then it must be admitted that the distinction between combatants and non-combatants and the justification of waging a war in the putative interests of a given nation, country, socioeconomic class, ethnic community, people, state, or the like cannot but be the expression of the very ideology in terms of which such collective entities are thought to exist.

People act. They may do so singly or in aggregations, that is, aggregatively—cooperatively, competitively, congruently. To talk of collective action is to risk equivocation: to act collectively, as in marching, is merely to act aggregatively; but it may be held, as by way of our ideology, that to act collectively signifies that a collective entity acts and that the actions of individual people are merely the events that embody the action of an actual collective entity. The United States declares war on Japan, for instance, but it does so through the speech of President Roosevelt. Obviously, the attribution of intentions, beliefs, convictions, actions to collective entities presupposes a doctrine or ideology in terms of which the intentions, beliefs, convictions, actions of individuals and aggregates of individuals may be interpreted as the state or behavior of those collective entities. When such doctrines or ideologies are embedded in the habits of mind and action of given aggregates, people quite spontaneously refer, and commit their energies, to the "interests" and "objectives" of selected collective entities. But—unless we confirm such so-called idealist doctrines as those of the organic state or such so-called (dubiously so-called) materialist doctrines as that of the existential priority of socioeconomic classes to human individuals—it is not literally true that there actually are collective entities that *have* interests, beliefs, convictions, and the like and that *act,* in an entirely non-metaphorical sense.

The point is central to the argument and cannot be softened. Collective entities are, on the thesis, merely intentional objects, that is, "objects" that need not exist in order that relevant activities on the part of aggregates of people obtain. For instance, we say that a man *serves his country* in war. But he may do so if he only believes that his country is an actual entity *whose proper interests* (not to be confused with his own) he serves: he serves his country, in this respect, in precisely the same sense in which Ponce de Leon sought the Fountain of Youth. And the reason that we must say that collective entities are fictional entities is precisely that we can only, in speaking of such entities, imagine them to *have* interests and objectives and to *commit* acts, in the paradigmatic sense in which human beings have interests and commit acts.[6] Nothing can perform an act or have an interest that is not at the very least alive, sentient, intelligent. Human beings, singly or aggregatively, satisfy these conditions. But a collective entity—a corporation, for instance—can only have interests imputed to it by human agents (can only be the intentional object designated as the beneficiary or even as the agent of certain actions performed by individual human beings). The argument is just that simple. But to say this much, of course, is neither to deny that people actually believe—or at least act as if they believe—that certain favored collective entities are real, actually exist; nor is it to deny that aggregates of human beings are really caught up in relationships that, given their ideologies, have a distinctly collective import. Thus, to say that there is no such *entity* as a socioeconomic class (in the literal sense in which a class is said to *have* its own proper interests) is not to deny that human beings enter into class *relationships* with one another or to deny that they may, at times, seriously claim that this or that serves, say, the interests of the capitalist class.

Still, war is an instrument of external policy on the part of collective (intentional) entities. So it is impossible to separate the appraisal of war from the admission of the fictitious entities that engage in war; and it is impossible to acknowledge such entities without some substantial commitment to ideologies in terms of which they are said to exist (but do not actually exist) and in terms of which their behavior may be appraised. Most briefly put, the very admission of war—ranging over the variety of forms already sketched—entails the admission of collective entities, for it is of the nature of war that it is conducted only by collective entities. Deny that we refer to such entities, however fictional, and we must interpret in radically different terms the recognition of war itself. Change the conception of what fictitious collective entities

6. There is an ulterior question concerning reference to fictional and intentional entities and concerning what there is or exists. For a sustained discussion, cf. Joseph Margolis, *Knowledge and Existence* (New York: Oxford University Press, 1973), Ch. 4.

collect our allegiance and you risk changing our convictions about the conduct of those alleged entities—including their conduct in war. The entire idiom of speaking of harming the interests of, or destroying, nations, for instance, is figurative, in the sense in which, only in accord with some prevailing ideology, can one even interpret the behavior of *aggregates* of men as the behavior of given *collective* entities impinging on the interests and life of other collective entities.

It is in this sense that other well-known problems of war are rendered much more difficult than they are ordinarily thought to be. For example, modern technological warfare, that cannot readily confine destruction to pinpointed targets, not only threatens to make an effective shambles of every distinction between combatants and non-combatants but also threatens to make utterly inoperative any distinction between intended and merely foreseen consequences—that is, the distinction covered by the Principle of Double Effect.[7] It is simply naive to insist that, in war, human combatants have no right to inflict death and harm on these or those innocent parties; for that entails that one's own ideology properly designates who and whose behavior embody the combatant interests and conduct of the hostile collective entity opposed. And it is equally naive to insist that a fair line can be drawn between the intended (and therefore, putatively defensible) consequences for some *aggregated* population and the merely foreseen consequence for that population, either defensibly allowed (as inescapable) or defensibly censured (as cancelling or even overriding the merit of the intended consequences); for that entails that one's own ideology properly specifies how the effects of war on given *aggregates* of people embody the defensible effects of war on the *collective* entities that are actually at war. The very same issue arises in the difficult matter of war crimes and regarding the responsibility of functioning agents of the state to obey superior orders—say, men and officers in an army, or clerks and guards in a concentration camp—when the actions of indi-

7. Cf. "Double Effect, Principle of," *New Catholic Encyclopedia*, Vol. 4 (New York: McGraw-Hill, 1967), 1020-22. Cf. also, Anscombe, *op. cit.*; and Ford, *op. cit.*

vidual men are said to constitute crimes against humanity.[8] For, apart from the issue of so-called victors' trials (Nuremburg, for instance) and apart from the pragmatic difficulties of avoiding or resisting superior orders during wartime—regardless of one's conscience—there remains the conceptual difficulty of justifying imposing one set of ideological constraints on what is admissible under an alternative doctrine regarding relationships between individual combatants and the collective entities they may serve and regarding the legitimate objectives of such collective entities.

The point is that the usual humane criticism of slaughtering the innocent, of technological warfare, of persons committing horrid acts in the name of their duties in war normally fails to address itself to the conceptual question of the grounds on which the *acts of collective entities* may be justifiably constrained or censured or resisted as by war, and of the grounds on which responsibility for *those acts* may be distributed to *aggregates of persons whose own individual acts embody the former*. It is, for instance, a conceptual oversight that conflates the question of assigning individual responsibility, given collective responsibility, with the question of assigning individual responsibility, given aggregative responsibility. For, in the first instance, the conduct of individuals is taken to *embody* the "conduct" of collective entities—in accord with a favored ideology; and, in the second instance, the conduct of aggregates is a *summation* of some sort of the determinate conduct of individuals—in accord with various parameters. There will, obviously, be competing principles on which the assignment of individual responsibility will be defended in either context; still, there is no obvious way in which to reduce assignments of the first sort to assignments of the second, without the intrusion of a favored ideology. As a matter of fact, the confusion of these two ways of viewing responsibility is characteristic of certain utilitarian arguments, that advocate sacrificing these or those values for individuals or aggregates of individuals for the sake of values putatively serving "the greatest

8. Cf. the well-documented study by G. Lewy, "Superior Orders, Nuclear Warfare, and the Dictates of Conscience: The Dilemma of Military Obedience in the Atomic Age," *American Political Science Review,* Vol. LV (1961), 3-23.

good for the greatest number"; but the confusion is by no means confined to explicitly utilitarian doctrines.[9]

Furthermore, it is of decisive importance whether, in judging the behavior of individual combatants, the appraisal is *internal* to the very ideology in terms of which they acted as agents of the state, or whether the appraisal is *externally* applied in terms of an admittedly inimical or alien ideology or in terms of some allegedly independent principle. In the first case, the sole question at stake is one of coherence and consistency vis-à-vis given rules and principles; in the second, an ulterior question arises as to how to justify objectively the governing rules and principles of any collective entity. Presumably, as in charging crimes against humanity, the argument would require that we show how the activities of collective entities legitimately further the proper rights or ideals or values of men *qua* men. And that entails a cognitivism or a theory of normative constraints essential to human nature as such, for which there is at present, in my view, not the slightest prospect of confirmation.[10] Also, in the absence of any discovery of this last sort, the competing ideologies themselves generate their own favored claim about the norms that allegedly do, or ought to, govern the behavior of men *qua* men. So it is practically impossible to break through the circle of competing ideological justifications, to some putatively objective and non-tendentious standard by which all of those ideologies are or ought to be governed. In fact, if it could be done, then, rationally, either there would be no need for the projection of collective entities with their various and competing overriding values or else collective entities would, in effect, be no more than social instruments by which we abbreviate in practice our commitments and judgments regarding the entire human population.

With these distinctions in mind, we may say, fairly, that the argument advanced is doubly conditional. For one thing, it needs to be shown that there are or are no cognitive grounds by means of which to discern the proper moral constraints on political and

9. Cf. Stuart Hampshire, "Morality and Pessimism," *The New York Review of Books,* XIX, Nos. 11-12 (January 25, 1973), 26-33.
10. Cf. Margolis, *Values and Conduct,* chs. 4-5.

other forms of behavior (as opposed to mere agreement about moral matters—a prospect that the history of war itself makes very unlikely). And for a second, it needs to be shown how, if war is primarily the work of collective entities, it is possible to provide cognitively objective grounds for constraining *such* entities and human beings insofar as they are acting as their agents. We have explored the second condition primarily and allowed the first, as a more general consideration, to stand as an unsupported assumption;[11] for, if collective entities are fictitious entities despite their being the putative agents of war, it seems impossible—regardless of whether or not we can provide, independently, a favorable account of moral cognition about the behavior of individuals or aggregates—to provide also an ideologically neutral and objective appraisal of the "conduct" of collective entities and of their agents *qua* agents.

Consider, now, the details of censuring the behavior of individual persons who, presumably, are acting as agents of states or of other collective entities at war—even in instances like that of the My Lai massacre or of the Eichmann atrocities. There is, first of all, the purely internal question of whether the acts of given individuals were authorized, in the procedural sense, by the proper authorities, or fell, as a discretionary option, within some authorization. If there is no sense in which they were authorized, then of course the acts in question may not really have been the acts of warring agents as such but only the acts of individuals that, contingently, took place in the context of war or the acts of warring agents not acting in their capacity as such. The man who takes his neighbor's life under cover of an enemy attack is guilty of a crime but not for waging war criminally. The charges against Lieutenant Calley and Adolph Eichmann concern, at least provisionally, the criminal status of what they did *as agents fulfilling their duties in prosecuting the war.*

The conceptual options are straightforward, though the resolution of the alternative legal and moral issues is incredibly complex. They may not have been authorized, in any fair sense, to

---

11. But see *Values and Conduct*, for a sustained discussion of the prospects of a cognitive basis for discerning the normative values binding on human beings.

act as they did; but, resting their defense on an alleged authorization, they may be criminally responsible for pursuing their war duties as they did. In this sense, the question is an internal question, a question internal to the workings of some legal system; or, the moral analogue may provide for a larger and more informal context of political authorization and responsibility. Internally, then, there are two options open: Calley or Eichmann could have been judged to have acted utterly without authorization and without any plausible link to due authorization, so that, under the cover of their proper duties in pursuing the war, they committed crimes as private persons; or, they could have been judged to have pursued their duties with respect to the war—criminally. Interestingly, Calley and Eichmann were judged to be criminally liable in the latter sense and judged so, respectively, by an internal and an external judicial review. Still, however fair or unfair we may suppose Eichmann's trial to have been, the man was judged either in accord with the external Israeli conception of the duties of agents in war (which obliges us to weigh the partisan nature of ideologically alternative visions of political life and political duties) or in accord with putatively higher, objective moral obligations that take precedence over duties authorized by any state or any other relevant political entity (which obliges us to weigh the prospects of formulating such obligations nontendentiously, that is, where war itself is not, merely as such, disallowed). The point is worth pressing, because, *if* the higher moral obligations alleged to obtain are genuinely objective, then such criticism cannot be said to be merely external to the Eichmann case—even if managed through an external court: this is the import of speaking of "crimes against humanity"; but *if* such obligations cannot be shown to be objective in the sense required, then the pretension of resting charges of criminally pursuing one's war duties on these grounds is nothing more than the intrusion of an alternative and inimical ideology. It must be stressed, of course, that, in accord with distinctions already provided, the objectivity needed concerns duties and rights *in war*—hence, the duties and rights of collective entities and of their agents *qua* agents.

Now, what is true of the acts of the agents of collective entities is even more obviously true of the "acts" of those collective entities themselves. Individual men cannot wage war except *as* agents of collective entities that are at war (even if war is sometimes acknowledged only unilaterally). But what may be said to be the political and moral ideals of given collective entities cannot be challenged by the "beliefs" and "interests" of other collective entities, except on a partisan basis; and, where the policy and practice of a *collective entity* is judged or censured by *individual* men, presumably not as such committed to the ideology favored by any other collective entity, there is no other basis for appraisal than some alleged moral consensus of mankind or some alleged discovery of the normative and natural constraints on human behavior involving putative relations with collective entities. But it is a foregone conclusion that, since there are radical ideological conflicts among states and other political entities precisely on the matter of the overriding duties, values, ideals appropriate to human beings, there cannot be a realistic expectation of moral consensus, except perhaps within the range of a family of related or congruent ideologies, and that's just the trouble. Is there any reason to think, for instance, that the killing of the Israeli athletes was not sincerely viewed, on the part of the guerrillas, as a justified act of war in a just war? Or, that the technique of gradual starvation used by the Nigerians against the Biafrans—notably effective against children—was not, under the circumstances, viewed as a justified act of war in a just war? Or, that the Soviets' crushing of the Hungarian uprising was not viewed as a justified act of war in a just (however brief) war? Or, that the American bombing of Hanoi and Haiphong was not viewed as a justified act of war in a just (however undeclared) war? Or, that the Chinese annexation of Tibet was not viewed as a justified act of war in a just (however improbable) war?

This is not, of course, to concede every ideological conviction as self-validating or to deny the possibility of rational grounds for censure and judgment regarding war and, especially, regarding the putative justification for particular wars and particular acts committed in pursuing a war. But it is to emphasize that there is no ready moral consensus about the conduct of war that is not itself substantially the reflection of the conventional views of states (themselves challenged by the emergence of political forces committed to quite different conceptions of war); and to emphasize that the usual appraisal of the conduct of human beings in war neglects the dialectical relationship between the "acts" of states, or of other collective entities, and the acts of individual persons.

There is a further complication. For, even if it is conceded that international instruments governing the conduct of wars have been formulated and agreed to by participating *states* (for instance, as in the Geneva Convention or the Kellogg-Briand Pact), such instruments presuppose the legitimacy of the participating powers, the powers themselves are constrained only within the limits of their agreement, non-signatory powers are not bound by the agreement, and the signatory powers themselves have no relevant means of appraising the alternative practices and policies of non-signatory powers—particularly those organized in accord with entirely different principles and ideals—that are not determined by their own converging ideologies. Even admitting the repugnant and irrational nature of Hitler's general claims, was the ceding of the Sudeten territory to Germany justified or utterly unjustified and would Germany have been justified, on being refused at that point, in going to war with Czechoslovakia? Or, given the Soviet version of the Marxist ideology, was the crushing of the Dubček Spring justified? If Jordan were prepared to make a separate peace with Israel, would Syria be justified in invading Jordan, in order to forestall the failure of a putatively just and larger cause? Given the North Vietnamese picture of American aggression in Southeast Asia, were the North Vietnamese justified in invading the apparently sovereign territories of Laos and Cambodia?

The very admission of collective entities depends, as we have seen, on the habits of mind and conduct of given aggregates of men. Seen internally, the state or surrogate entity provides the political context within which the preferred values of some aggregate—both their political and non-political values—are most effectively pursued. Being a fiction in the sense supplied, collective entities cannot but be committed to their own survival and to the maintenance or enlargement of their power, because only in that way—on the interpretation of any ideology that admits competing powers—could they "act" to achieve or make accessible the objectives of their home population. Even the Marxist "withering away of the state" presupposes the intervening agency of the proletariat as a collective entity and is to obtain only in the limit in which class differences themselves are effectively erased. So there is no clear demarcation line, internally viewed, between the prudential and the moral or political objectives of *given collective entities*. The external insistence on such a demarcation is simply the expression of an alien and non-converging ideology. And the internal admission of such a demarcation is simply the expression of a provisional ranking of a collective entity's own priorities. In any event, we must not confuse the constraints a collective entity "imposes" on itself and the constraints human aggregates impose on themselves within or with respect to given collective entities. When, say, aggregates within a state effectively insist on such a demarcation, when they are prepared to risk the "survival" of the state in the name of allegedly higher values, to that extent—as in civil war and revolution—they correspondingly change those habits of mind and conduct on the basis of which alone the state effectively "exists"; also, characteristically—as in civil war and revolution—they fully expect to be able to constitute a new state in place of the old and, in fact, have already assigned their loyalties to alternative entities. This is the point of the limited, separatist movements of Bangaladesh, Northern Ireland, Biafra, South Vietnam, the Kurds, the Croatians, the Ukrainians, the Black Muslims, as well as of the deeper upheavals of the French and Russian Revolutions. Viewed externally by other effective collective entities, given states or surrogates are viewed prudentially, that is, as impinging on the policies and practices of a particular collective entity and as committed or not committed to compatible objectives.

In a sense, these considerations vindicate Hobbes's well-known thesis that political states are in a state of nature, that is, a state of war, vis-à-vis one another. For, this is simply to say that collective political entities, *given* their ideologies and overriding values, see themselves potentially threatened by the existence and commitment of every other collective entity. Political states are not viewed, relative to their native ideologies, as mere instruments for securing certain overriding values; they are viewed as essentially providing the ongoing system of life in which those overriding values are or are to be embodied. Individual persons may construe the existence of political states instrumentally. But in order to make their appraisals convincing, they require an independent and objective moral or political principle by which to constrain collective entities as such and relations that may hold between individuals and collective entities; and that, as has been argued, seems to me most unpromising to defend.

Effectively, then human beings tend to judge the behavior of their own states and of others (or of other collective entities) in terms of their own ideological loyalties (which does not preclude considerations of fairness, arbitrariness, consistency, plausibility, self-criticism, relevance, strictness, tolerance, and the like). It is quite likely that individual persons, attempting to justify their allegiance to a given collective entity on rational grounds independent of that or another entity's internal ideology, would be utterly baffled; on the other hand, the problem does not arise for people who already regard themselves as member parts or agents of such entities. The point of Hobbes's thesis that individuals in a state of nature (outside of political organization) are in a state of war "of all against all" is clear enough. But Hobbes's use of the term 'war' to characterize the behavior of individual persons as well as of collective entities and Hobbes's failure to distinguish carefully between the conduct of aggregates and of collective entities obscure the conceptual relations involved in appraising wars and the acts of agents in war. The argument, of course, is a conditional one; also, we may reasonably restrict the use of 'war' to distinctly violent behavior of the sort already indicated. But if there is no independent cognitive basis for discerning normative constraints on political behavior, essentially required by human nature itself and addressed to the conduct of, and relationships involving collective entities, then—in politics as in morals—the best that human beings can do is to act as rational and informed partisans. And then, in the Hobbesian sense, aggregates of human beings, acting as political agents, are actually in a state of war against one another, in that the states (or other such entities) to which they are loyal are themselves in a state of war.

The critical issue, then, is that war is properly ascribed to collective entities, not to individual persons or to aggregates of persons—except derivatively, as agents or "member parts" of a given collective entity, so designated in accord with the very ideology by means of which aggregates intentionally direct their efforts to the "interests" of such an entity. Collective entities "exist," then, in the sense in which they are the intentional objects of sustained human endeavor not otherwise relevantly characterized (as waging war, making treaties, and the like). The dialectical difficulties involving determining the responsibility of individual agents in war does not actually require that collective entities be fictions. That they are fictions depends on ulterior ontological considerations regarding, say, the ascription of personal predicates to putative entities that lack brains and minds; also, their being fictions affects the very possibility of a cognitive basis for constraining "their" behavior. Their being fictions, of course, dramatizes the hypnotic power of ideologies, in virtue of which individuals spontaneously direct their own activities to the interests and objectives of enveloping states, races, socioeconomic classes, peoples, and the like. What has been stressed here is the sense in which—apart from formal constraints of coherence, relevance, avoidance of arbitrariness—the justification of war and the justification of the conduct of aggregates of individuals in war are essentially inseparable from matters of ideological conviction. Given policies may be shown to be indefensible on formal grounds; but the positive justification of such policies cannot be freed from some governing ideology. To block the conclusion, we should have to show both that the proper norms of human conduct are cognitively discernible and that collective entities are actually existent and natural norms, assignable to them. But, on the condition that the countermoves fail, at least with respect to the actual existence of collective entities, the very designation of particular conflicts *as* wars (rather than as insurrections, revolts, civil disturbances, palace coups, police actions, anarchy, and the like) is itself a potential instrument *of* war.

10

Morally Blaming Whole Populations

PETER A. FRENCH

Whenever wartime atrocities are revealed to the general public issues of legal and moral responsibility arise. The legal questions are surely complex and important, especially when the plea of superior orders is involved. On the moral side, however, arise other questions which are often shrouded in confusions and yet, I think, they are at least as important as whether or not a specific number of soldiers and their officers are guilty of crimes against humanity or against peace. I am most concerned with the justification of ascriptions of moral blame to collectivities. I am particularly interested in ascriptions of blame to whole populations (or ethnic groups). We have been told by some writers that the American people are to blame for the Vietnam atrocities.[1] After the Second World War the collective "German people" or just "the Germans" were frequently blamed for the atrocities of the concentration camps. I shall attempt to expose the moral foundations which support such ascriptions of collective blame. If, as I hope to demonstrate, blame is in some cases justifiably placed on collectivities, many of our ethical standards may need reconsideration.

The etymological roots of 'to blame' lie in 'to blaspheme' ('to

---

1. Even Lt. Calley has made such a claim. "The guilt: as Medina said, we all as American citizens share it. I agree . . . I say if there's guilt, we must suffer it." From "The Concluding Confessions of Lieutenant Calley," by First Lieutenant William L. Calley, Jr., interviewed by John Sack, *Esquire*, September 1971.

speak evil of'). Although there are numerous everyday occasions where the sole function of blaming seems to be identifying the cause of unhappy or untoward events (for example, "Blame the weather for ruining the vacation"), there is more to blaming than the determination of causes or faults. There are at least two major senses of 'blame.' In the first, to blame is to fix responsibility, to identify the cause or causes of an untoward or disvalued event: the weather is to blame for a ruined vacation, the dead battery is to blame for the flashlight's failure, etc. In the second sense, to blame is to hold responsible. It is a key to our various uses of 'blaming' that we cannot hold the weather responsible or the dead battery responsible for the unhappy events for which they are to blame. It is a fact in both our legal and moral institutions that some things and some people[2] may be *to blame* for certain unhappy events, though they are not *to be blamed* for them.

Where blaming is an expression of displeasure directed without distinction at animate and inanimate objects, persons and things, I shall call that type of blame "non-moral." Surely there are many distinguishing characteristics of such non-moral blame over and above the mere expression of displeasure at the untoward event and its alleged causes, though often non-moral blaming is just dispraising. Expressions of disapprobation are central to all blaming episodes. It is a characteristic of non-moral blaming that it is used in cases of accident, mistake, and often where the blamed party is not believed to be capable of helping what it does. My son, for example, is to blame for breaking his toy train, even though he is only four years old and it was surely an accident. To resurrect one of Austin's famous illustrations,[3] I am to blame for killing your donkey even though I shot it in the mistaken belief that it was my donkey. Non-moral blame does not necessarily occasion evaluations of intelligence, states of mind, intentions, or responsibilities. In the case of persons, we only need

2. See my "On Blaming Psychopaths" in D. E. Cooper, ed., *The Manson Murders: A Philosophical Inquiry* (Cambridge: Schenkman Publishing Co., 1973).
3. J. L. Austin, "A Plea for Excuses," The Presidential Address to the Aristotelian Society, 1956, *Proceedings of the Aristotelian Society*, 1956-57, Vol. VII, 1957.

to know (some of us need only to suspect) that an individual did bring about the unpleasant or unwanted circumstances in order to blame him. As I have stressed, there is no difference in kind between blaming persons and blaming such things as inanimate objects and the weather, as long as blame is of a non-moral sort. A further characteristic of non-moral blaming (though I think this may be the case with blaming in general) would seem to be that occasions of its use are not necessarily directed at altering future behavior. This is most obvious in the example of blaming the weather.

We ascribe non-moral blame even when most people would admit that the person or thing blamed could not have effected the outcome of his (its) actions by intention. This type of blame does not involve us in issues of whether or not the blamed could have done something other than he did. We make no assumption that the blamed acted freely (that the blamed has free will) when we non-morally blame. It is entirely consistent with this type of blaming to blame sociopaths and psychopaths for their anti-social behavior and to blame children for breaking toys in so far as a causal relationship can be shown between the occurrence of the disapproved event and the thing blamed.

To non-morally blame is first to identify the cause of an untoward event. It is not so much to grade the cause as it is to single it out as having fallen below expected standards. It is like answering the question "Who (or what) is to blame for this (disvalued event)?" To blame the December weather in Minnesota for my automobile accident is not necessarily to grade the December weather. After all, it is standard for the weather in December in Minnesota to be violently snowy and icy, and many of the residents like it that way. It is to say that the weather conditions were a major contributory factor in the disvalued outcome, and it might be to say that the weather was the cause of substandard road conditions. The brakes are to blame for an auto accident if the brakes should have worked, if it would have been standard for them to work, but because they did not the accident occurred.

Non-moral blaming does, however, differ from just citing the causes of disapproved events in so far as it is not dispassionate. It is to use animadvertives in an objurgatory way toward the thing, event, or person blamed.[4] Consider the following contrasting examples:

(A.) While driving at a legal speed down a residential street, Mr. X is shocked to see a young child dart in front of his car. The shock of what is about to occur is too much for Mr. X's heart. He suffers a massive attack. The car swerves directly at the child. She is dead on impact, but later Mr. X recovers.

(B.) While driving at a legal speed down a residential street Mr. Y suddenly is shocked to see a young child dart in front of his vehicle. Mr. Y panics and instead of braking slams his foot on the accelerator. The child is killed instantly.

Surely both X and Y caused the deaths of children. But we would be inclined to blame Y for the child's death and reluctant to do the same in X's case, though we surely might blame X's heart for the accident. For that matter automobiles also caused those deaths. But in neither case are we likely to blame the car or its manufacturer. After all, the car operated as advertised, as cars are expected to operate. Had there been some mechanical fault in the construction of the car which made emergency stopping impossible, we would blame not only the car but its manufacturer or perhaps the most recent mechanic to have serviced it. Cars are expected to perform according to a certain automotive standard, and when accidents occur because of failure to meet that standard, we (and Ralph Nader) are entirely justified in blaming the

---

4. There is a whole class of expressions and idioms which might be called animadvertives (utterances of criticism, censure, or reproof) including 'despicable', 'detestable', 'diabolical', 'evil', 'insufferable', 'reprehensible', etc. Animadvertives might best be described as the verbal expression of what might be called disapprobatives ('disapproval', 'disvaluation', 'dislike', 'disfavor', 'dispraise', etc.). The boundaries of and relationships between disapprobatives, animadvertives, abusives, and possibly objurgatives need to be clarified in the map of blame.

car for the accident and often exonerating the driver. Notice, however, that where standards are harder to determine, as in the case of the weather being to blame for an accident, there is a reluctance to exonerate the driver completely. Unless the weather unexpectedly changed, we are likely to say that the driver is to blame for having ventured out at all, "He should have known better."

In regard to (A.) we might find ourselves blaming the child for her own death, but that likely would be contingent upon the age of the child. If she were only one or two years old, it would seem unlikely we would say she was to blame for her death, unless we were consoling Mr. X. If the child were somewhat older, say four or five, and of normal health, we might be more inclined to include her in the blame. Our reluctance to ascribe even non-moral blame to the very young child is due to our expectations and standards of performance. Seldom do we blame those persons who should not be expected to comprehend the possible disastrous consequences of performing certain acts. It makes no sense to say, "She should have known better," nor does it make sense to speak with objurgation toward or about her.

Returning to the drivers, I think that we would say that X is not to be blamed for the child's death. It makes little sense to talk of standards in regard to heart attacks. Perhaps we might say that X's heart was to blame for the child's death; in so far as it malfunctioned it tragically fell below the standards customarily applied to hearts. But, assuming X does not have a history of heart ailment, that he should not have been expecting an attack, X would seem to be blameless, even in the non-moral sense of blame, for the child's death.

Y, on the other hand, is to be blamed, non-morally, for the child's death. Y's performance behind the wheel was substandard. Panic is not sufficient exculpation for driving at top speed directly at the child. Most drivers do not do that; they are expected not to do so. Keeping the car under control is the first rule of the road. Y should have known which pedal was the brake, and he should have swerved to avoid the fatal accident. Y is more than just the cause of the child's death; he merits blame (in the non-moral sense) even if it is claimed that he was so gripped with panic that he could not have acted other than he did. It should by now be evident that primary in blaming is the notion of *should have*, not *could have*.

To begin with, we must distinguish between 'should have' and the rather more often discussed 'should have if I had chosen'.[5] Although I agree with Austin that Moore is confused when he appears to hold that 'should have if I had chosen' may be substituted for 'could have if I had chosen', I find a different distinction more important for the present purposes. Consider the following:

> (C.) Teacher to pupil: "You should have written more on *natura naturans*. I'm afraid I can't give you a very good grade."

Two elements are worth noting: (1.) 'should have' refers to a standard (explicit or implicit) and (2.) 'should have' does not depend for its sense upon the capacities, dispositions, or abilities of its subjects. Suppose the pupil in (C.) has no capacity or ability to understand or comment on *natura naturans*. He could not have written more on it in his essay without producing gibberish. Would we then say that he should not have written more? I think not. It is appropriate then to blame the pupil for his poor grade although blame, it must be reminded, is surely not at this level of a moral sort. When one says of the pupil in (C.) that he "should have" written more on *natura naturans,* one is *not* prepared to say that "if (such and such) he would have." What has been said is simply that he failed to reach a certain expected standard, one which is involved when judgments are made within the type of activity in which he was engaged.[6]

Our practices of blaming rest upon the existence of certain

5. See P. H. Nowell-Smith, *Ethics* (London: Penguin Books, 1954, 1964), pp. 239-243. Also J. L. Austin, "Ifs and Cans," *Proceedings of the British Academy,* XLII, 1956.
6. There is, I suppose, a hypothetical suppressed in the notion of a standard of the sort that if he had satisfied the criterion he would have been successful, but I do not think that is an important element in the logic of "should have."

standards and expectations relevant to our various activities and the events of our lives. It is not here important to discuss the genesis of those standards and whether or not they stand in need of justification. Someone or something is to blame when the major criterion of our adverse judgment of him or it is of the "should have" variety. This might be only an attitude that it "should have" (what J. L. Austin called the behabitive sense of blaming). Hence to say the weather should have been better, i.e. to blame the weather for our ruined vacation, is to express the attitude that we disvalue the weather. We had counted on sunny days and it rained for a week. 'The weather should have been better' is then 'We had in mind a standard of acceptable weather which was not met when it rained for a week'. Obviously some types of non-moral blaming are like scolding or rebuking or chiding, while others are merely expressions of attitude.

In regard to justifying collective non-moral blame to whole populations let us consider the case of war crimes. The ascription of non-moral blame for war crimes in Vietnam to the American people can be justified, if the blamer can cite (1) reasons for treating that particular section of humanity as a collectivity, i.e. there is a solidarity (to use Feinberg's term) to the group; (2) evidence that the perpetrators of the war atrocities, those strictly liable for them, would not have had opportunity to perform them had not the collecivity acted in such a way as to have allowed themselves to be led or misled by political leaders, paid taxes without protest, failed to question governmental decisions, etc.; (3) standards or behavioral norms by which the conduct of a people in relation to their government is judgable (the American people in relation to the American state); and (4) a demonstration that those acts (as in (2)) of the collectivity did fall short of the standards (as in (3)) regardless of whether or not anyone or all of the members of the population could have altered the whole population's pattern of behavior or their government's policies, even if they had had the mechanics for such alteration. By claiming in the non-moral sense that the American people are to blame for the Vietnam atrocities, events which aroused in him feelings of disapprobation, one is saying that he believes that the American people should have done x, y, and z, and of course, that they did not do x, y, and z.[7] However, moral condemnation of the American people is quite another matter.

The types of judgments which signal the practice of moral blaming are first, "should have's" of a particular kind, i.e. moral judgments based on our moral standards, and secondly "could have's." It would not be profitable or justifiable in a paper of this length to compare and contrast the various positions taken in the discussion of whether responsibility may be reconciled with some form of determinism.[8] I take it to be a fact of our ordinary language and everyday behavior that we do hold certain individuals morally blameworthy for some, though not all, of their actions.[9] That is, we hold ourselves and others morally responsible for some of our behavior and its consequences. It is also a fact that we refrain from holding morally responsible some human beings no matter what they do: certain mental defectives and infants. And we never literally hold animals or mechanical devices morally responsible. What distinguishes those cases where we are inclined to hold people morally responsible (blameworthy) from those where we are reluctant to do so?

It should by now be clear that an essential element of all blaming is the existence of standards, either implicit or explicit. The standards in question where non-moral blaming is involved are standards of performance. When moral blaming is at issue 'He should have done something other than he did when he fell below standard', is a moral judgment and we are concerned with whether or not "he could have. . . ."

'Could have', as many writers have pointed out,[10] is problematic. Clearly though, if it is said of someone (Lt. Calley, for ex-

---

7. Clearly this is far more complex than a series of things not done: a time element would be necessary, etc.

8. I suggest that J. Glover, *Responsibility* (London: Routledge and Kegan Paul, 1970), be read in this regard.

9. Austin, I believe, would call this type of blaming verdictive. See *How To Do Things With Words* (Oxford: Clarendon Press, 1965), p. 152.

10. See Nowell-Smith, *op. cit.*; Austin, "Ifs and Cans;" J. J. C. Smart, "Freewill, Praise and Blame," *Mind*, 1961; Kurt Baier, "Could and Would," *Analysis*, Supp. Vol., 1963, pp. 20-29.

ample) that "He could have prevented the atrocity," we are generally aware of what the speaker believes about Lt. Calley and the
situation. In the first place, he believes that Calley did not prevent the atrocity. Secondly, he believes that Calley possessed a
certain amount of power relative to the situation, that Calley had
opportunity to alter the situation (he was in command of Charlie
Company.) Also he believes that Calley was in possession of his
mental faculties and thereby capable of assessing the situation
and drawing upon and acting upon those assessments. In brief, to
say "He could have prevented the massacre at My Lai," is to make
implicit reference to Calley's abilities and opportunities. I take
'could have done n' to mean 'There is something such that if he
had tried to do that (and that was not what he did do) he would
have done n'.[11] Calley is to be morally blamed for the My Lai
atrocity because there were many conceivable alternative courses
of action, which had he tried to do them he would not have led
Charlie Company to massacre innocent villagers (which is not to
say that the massacre would not have occurred had Calley tried
to do something other than he did). Assuming that mitigating
circumstances relative to Calley's mental health are not demonstrable, we have grounds for the belief that Calley "could have
done something other than he did," and he is thereby blameworthy for the massacre.

There is an important sequential relationship to be drawn between "should have's" and "could have's" in the practice of blaming. "Should have's" are the primary grounds for judgments of
blame for untoward or disvalued events. "Should have's" express
our standards, moral or non-moral, usually by citing specific
courses of action, that have not been met. A natural progression
from the recognition of the event as substandard, the determination of the cause or causes and the expression of our disapprobation to the question of blameworthiness is indicated by the passage to consideration of "could have's." Hence the expressions 'I
know he did it, but you can't blame him' or 'Well, yes, he is to
blame for it, but how can we blame him'? indicate that mitigating

11. I owe much here to the work of Roderick Chisholm, "J. L. Austin's Philosophical Papers," *Mind*, 1964, especially pp. 20-25.

circumstances have affected the secondary "could have" evaluation: where moral blame is not justified some conditions must be believed to exist such that there is really nothing conceivable in his province that if he had tried to do that he could not have caused or participated in the production of the untoward (disvalued) event. In effect, "could have" questions arise only in light of "should have" questions where blaming is concerned.[12]

Simply then, moral blame is justifiable when no mitigation or exculpation is demonstrable in the secondary "could have" evaluation of an individual already to blame for failure to meet a moral standard. We need not consider here what might be sufficient grounds for mitigation,[13] though I think we should expect that most if not all examinations into mitigation would begin with the question, "Was he capable of doing anything that we would normally expect would have resulted in different (i.e. not untoward) consequences?" After that question might then follow, "Was he capable of appreciating alternative courses of action to the one he pursued?" The relationship which I am herein emphasizing is typified by a statement by Daniel Ellsberg in which he was blaming Robert McNamara for the Vietnam war. Ellsberg said, "It must occur to him that the things he did not know were things he should and could have discovered."[14]

When the criteria above are applied to the driver in (A.) we see why no moral blame is due him. Also regarding (B.) we are not likely to morally blame the panic-stricken driver if only because there was nothing conceivable he could have tried to do which would have prevented the accident (assuming we understand his state of panic to be a mitigating circumstance—he did not "willfully panic"; perhaps anyone would have panicked in such a situation, although most people would have had better bodily reactions and hit the brake). If the pupil in (C.) simply lacks the ability or the capacity to succeed at his task, again he could not have learned more and thereby could not have written more and

---

12. "Should have's" of course are not prior to "could have's" in normal non-blaming usage. For example, "He could have run a mile today."
13. See my "On Blaming Psychopaths," *op. cit.*
14. J. Robert Moskin, "Ellsberg Talks," *Look*, Oct. 5, 1971, pp. 31-34, 39-42.

thereby he is not blameworthy for his failures. Contrary to "should have's," "could have's" are suppressed hypotheticals, though as Austin rightly points out,[15] they are not causal conditionals.

It is necessary, however, to make clear that where judgments of blameworthiness are concerned, the blamer is justified only if he is able to cite some specific action which if the blamed could have done that he would have acted differently. 'He could have done n', if n stands for a normal verbal expression such as 'written more on *natura naturans*' or 'paid his debts', needs to be supported by demonstrating the satisfaction of a number of conditions regarding his rather special abilities. 'He could have done n' is true then only if those conditions are satisfied and not true if conditions favorable to his doing n are only a mattter of happenstance, chance, or luck. On the other hand, the broader statement 'He could have acted differently' is true just in so far as 'He would have acted differently if he had chosen' is true, and that might be true when his abilities and skills are not essentially involved in the act. 'He would have run the four-minute mile if he had chosen' leaves open whether his success would have been the result of his skills or of the luck of having a brisk wind at his back. Hence the expression 'done something other than he did' is not to be simply equated with 'acted differently'. This is, of course, to elaborate upon the relationship in blaming between 'should have' and 'could have'. 'He should have acted differently' is incomplete. It must be supplemented by reference to the standard of behavior, which is generally, as I have maintained, to cite a specific norm of action.

I have spoken at some length of the different senses of blame, and I have indicated how collective blame may be justified in the non-moral senses of blaming, i.e. if 'they should have done something other than they did' is not a moral judgment. In that sense, a whole population which aided, even by their acquiescence, the perpetration of the untoward events is to blame for those events. But when the "should have" judgment is a moral one and its subject is a collectivity such as the American people, a number of

15. J. L. Austin, "Ifs and Cans," *op. cit.*

further problems arise. I shall examine some of those problems with reference to war crimes.

Three issues must be met head on: (a) Can one be morally to blame for the acts of another? (b) Can a collectivity such as "the American people" be the bearer of moral blame? and (c) Is "vicarious collective moral blame" reducible to individual vicarious liabilities? Many philosophers have rejected the whole idea of collective responsibility because they feel compelled to answer (a) in the negative.[16] Common usage, however, suggests that there do exist cases in which not only persons *can* be held, but in which we *do* hold people morally responsible (blameworthy) for the acts of others. Possibly underlying the negative answer to (a) is a confusion of the concept of guilt with that of blame.

'Guilt' is generally applied in cases of willful breach of legal codes. If Mr. X is guilty of *y*, he is a perpetrator, inciter, abettor, or accomplice, etc. in the performance of the untoward or unpermitted *y*. (I am not here interested in the legalistic sense of guilt as 'having been found guilty'.) No one, to be sure, can be guilty of the illegal acts of another, though as history has painfully shown, one can be found guilty of the acts of another.

If my child steals a car, he is guilty of stealing. I cannot be guilty of his stealing, but I may well be held to blame for his stealing. I may, of course, be guilty of raising my child a thief, but that is not to be guilty of his thievery. For me to be guilty of stealing the car it must be shown that I was an abettor, accomplice, inciter, etc. Even then, however, I am not guilty of his stealing. I am guilty myself of stealing. Considering such examples it should be evident that 'guilt' and 'blame' are not synonymous (cannot always be used interchangeably) and furthermore that blame can be vicarious (I am to blame for the child's thievery, even though I am not the thief). As I have argued, moral blame stresses the censure that is coincidental with one's being held liable for substandard behavior. As there are a number of things I might have tried to do which would normally be expected in

16. See, for example: H. D. Lewis, "Collective Responsibility," *Philosophy*, Jan. 1948, Vol. XXIII, No. 84, p. 3; R. S. Downie, "Collective Responsibility," *Philosophy*, Jan. 1969, Vol. XLIV, No. 167, p. 66.

order to raise a child with a greater respect for private property and as I do not qualify for any acceptable exemptions, others are justified in morally blaming me for my child's thievery. I might even blame myself. It is not simply that I should have raised him better than I did, I could have done so. It might be objected that I am really only morally to blame for being a poor parent and not vicariously to blame for my son's thefts. I think, however, such an objection misses the point of expressions such as 'The boy stole the car, but the parents are to blame'. When we are speaking of moral blame, guilt is not the major problem. I am inclined to the view that to be guilty is to have done the disapprobated deed, that the paradigmatic use of the word is its legalistic use. I assume then, that to be "morally guilty" is to have transgressed a moral code, but that is only the first step in determining moral blameworthiness. After all, psychopaths, mental defectives, young children, and idiots are constantly transgressing such codes. The notion that such persons cannot transgress moral codes because they cannot appreciate the moral nature of such codes begs the question. To argue that "moral guilt" is the willful transgression of such codes will not do either. Surely some of the above-mentioned transgress those codes not only willingly but with finesse.[17]

What the illustration of the thieving child shows is that moral blame is transferable. There is nothing out of the ordinary in the notion of vicarious liability. Another example may be made to bear more specifically on the issue of justifying the blaming of collectivities. We have all seen science fiction movies in which a scientist attempting to probe the limits of knowledge in search of the "secret of life" (and often for some humane reason) creates a human-looking monster which soon goes berserk and indiscriminately ravages the countryside. The scientist is beset with overwhelming pangs of self-blame, and the good people of the town also blame him for the monstrous evil deeds.[18] Despite the fact that

17. Charles Manson might well be a case in point.
18. I have elaborated upon such an example in "Monsters and Their Makers," in Peter A. French, ed., *Individual and Collective Responsibility: Massacre at My Lai* (Cambridge: Schenkman Publishing Co., 1972).

the scientist has no control over the monster, despite the fact that he had only good intentions at its creation, I think we are justified in holding him morally blameworthy for the monster's deeds. He should have expected dire consequences to occur when he created a super-human monster. But not only should he have refrained from creating the monster; he could have, in the relevant sense, so refrained, assuming, of course, that he was not a mental defective, psychopath, etc. The scientist I have in mind is not of the "mad" variety, though he may be obsessed with his theories. Obsessions of this sort do not alter what he "could have done"; after all, an obsession is not unalterable.[19]

Now let us expand this science fiction example in order to examine the issues of collective moral blame. Suppose our scientist were not working in isolation, that he was one of a team of scientists. I think that we would not be reluctant to morally blame the team of scientists for the monster's deeds; we can make perfectly good sense of the expression 'The whole team of scientists is to blame'. First let us assume that the team of scientists was organized in such a way that they could make group decisions on the value and advisability of various avenues of research in their project, that as a team they were capable of making judgments including moral ones and of putting them into practice.[20] Let us also assume that no one was forced to join the team and that they all knew that they were "searching for the secret of life." This would fulfill certain requirements for identifying them as a specific collectivity and not just a gathering of scientists. As a team they would then satisfy the criteria for moral blameworthiness in

19. The great tragedy of *Moby-Dick* is not that Ahab has no choice but that he indulges his obsession to pursue the white whale. It is precisely Ahab's failure to alter his fatal course (i.e. he could have gone to the aid of the *Rachael*, etc.) that seals his tragic fate, making him morally to blame for his and his crew's untimely deaths.

20. Virginia Held convincingly argues that a collectivity is distinguishable from a random collection of individuals by its possession of a decision method for action. See her "Can a Random Collection of Individuals Be Morally Responsible?" *Journal of Philosophy*, July 23, 1970, pp. 461 ff, and "Moral Responsibility and Collective Action" in my *Individual and Collective Responsibility: Massacre at My Lai, op. cit.*, pp. 101-18.

the case of the monster's acts. Not only should they have chosen a different avenue of research, they could have done so.

But once we have blamed the team, we have not necessarily blamed each scientist individually for the monstrous deeds. If X, Y, and Z form collectivity A, and if A can and does act as a collectivity, e.g. it has and makes use of its decision methods for action, then we may be justified in finding A morally blameworthy for its acts; though the sum of X, Y, and Z's liability is not equivalent to that we ascribe to A. 'Collectivity A is blameworthy for event n and A is composed of individuals X, Y, and Z' does not entail 'X is blameworthy for n, Y is blameworthy for n, and Z is blameworthy for n'. Herein, of course, lies one of the stickiest problems with the notion of blaming collectivities: how can a collectivity be held morally to blame for event n when not all of its members are held morally blameworthy for n? The approach I am suggesting for blaming collectivities appears to make the collectivity an entity capable of bearing moral blame over and above the sum of the blame due each individual member. I think that there are good reasons for holding such a view. Collectivities are, in fact, often organized in such a way that they may shoulder blame for the failure of their projects without reflecting on individuals. For example, the Honeywell corporation is said by many to be to blame for the damage done by its anti-personnel bombs in North Vietnam.[21] Most people, however, would recognize as unjust blaming every Honeywell worker individually for that destruction.

It should be noted, however, that from 'Collectivity A is blameworthy for event n and A is composed of X, Y, and Z' it would be presumptuous to conclude that X, Y or Z do not warrant any blame for n or that either X, Y, or Z is not himself blameworthy in the case of n. My point is that such judgments assessed on members of the collectivity do not follow necessarily from judgments of collective blame. Indeed, we may expect that at least one of the scientists in the team merits individual blame for n, but the

21. Honeywell disputes this, however, by claiming that they only make the bombs for their government as a patriotic service. They do not drop them on Vietnamese citizens.

grounds for justifying such blaming are not those by which the collective blame is justified. It has been argued by Virginia Held[22] that the assessment of moral responsibility on a collectivity is not distributive but that it can be concluded from such an assessment that at least some members of the collectivity are responsible for the act in question. I shall argue that although such is often the case, it is not a defining characteristic of morally blaming collectivities that one is able to conclude from the ascription of collective responsibility that some member or members of the collectivity is/are liable for the act in question.

Three questions bear most significantly on the question of justifying morally blaming collectivities: (1) Can collectivities act in ways not simply reducible to the acts of their members? (2) Does it make sense to say that a collectivity should have done something other than it did do? (or Do standards of collective action exist?), and (3) Are collectivities capable of trying courses of action different from those they actually took? There are any number of things one can say about the actions of a collectivity which cannot be said of or cannot be reduced to statements about the acts of individuals, or at least such reductions destroy the sense of the original statement about the collectivity. In the case of the team of scientists, it might be said that they created a monster, though no individual scientist on the team could have done so alone. 'The X, Y, Z team of scientists made a monster' does not entail, 'X made a monster, Y made a monster, and Z made a monster'. If the point is not yet clear, compare the above to the statement, 'The team lost the big game', which does not entail 'The quarterback lost the big game' or 'The middle linebacker lost the big game', etc. It does not even entail that any of the players played poorly as individuals. The team effort was just not up to the occasion, perchance a general spirit was lacking; or perhaps the team, through circumstances for which no individual could be cited, is so constituted that even when all members play as well as they possibly can, the total performance is dismal. The team simply lacks a certain complementarity.

22. Held, in my *Individual and Collective Responsibility*.

Some have argued[23] that although fault may be collective, group liability is always distributive. I think that in such a view is embedded a confusion. Let us take the example with which we are basically concerned:

> (D.) "The American people are to blame for the Vietnam atrocities."

Assume that we are dealing with moral blame. How is (D.) to be justified? Anyone sincerely saying (D.) must be able to show (1) that there exists a recognizable or referable collectivity designated by the term 'the American people'; (2) that events describable as "atrocities" took place in Vietnam;[24] (3) that a causal relationship can be drawn from acts of the collectivity to the "atrocities" in question; (4) that the American people should have acted (collectively) in a manner different from the manner in which they did act; (5) that the American people were not completely unaware of the nature of their behavior (that is, the American people did not believe they were authorizing a cultural exchange of ballet troupes with the Vietnamese); and (6) that the collectivity could have acted (had the ability and opportunity of acting) in those alternative ways cited in (4), that is, there were conceivable alternative courses of collective action which had they been tried would have made less likely the perpetration of atrocities in Vietnam (the untoward events).

Now it might be argued that my position seems to ignore the fact that collectivities are collections of individuals, that "the American people" is a composition of all Americans (compared to "Mankind is a composition of all men"), and that it seems intuitively unjust to morally blame the American people (all Americans) when a goodly number evidence their lack of support for the war effort. But far from having ignored such a view, I have shown that it rests on a misunderstanding; collectivities are not *just* collections of individuals.

23. Joel Feinberg, *Doing and Deserving* (Princeton: Princeton University Press, 1970), p. 249.
24. Clearly the word 'atrocity' is an implicit blaming expression.

The terms 'the American people' and 'all Americans' are not equivalent. In 'all Americans' 'Americans' acts as a general term. What is true of all Americans is true of each and every American. If we were saying "All Americans are to blame for the Vietnam atrocities" then we would have to justify blaming each American, a task which would be most difficult in the case of some Americans. On the other hand 'the American people' is not a general term. It is a singular term which names or purports to name a collectivity. What is true of "the American people" need not be, and actually often is not true of each and every American. For example consider the statement 'The American people have the highest standard of living in the world', which certainly does not mean that each and every American has the highest standard of living in the world. Notice also that the statement 'The American people grew tired of hearing about the Vietnamese war' may be true when the statement 'American John Doe grew tired of hearing about the Vietnamese war' is false. There is therefore no question of justifying ascriptions of blame for the war to each and every American citizen.

Those who might seek to preserve the notion that responsibility is primarily an individual matter might propose we treat statements such as (D.) as a shorthand version of

> (E.) "All American citizens who did not overtly behave in ways which manifested their non-membership in the sub-collectivity 'American war supporters' are individually to blame (degrees of blame would probably be appropriate) for the Vietnam atrocities."

But (E.) as the above suggests, is not an acceptable substitute for (D.). They mean entirely different things. The membership of a blamed collectivity (like the American people) cannot be defined, *ad hoc,* in terms of individual participation (overt or covert) in the untoward events which were the occasion of the blaming episode. When someone blames "the American people" or "the Honeywell corporation" or the team of scientists or the football team he is not usually adding (softly under his breath so that he and a few methodological individualists can hear) some qualification to the effect "except those who did. . . ." The collectivity would soon die the death of "a thousand qualifications."[25] "The American people" is a collectivity of which action is predicable and to which blame (moral responsibility) is ascribable. If it were the case that the meaning of a statement about "the American people" were identical to the conjunction of a number of statements about the members of the collectivity "the American people," then had one of the individuals belonging to the American people (collectivity) not in fact been a member, the meaning of the original statement would have been different. It is a mistake thereby to seek grounds for exculpation for individual collectivity members, when (D.) is not individually blaming anyone (which is not to say that individuals are not morally to blame). The only issue of exculpation in regard to (D.) is that of whether or not in the relevant sense one is justified in saying that "the American people" could not have tried to do anything other than it did in the circumstances even if it should have.

Membership in "the American people" or "the Honeywell corporation" or "the football team" is not determined by whether one materially contributed to the particular untoward event for which the collectivity is being blamed, but instead whether one has the "credentials" of membership in the collectivity that can act in such a way as to be productive of such an untoward event. The credentials of membership in "the American people" would seem to include at least citizenship, perhaps maturity, common descent, language, or history, if you like. But the expression 'the American people' surely does not mean 'only those people of American citizenship who support program x or y or z of their government'. In fact, 'the American people' is used in ordinary discourse to name not only a collectivity of individuals but also the nation for which the President of the United States speaks and in whose name the armies of the United States march. It should not be forgotten that, theoretically at least, "the American people" are sovereign in the United States.

There remains another possible objection; it might be argued that we are not justified in morally blaming whole populations

25. This term is borrowed from Antony Flew.

without blaming individuals because there is really no point in it; that there is no reason to expect our blaming to alter the future behavior of the collectivity. Certainly few national populations alter their actions because of a fear of blame or censure. Perhaps, however, such a statement as 'The German people are to blame for Dachau' has had some impact at least as a kind of warning (the plaque at Dachau reads, "For the past, honor, for the future a warning.") The confusion here, however, is in treating the efficacy of blaming as the grounds for blaming.[26] Whether or not blaming X for n is or should be expected to be productive of desired results is not the same problem as whether or not X merits moral blame for n. It must be remembered that moral blaming is "to hold responsible," "to deem blameworthy." It is not "to punish." The only justifiable reason for morally blaming a whole population is that that population merits moral blame, and the determination of blameworthiness is first a question of standards and then one of abilities and opportunities.

To the question, "Why should we blame the American people?", the answer "Because it will make the American people act differently in the future" rests only on the vaguest of hopes and goes counter to most of what we know of history. But then history gives us little precedent for morally dealing with the powerful technological conglomerates and political machines which now proliferate at a blinding rate of speed. Standards for individual behavior and standards of collective behavior should not be thought *a priori* to be ineffably linked. What is needed is not a reversion to traditional theories of individualism but a realistic approach to the problem of standards of behavior for both individuals and collectivities.

26. This appears to be the view of Nowell-Smith, *op. cit.*

11

Social Science and American Foreign Policy

KAI NIELSEN

I

Noam Chomsky has made a trenchant and much discussed radical assessment of America's role in the world. His critique is distinguished both by his careful attention to the facts and by his willingness to make a radical moral assessment of United States foreign policy and America's stance toward the world. His work brilliantly exemplifies C. Wright Mills's contention that objectivity and moral commitment can ride tandem. Yet given Chomsky's forceful criticisms of United States government policy and given his exposure of the liberal establishment subservient to the American government, it is no surprise that his work has been extensively and indeed sometimes even abusively criticized.

What I am concerned to do here is to see, by looking at some of Chomsky's central critical claims concerning American foreign policy, and some of the responses to them, whether it is the case that Chomsky and his critics could have available to them some plain empirical facts which would confute or refute their central claims such that we could at least in principle establish or disestablish their positions by an appeal to the facts without relying on a set of norm-laden interpretive claims which may indeed even suffer from ideological distortion.[1] My underlying interests and

1. Noam Chomsky, *American Power and the New Mandarins* (Harmondsworth, Middlesex, England: Penguin Books, 1969); Noam Chomsky, *At War with Asia* (New York: Vintage Books, 1970); Noam Chomsky, *Problems of Knowledge and Freedom* (London: Barrie and Jenkins, 1972); Noam Chomsky,

concerns are actually much wider than merely to examine the argument between Chomsky and his critics. I use this important dispute as a crucial test case to see whether it is possible over foreign policy disputes of this magnitude to confirm or disconfirm the fundamental claims involved by an appeal to "the empirical facts" or whether in such disputes we are unavoidably caught in an interpretive hermeneutical circle in which there can be no "value-free," "interpretation-free" appeal to the facts.

There is an increasingly influential account of social science which maintains that the social sciences are irreducibly interpretive (hermeneutical) and that they cannot and should not be normatively neutral. If this account of social science is correct, there can be no such an "appeal to the facts" to resolve such foreign policy disputes as obtain between Chomsky and his critics, yet both Chomsky and his critics (conceptually sophisticated as they are) are convinced that there are plain appeals to the facts, which, if their opponents would only attend to them, would refute what they claim. I shall try to ascertain whether "the logic of the situation" is such that there can be such an appeal to "the facts" or whether it is more plausible to maintain that we are caught in

"Philosophers and Public Philosophy," *Ethics*, Vol. 79, No. 1 (Oct. 1968); (Note responses in the same volume by William Earle and John R. Silber.) Noam Chomsky, "The Student Movement," *The Humanist*, Vol. XXX, No. 5 (Sept.-Oct. 1970); Sidney Hook, "The Political Fantasies of Noam Chomsky," *The Humanist*, Vol. XXX, No. 6 (Nov.-Dec. 1970); Noam Chomsky, "Response to Sidney Hook," *The Humanist*, Vol. XXXI, No. 1 (Jan.-Feb. 1971); Sidney Hook, "The Knight of the Double Standard," *The Humanist*, Vol. XXXI, No. 1 (Jan.-Feb. 1971); Noam Chomsky, "Response to Sidney Hook II," *The Humanist*, Vol. XXXI, No. 2 (March-April 1971); Sidney Hook, "The Knight Comes a Cropper," *The Humanist*, Vol. XXXI, No. 2 (March-April 1971); Antony Flew, "New Left Isolationism," *The Humanist*, Vol. XXXI, No. 5 (Sept.-Oct. 1971); Arthur Schlesinger, Jr., "Review of American Power and the New Mandarins," *Book World* (March 23, 1969); Lionel Abel, "The Position of Noam Chomsky," *Commentary*, Vol. 48, No. 2 (May 1969); Noam Chomsky and Lionel Abel—an exchange, "Vietnam, the Cold War and Other Matters," *Commentary*, Vol. 48, No. 4 (Oct. 1969); Noam Chomsky, "Scholarship and Ideology," *The VAG Magazine*, Vol. 2, No. 1 (Winter 1973), pp. 31-43. This last essay together with others on similar themes is published in Chomsky's collection of essays, *For Reasons of State* (New York: Pantheon Books, 1973).

such a hermeneutical circle—that is to say, we are enmeshed in an interpretive account of social phenomena from which there is no independent appeal to the facts.

My strategy shall be as follows: I shall first set out a central part of the dispute between Chomsky and his critics, then elucidate an interpretive account of social science, and finally, in the light of such an account, see if there is any reasonable way of setting out the dispute between Chomsky and his critics such that it would serve as a disconfirming instance of this interpretive account of social science. In doing this I shall try to achieve two closely related aims: (1) to see what kinds of tests we can expect for such foreign policy claims and (2) to test, against an important case, the plausibility of such an hermeneutical conception of social science.

In doing this I shall fasten on a particular statement of that hermeneutical account of social science, namely, the one given by Charles Taylor.[2] I do this because it is a succinct, plausible, and powerfully articulated statement of this view. In section III, I shall expound it and elucidate it, trying to bring out its force, for on the above summary statement it may have sounded implausible. I should add that it has been remarked to me that it is unlikely that Taylor would disagree very much, if at all, with Chomsky's political assessments. Taylor, after all, is a distinguished advocate of a kind of libertarian socialism, and his politically important *Patterns of Politics* involves a critique of American imperialistic foreign policy *vis-à-vis* Canada. However, notwithstanding all this, and independently of how much or how little Taylor would side with Chomsky's particular political views, it seems to me, for reasons that I shall set out, that Taylor's theoretical views concerning social science are in conflict with some of both Chomsky's and his critics' core claims. On my reading of Taylor's account, neither cluster of claims, if Taylor is correct, should be taken at face value. If any such cluster of claims, as either Chomsky or his critics make, is to be made out, they must be radically

---

2. Charles Taylor, "Interpretation and the Sciences of Man," *The Review of Metaphysics,* Vol. XXV, No. 1 (Sept. 1971).

reconstrued, if such an hermeneutical account of social science is accepted.

II

The debate between Chomsky and his liberal and conservative critics is sharp and often acrimonious. That these disputes are extremely bitter seems to me perfectly natural, given the different beliefs involved and the obvious centrality of the issues raised to ourselves, our children and to mankind generally. The fight is about the very quality of our lives and over what kind of social reality we want to see come into being. Over such really staggering issues, the disputants tend to see each other as blinded, hopelessly irrational, morally fanatical and politically evasive. Perhaps such abuse in some cases is warranted, but be that as it may, I do not want to take sides on this or indeed even consider it. What is evident, however, is that on all sides of the dispute we have philosophically literate, informed, and politically aware individuals in fundamental disagreement concerning central moral and political phenomena. I want to isolate the crucial claims made by Chomsky and the crucial counterclaims, to try to see what they are like and what kind of considerations are at issue between Chomsky and his critics. I want to try to ascertain to what extent we simply have rival readings of meanings which themselves are not exclusively brute identifiable data and I want to try to determine what, if anything, would count as a more adequate reading here.

The central substantive issues deeply concern me, as they must any aware and humane person. But I shall not try here, except perhaps by indirection, to push them further toward a resolution. Rather I am concerned with understanding the structure of the argument and with trying to understand what, if anything, would count as a rational resolution of such disputes. Since what I must be doing here is offering an interpretation of interpretations, I should like to make my own substantive beliefs concerning these matters explicit, for *if* they will skew my own understanding of the logic of the situation or of what is crucially at issue, it is well to have them out in the open. Then, if there is unwitting bias or blindness in what I say, it will be somewhat easier to spot the direction it will take. So I should say at the outset that my sympathies here are with Chomsky. I think that some of the things he says are overstated and I take this (though this is my surmise) to be partly a deliberate attempt at a shock effect by use of hyperbole. But I do believe, rightly or wrongly, that the central thrust of what he says is not political fantasy or paranoia but is for the most part a correct and absolutely vital cluster of claims about contemporary political and social reality. But I am not out to argue this here, though I do believe that it is vital that the argument go on and that the unmasking of liberal ideology and the articulation of critical rival analyses proceed beyond the point where Chomsky has taken his analyses of America's role in the world. Be that as it may, what I want to do here is to lay out some of these arguments and see what can be seen about their logic and what criteria can be given for their rational resolution.

Chomsky developed his radical critique of American society from his analysis of the war in Vietnam. Writing in 1969, he remarks in the introduction to his *American Power and the New Mandarins* that "anyone who puts a fraction of his mind to the task can construct" an "overwhelming case against the American war in Vietnam."[3] This we can take as his first central claim. Examining this situation and the reasons why this should be so, Chomsky is led to some radical theses which have offended and distressed many Americans. Chomsky stresses again and again that what Americans should come to see is not merely that they made a mistake in terms of cost and utility in going into Vietnam but that what they "have done in Vietnam is wrong, a criminal act," and "that an American 'victory' would have been a tragedy."[4] To this, it is responded by some liberal critics, that America did what it did in good faith: that it went into South Vietnam initially to protect it from Communist aggression and to modernize the country in order to create a better life for the Vietnamese. The United States has, as they see it, tragically been forced to remain to honor its treaty commitments and to prevent a blood bath by a precipi-

---

3. Noam Chomsky, *American Power and the New Mandarins*, pp. 11-12.
4. *Ibid.*, p. 13.

tate withdrawal which would, as well, encourage Communist subversion throughout the underdeveloped world. They admit that
things have gotten so out of hand, the war has become so plainly
unwinnable, except at a cost in destruction that Americans will
find unacceptable, that America must gradually wind down the
war. But, they contend, the United States is not behaving in the
war in a criminally wrong way. It is not, they claim, an evil imperialist power brutally and genocidally attempting to destroy a
small country that will not bow to its will.

Chomsky responds that this is not so and that in the case of such
informed men as Schlesinger and Hook, for instance, the taking
of such a line is just out and out intellectual counterrevolutionary
misrepresentation. In short, these men in their public stances
at least, are either making claims that they know not to be the
case, or are omitting to consider phenomena, or covering up
phenomena, which plainly establish the imperialist stance of
the United States. They are in short apologists for the American
capitalist and imperialist system, using their skills, their knowledge, and their argumentative capabilities to defend the American system and dampen down disquietude with it. Such intellectuals do not accept the traditional role of intellectuals as persons
who must attempt "to speak the truth and to expose lies."[5] Rather,
they will not over a crucial matter challenge in any fundamental
way, the government or the powers that be, but will always provide an ideological justification for the use of American power
and the defense of the American way of life.

Chomsky believes that these ideological apologists for American
power can be refuted by people who will give careful attention to
the "bare and inescapable facts." Such an attention, he believes,
will vindicate the core of his position. Knowing where to stand
here is not a matter of "existential decision" to which no knowl-
edge-claim is relevant or even in certain circumstances decisive and
it is not a matter of adopting some problematical ideological
framework but rather it is a matter of patient and careful attention
to the empirical facts. Chomsky asserts that certain "basic facts"

5. *Ibid.*, p. 257.

about Vietnam, the United States, China, and Russia are clear enough to make the truth of the following claims evident.[6]

1. The United States is the primary agent of repression and counterrevolution throughout the world.[7]

2. By any objective standard, the United States during the past six years at least has been and still continues to be "the most aggressive country in the world, the greatest threat to world peace" and "without a rival today as an agent of international criminal violence."[8]

He then goes on to make what he takes to be the following more controversial claims. Yet they are claims which he believes we can know to be true.

3. The pragmatic attitude toward the war in Vietnam is "a sign of moral degeneration so severe that talk of using the normal channels of protest and dissent becomes meaningless and the various forms of resistance provide the most significant course of political action, open to a concerned citizen. The American political consciousness does not see Vietnam policies as wrong but as policies which should be abandoned because they are failing."[9]

4. There is no more powerful force that can call the United States to account. If there is to be a change, it will have to come from within. ". . . the fate of millions of poor and oppressed people throughout the world will be determined by our [the American] ability to carry out a profound 'cultural revolution' in the United States."[10]

6. *Ibid.*, p. 11.
7. Noam Chomsky, "Philosophers and Public Philosophy," *Ethics*, Vol. 79, No. 1 (Oct. 1968), p. 1.
8. *Ibid.*
9. *Ibid.*
10. *Ibid.*, p. 3.

5. To carry this cultural revolution through in the United States, given the truth of the above four propositions, requires a kind of denazification.[11]

6. To carry out this cultural revolution, we must modify political and moral consciousness and "construct alternative institutional forms that reflect and support this development."[12]

Now all these claims are on Taylor's standards interpretive. And I would surely not wish to challenge that, but I would ask whether, in trying to confirm them or disconfirm them, in trying to tell it like it is, in trying to say something which is plainly and objectively so, are we actually caught up in a kind of hermeneutical circle, so that we can never, without an appeal to contestable insights or intuitions, or just insight or intuition *sans phrase,* empirically establish what is the case with respect to any of these propositions? I would think that the crucial cases here are propositions 1 and 2. Propositions 3, 4, and 5 might indeed, *in some fashion* be propositions we could objectively establish or disestablish, but surely they are so heavily interpretive that, without certain tolerably complex moral arguments and the establishment of a definite linkage between government atrocities and the morality of the perhaps largely duped population, they could hardly—just like that—be said to be true because of certain basic facts, just there to be recognized for anyone who will but honestly observe what goes on around him. Six (6), by contrast, is a truism, though in the context in which Chomsky employs it, it is a truism which should be uttered and indeed stressed, if he is justified in making the first four claims. Note further that in their association with them, 6 comes to have a certain content, but just taken by itself, it is a truism, though we should not forget that even truisms can be true.

So it is propositions 1 and 2 that are crucial for my case. Chomsky thinks they are plainly and evidently true, that there are plain

11. *Ibid.*
12. *Ibid.*

inescapable facts which establish their truth, while his liberal and conservative critics are equally convinced that they are plainly false—that Chomsky is a political fanatic or paranoid who is "flying in the face of the facts."

Given a thoroughly hermeneutical account of sociology, the claim should be that they are—if we take Chomsky and his critics literally—both mistaken: that in the nature of the case there can be no brute data—no empirical facts—there for every honest observer and logical inferer just to take note of. Rather with different interpretive accounts of man, society, and human potentialities—ultimately resting on human insight and self-definition —we will take different sides here, be committed to different political philosophies and *Weltanschauungen*. On such an account, we do not have anything crucial in such disputes that we can settle by (1) getting straight on what the empirical facts are and (2) by holding and reminding ourselves of—taking to heart—some obvious, truistic, and cross-culturally accepted moral norms, viz. pain is bad, human oppression and degradation evil, suffering to no point is to be avoided, and freedom and self-determination are good. We remain here, as with all important social determinations, within the hermeneutical circle.

III

It is at this point that I want to interject Taylor's interpretive account of sociology. An articulation and elucidation of it can provide a theoretical rationale for the perhaps not uncommon conviction that Chomsky and his critics are locked in an ideological battle, involving conflicting interpretive stances, which cannot be resolved simply by "clear thinking" and "getting straight about the facts."

Social sciences—indeed all the human sciences—are on Taylor's account irreducibly hermeneutical. That is to say, they are interpretive sciences whose most primitive data are readings of meanings. Such a science is not essentially predictive; its aim is not or at least should not be to state causal laws from which predictions or retrodictions can be derived. Hard prediction is out in the social sciences, for "really to be able to predict the future would be to have explicated so clearly the human condition that one would already have pre-empted all cultural innovation and transformation."[13] Rather its aim is to make clear—to make intelligible—its object of study. Thus whatever we are talking about in a hermeneutical science must be describable in terms of sense and nonsense, coherence and its absence. Moreover, there is no breaking out of this web of interpretations, getting utterly beyond interpretations altogether and utilizing some brute data, checking—without making interpretations oneself—the correctness of the interpretations by verifying in an empirical and non-interpretive way the social science claims in question. There is no breaking out of the hermeneutical circle so that independently of some challengable, hermeneutical stance we can verify any significant social science or political claim. Social science is a science of interpretation and not a science of verification.

In such a science we cannot escape in the last resort an appeal to insight and to a common understanding of the expressions we use in our characterization of social reality. We have, that is, forms of language which are also forms of life and to have an understanding of them is to have a participant's grasp of how they function. To understand them, they must be meaningful to us as subjects by being part of our way of life. If we are not actually participants, if the way of life is not actually our own way of life, we must have the kind of insider's understanding and feel for it which is close to that of a participant. This is what I mean by 'a participant's understanding'; but, as understanding admits of degrees, so does being a participant. But the essential thing to see here is that there is no understanding of what is involved without having the sort of understanding a participant would have. There is no stepping back from or "out of" these forms of life and language and just seeing or observing how society is and what "human beings are really like" independently of these forms. There is and can be no such Archimedean point.

The concept of social reality is a key concept for Taylor. He is concerned to deny, what many empiricists affirm and what main

13. Charles Taylor, "Interpretation and the Sciences of Man," *loc. cit.*, p. 50.

line social science simply assumes, namely, that in speaking of social reality we are speaking of something which is just there and
brute-fact-identifiable, independently of human conventions, vocabulary, and conceptualizations. This understanding of what is
meant by 'social reality' is not a pellucid notion, and yet it is for
Taylor—and I believe rightly—a central notion. It is imperative
then that we clearly display his argumentation for it.

Social reality, on Taylor's view, is not like the heavens which
exist whether or not we have a set of concepts in accordance with
which we have some understanding of the heavens. Different peoples more or less adequately conceptualize the heavens. But there
is no mutual dependence between their descriptions of the heavens and the heavens. The heavens are what they are independently of any description of them. By contrast, the realities we are
talking about when we talk of 'social realities' are for the most
part and indeed essentially social practices and they cannot be
identified in abstraction from the language we use in invoking
them or characterizing them. Language and reality in such a context are not mutually independent of each other.

Taylor does not say what he means by 'a social practice' but his
treatment of his examples, e.g. bargaining and voting, make it
evident enough that he is talking about a human activity contain-
ing, but not exhausted by, a cluster of rules which specify or at
least partially specify permissible and impermissible steps and appropriate and inappropriate ways of acting, if one is to engage in
the activity in question. Practices, he tells us, are essentially modes
of social relations. They do not, as it might at first be thought, express community consensus, for without them there could be
neither consensus nor polarization; indeed there could not even
be a community without social practices. If we vote there are certain things we must do if we are to engage in such an activity.
And if someone does not recognize that he must act in a certain
way, he just does not understand the activity in question, and indeed if people do not act in certain ways, follow certain rules,
there would be no such activity.

Such activities are practices. The key vocabulary involved in
them would not make sense without the activity, and the activity

could not exist without that vocabulary or a vocabulary equisignificant or nearly equisignificant to it. They exist in mutual dependence; and indeed the very language or a language equisignificant to it is "constitutive of the reality, is essential to its being the kind of reality it is."

In elucidating this claim, Taylor extends Searle's conception of a constitutive rule. An example would be that when playing basketball, if one shoots when the ball is in play and if one has not broken other rules—such as having run with the ball—and the ball goes through one's own basket, one has scored. Without such a rule, basketball, as we understand it, or in a way even remotely like we understand it, simply would not be; so that it is now appropriate to call such a rule a constitutive rule of basketball.

Taylor extends the notion of "being constitutive" to practices. Just as there are rules such that the behavior they govern could not exist without them, so there are other constitutive ranges of language such that they too are inseparable from certain ranges of behavior. The one simply could not exist without the other. Social practices and indeed even institutions are diverse but they all are such that for each of them there are certain distinctions—demarcations that we make by the use of language—which are constitutive of them.

It should be added, that the very drawing of these distinctions imputes a certain significance to the behavior that it would not otherwise have. What is essential to the practice of voting is that some verdict or decision be achieved. Without it there is no point to the passing around of ballots, the raising of hands and the like. Indeed these activities are not even intelligible as voting activities unless they are integral to a way of coming to a decision or verdict about who is to hold a certain office or what measures are to be passed. There can be no practice of voting unless some such distinctions have application.

Implicit in these very practices are certain norms and, as Taylor puts it, "a certain vision of the agent and his relation to others and to society." The practice of negotiation, for example, has a certain conception of autonomy, of interest, and a certain understanding of how clashes of interests are to be resolved. Likewise the practice of voting also has a certain conception of autonomy, of rule by some kind of majority, and a conception of the importance of human choice. To operate willingly with such practices is to define yourself in a certain way; it is to commit yourself to a certain way of living.

Social scientists in the mainstream and out of an empiricist tradition, that Taylor opposes, take (by contrast) social reality as something just there in the world, brute-fact-identifiable and characterizable. Just as we recognize by observation that a hand has been raised, so we can, these empiricists argue, come adequately to grasp, also as something which is brute-fact-identifiable, what, in a given context, is identified as social reality. In short, mainstream social science takes social reality to be something which, with ingenuity, could be reconstructed out of brute data alone—data which are just there to be observed, require no interpretive understanding, and are not constituted by certain rules or categorial distinctions. But as our discussion above of constitutivity has shown, social reality, in part constituted by social practices, is not and cannot be brute-fact-identifiable.

In thinking through the implications of this, we can come to see how (1) social science cannot but be an interpretive science and (2) how it is not a normatively neutral science. Let us see how Taylor argues for these theses.

If we take 'social reality' as Taylor does, social science cannot fail to be interpretive, for understanding social reality necessarily involves having a participant's grasp of a certain language. Without a *knowledge by wont* of the practices of a certain culture, the actions of the people of that culture must remain utterly opaque to one. But this knowledge involves understanding how to operate with certain concepts embedded in a certain language and this in turn involves the understanding of certain norms which are part of a certain cluster of practices.

Granting that this is a form of practical knowledge—a knowledge of what to do and not simply a knowledge of what is the case —why should we say that it must be interpretive? It must be interpretive because its most primitive data still involve the grasping of certain meanings which are constitutive of a distinctive social reality. But why exactly must such data be interpretive and what indeed does it *mean* to say that they are interpretive? They are interpretive in the way that understanding a text is interpretive, namely, they involve having a participant's grasp of a certain language, part of which involves understanding rules and distinctions, the having of which constitutes part of the social reality we are talking about and without which such a reality could not even exist. Indeed without such a language the very idea of such a reality would be so utterly problematic as to be unintelligible.

To understand here is to interpret, and any more systematic understanding, such as the one a hermeneutical political sociology might give, would still be one which would have to rely on this prior interpretive understanding, though this is not to suggest that it could not and indeed would not build on this to produce a more comprehensive systematic interpretive understanding with far greater explanatory force. But there is no breaking out, Taylor repeatedly reiterates, of this hermeneutical circle. Understanding in social science comes most centrally to making an interpretation of interpretations. Moreover, we can never, no matter how favorably we are placed, check our interpretations by reference to phenomena which are free of interpretation.

It is worth pursuing why exactly Taylor believes this to be so. It is (I believe) correct to give a short, though oblique, answer by saying that the rationale for this is implicit in his very idea of what is meant by 'social reality'. But it still remains the case that given the importance of this idea, it is worth spelling out exactly why Taylor claims that social science must be hermeneutical.

We have no brute data because we cannot understand the simplest politically relevant action except by relating it to a cluster of notions some of which involve knowledge of the intentions, purposes, conceptions of appropriate behavior, and aims of the agent. Furthermore, an understanding of this in turn involves an understanding of his culture, including its norms of rationality, credibility and, sometimes at least, its morality. Consider voting as an example. Suppose I take a Martian unfamiliar with our practices to a meeting in which I, among others, vote. He sees me raise my hand at certain intervals when certain things are said. What is readily recognizable is that hands go up when someone in charge of the meeting says certain things and this means, depending on when the hands go up, that the hand raiser is, at least as far as the public record goes, for or against certain proposals. Some of this and *perhaps* all of it is brute-data-identifiable. But someone who only understood what I have characterized above would still have a very inadequate idea of what voting consists in and what I was doing by voting on that occasion. One does not understand the practice of voting by noting how certain physical movements such as raising one's hand or marking slips of paper are tied to certain institutional rules of a quite explicit sort. My "political behavior" in voting could not be exhausted by such brute-data descriptions. Suppose I am voting in an academic setting over matters that arise in the university. In voting for a measure, I may also be working for long-range structural changes in the university, attempting to further progressive notions, standing by a certain set of moral principles, saving face, expressing my solidarity with a certain group, and the like. Until this is understood the Martian would have a very poor understanding of voting and a very poor understanding of certain bits of my political behavior. These notions are not brute-data-identifiable. Neither the institution of voting nor the long-term aims and goals of the voter are brute data. Neither could exist without certain constitutive rules or practices. What is clearly brute-data-identifiable is that certain hands go up, that certain noises occur, coming from someone sitting or standing in front, before and after the hands go up. These things require no *knowledge by wont* of constitutive rules or practices.

Moreover, the perspicuous representation in a political theory of such notions as saving face, expressing solidarity, and even such notions as voting or rioting would involve a complex interpretation which would require a good understanding of the political culture in question, a sensibility to certain practices, and an understanding of certain political ideals. This involves the making sense of a number of complex notions and the coherent setting of them together. And this, of course, is irreducibly interpretive. If, instead, we stick to what is brute-data-identifiable, we will have a very inadequate understanding of the political behavior in question.[14]

Many will respond that if we wish to be objective—to be really scientific—we must stick exclusively to what is brute-data-identifiable, even if that is not very much, for what is objectively real is brute-data-identifiable and this is what social reality really is, the rest—the evaluative part—is just ideology: the (in part) culturally defined *affective* responses of individuals and groups. That group X or individual Y so responds is again brute-data-identifiable but all questions about the legitimacy, adequacy, or correctness of this response are beyond scientific or objective determination. But this is (1) to involve (as we already have seen) a thoroughly myth-ridden and inadequate conception of social reality; (2) it involves what is at least arguably an inadequate idea of science modeled after a certain picture of the natural sciences; and (3) it simply assumes a conception of objectivity which identifies 'being objective' with 'being scientific' on the above possibly inadequate conceptualization of 'scientific'. Taylor rightly challenges all these notions and unless they can be justified there is no, even nearly, sufficient reason to believe that an adequate social science must, indeed should or even could, stick exclusively to what is brute-data-identifiable.

Again it is natural to respond that while, humanly speaking, values are important, a person's values after all are really his affective responses—his attitudinal stances—toward a given situation. Science can tell us that individual Y or group X or culture Z has such and such values, regards such and such as appropriate or thus and so good, but what it cannot do, while remaining scientific, is to say that such and such is appropriate and such and such is good. It can legitimately study the occurrence of values, i.e. study what affective attitudes people have, but it can make no judgments of value itself. Social science, to be science, must in the nature of the case be value-free.

Taylor shows that this is doubly a dogma. In the first place if I assert 'The American aggression in Viet Nam has been a disaster

14. *Ibid.*, p. 17.

to the Viet Namese people', 'Agnew is an unsavory character', or
'The War Measures Act was an inappropriate response to the
situation', it is indeed true that I am very likely expressing attitudes and I am likely to evoke an attitudinal response from those
who hear my evaluative remarks. But I am by no means *just* evok-
ing and expressing attitudes or *just* taking a stand or showing or
evincing an affective response to the situation. I am also referring,
though obliquely, to certain empirically determinable features of
the situations in question. This would come out if I were asked
to give reasons for my assessments. (If I am making what could
genuinely count as "assessments," I must be able in theory at least
to give reasons for them.) And in giving reasons I could not bring
in my attitudes or cite my tendency to have a certain affective response, but I would cite certain empirical features of the situation
as reasons for making the assessments I made.[15] If I could not do
that, my remarks would no longer be taken as value judgments—
as reasoned assessments of the situation—but as prejudices and
mere expressions of emotion. There is, of course, a link between
values and attitudes, and it is true that if human beings were
without attitudes and had no feelings about what is happening to
them and around them, they would have no values. But to make
a value judgment is not simply to express, subscribe to, adopt,
or evoke an attitude. Values are not just attitudes or affective
responses.

In the second place, the language of political science is not and
cannot become so aseptic as to become value-free, if it is to continue to characterize significant political behavior, explain political realities, or make sense of politics. In his "Neutrality in
Political Science," Taylor points out that traditional political philosophy (e.g. Aristotle, Hobbes, Hegel, Mill, and Marx) did give
us comprehensive normative theories with distinctive conceptual
frameworks. In each of these theories a general description of phenomena was couched in the crucial concepts of a particular framework. Empirical investigation and explanation went on but it was
always developed in and remained instrumental to the interests

15. James Rachels, "Reasons for Action," *Canadian Journal of Philosophy*,
Vol. 1, No. 2 (Dec. 1971), pp. 173-87.

of the comprehensive normative theory. The empirical descriptions of these theories are always made in accordance with the (in part) normative categorial set of a given over-all normative theory. Even independently of these theories, our observations, where they are reasonably complex, can never be neat theory-unencumbered descriptions of what is going on. In fact there can be no simple, theory-free just taking note of what is going on. And our theoretical vocabulary here, whatever it is, in turn reflects a certain conception of life. And such a notion is not, of course, free of normative conceptions.

Contemporary political science aspires to be normatively neutral. However, there are, Taylor contends, value consequences of central importance within the supposedly neutral accounts of such influential, empiricist political theorists as Lipset, Lasswell, and Dahl. And this is not accidental, for comprehensive political theories—including allegedly "scientific theories"—will have an over-all conceptual framework and this framework, as Taylor puts it, will "secrete a value position. . . ."[16] This is obviously metaphorical, for no framework literally secretes anything, but Taylor makes it evident enough what he has in mind. The conceptual framework in a political theory sets out how political phenomena are to be characterized. It tells us "how they can vary" and what "the major dimensions of variation"[17] are. Since these are matters of great importance to human beings, each framework will have its own built-in scale of values. "That is to say, a given dimension of variation will usually determine for itself how we are to judge of good and bad; because of its relation to obvious human wants and needs."[18] Moreover, the framework is linked, "to a given conception of the schedule of human needs, wants, and purposes, such that, if the schedule turns out to have been mistaken in some significant way, the framework itself cannot be maintained."[19]

16. Charles Taylor, "Neutrality in Political Science," *Philosophy, Politics and Society,* Third Series ed. by Peter Laslett and W. G. Runciman (Oxford: Blackwell, 1967), p. 40.
17. *Ibid.*
18. *Ibid.*
19. *Ibid.,* p. 41.

Human needs, wants, and purposes have an important bearing on the way people act. Given that type of importance, they must have an influence on the framework. If the conceptualization of the schedule of human needs is inaccurate, the framework will thereby be shown to be inadequate at least in some degree. Moreover, it is also always true that if something fulfills human needs, wants, or purposes, that this constitutes a *prima facie* reason for calling it good. There is a conceptual link between wants, needs and values. They are not just contingently linked.[20]

The underlying point to Taylor's remarks here is to make it evident that the adoption of a "framework of explanation carries with it the adoption of the 'value-slope' implicit in it. . . ."[21] The adoption of a conceptual framework restricts the range of normative positions that can be defensibly held.[22] Such a framework will explicitly or implicitly involve some conceptualization of a schedule of human needs, wants, and purposes and this will give the theory a certain normative orientation. This only can be avoided by restricting one's account to rather brute descriptions such as 'More Italians voted Communist in the last decade than in the decade immediately following World War II'. But so to restrict political science is in effect to make it a non-theory and a non-science. Science is not just a random collection of facts and thus political *science* cannot be just unconnected social description. It essentially involves theory. But to the extent that political science is theoretical, it cannot escape being normative. Political science to the extent that it is a science and has any genuine theory at all, does give guidance as to right and wrong.[23] As Taylor puts it, "A study of the science of man is inseparable from an examination of the options between which men must choose."[24] Theory and practice are inextricably joined here.

It is important to recognize in this context that a person's social theory also helps him define himself. A human being, as a chooser

20. *Ibid.*, p. 48.
21. *Ibid.*, p. 42.
22. *Ibid.*, pp. 56-57.
23. *Ibid.*, p. 48.
24. *Ibid.*, p. 47.

and an animal who forms intentions and has purposes, defines himself in the practices he creates and sustains. His theoretical errors are also his own illusions and false consciousness. With changes in his self-definition go changes in his practices which instantiate his conception of himself. These changes in self-definition are also changes in what he is. For his conceptualizations of himself are constitutive of his practices and his practices in large measure make him what he is.

The social sciences, Taylor concludes, are necessarily hermeneutical sciences; and indeed as hermeneutical sciences they are also moral sciences, "founded on intuitions which all do not share, and what is worse . . . these intuitions are closely bound up with our fundamental options."[25] He maintains that we sometimes at least have incommensurables here and what are perhaps unadjudicatable conflicting conceptual frameworks resting on what may well be a network of essentially contested concepts. It isn't that thinking makes it so here or that nothing can be said, but it does appear to be the case that we are caught in a kind of unavoidable relativism or at least historicism and that we are at a juncture where we simply *must* rely on insight.

Relativism, of course, is a vague notion and it has been variously conceived. Taylor does not believe that his account is relativistic in any significant way and he does indeed point out in "Interpretation and the Sciences of Man" that even though there are some differences which will be "non-arbitrable by further evidence" and each side can only make appeal to having a deeper insight into what is involved than the other, that this fact is not symptomatic of relativism, for, where there is such a conflict, one position can still be superior to the other. Its superiority consists in the fact that "from the more adequate position one can understand one's own stand and that of one's opponent, but not the other way around."[26] But this itself would seem to be an evidential matter, showing, pace Taylor, that the differences were after all arbitrable by further evidence. If, appearances to the contrary

25. Charles Taylor, "Interpretation and the Sciences of Man," *loc. cit.* (Sept. 1971), p. 51.
26. *Ibid.*, p. 47.

notwithstanding, it is not at all an evidential matter in such cases which account is the more comprehensive, then it appears to be the case that it is itself in turn a matter of non-arbitrable, conflicting interpretive insights as to which position has the more comprehensive insights. But this does appear to be a form of relativism. Yet this seems at least to be where Taylor is at, for he remarks, after making his statement about how positions of superiority are ascertained, that it "goes without saying that this argument can only have weight for those in the superior position."[27]

It seems to me, however, that we must allow that at least in principle it must be possible for there to be evidence which could be seen, at least by an ideal and impartial observer, to have greater weight than the evidence for the other position. If, as I suspect is the case for Taylor, such ideal, impartial observers are a conceptual impossibility in such a context, then we do seem to be landed or stranded in a tolerably important form of relativism.

Just how extensive this relativism is, is something which is far from clear, but Taylor does speak of a "gap in intuitions" and he is explicit in rejecting a verificationist model even as a test for the truth or credibility of conceptions arrived at intuitively. Such a model, Taylor argues, will not give us the objectivity and truth we are seeking. There are no hard predictions here, no appeal to data which are themselves not subject to interpretation and reinterpretation in virtue of which we could check the accuracy and truth of our claims. We have no hard data which would be sufficient to decide between rival accounts of society. We can never break out of the hermeneutical circle.

IV

I now want to return to a consideration of the dispute between Chomsky and his critics in order (a) to see if it is reasonable to believe—keeping in mind the account of social reality we have just articulated—that there could be a vindication of any of their

27. *Ibid.* I should add that Taylor—as he has expressly said to me—does not believe that he is committed to a form of relativism. But it seems to me that this is an implication of his conceptions.

conflicting claims by an appeal to the facts and (b) whether such a significant case could plausibly serve as at least a partial disconfirmation of such a hermeneutical account of sociology. I shall pursue these twin aims together.

Honest and knowledgeable persons radically conflict over the substantive issues Chomsky raises and the rare uncommitted onlooker is likely to think—in some pejorative sense of 'ideology'—that on both sides it is "all ideology." This inclines one to think that an interpretive sociological account of the matter is correct and that it is *not* an issue that humane persons, who can reason objectively about the matter, could settle quite conclusively or even with any kind of reasonable decisiveness, if only they could get clear about what the facts actually are. What I want to probe is whether such a hermeneutical account is actually justified. Can it be made out, against such an account, that there are factual considerations, if only we could know which actual plain empirical propositions are true, which—independently of one's ideology and ideologically formed consciousness and sense of relevance and significance—would lead a humane person to either affirm or deny the first or second Chomsky-propositions asserted in section II.

I would like to see if such a case could be made out. Remember that most, if not all, the partners to this dispute believe their opponent(s) to be wildly and plainly off the mark. They think that there are plain facts which establish their respective cases. Chomsky thinks that Hook is thoroughly irrational about such issues and has little respect for the facts, and Hook returns the compliment. Chomsky refers to Abel's "numerous falsifications" and remarks of one in particular that it is "nothing but a reversion to McCarthyism of the most vulgar sort."[28] And Abel responds by speaking of Chomsky's deliberate misrepresentations —"representations [which] are by no means careless . . . ," while Silber accuses Chomsky of a "McCarthyism of the Left."[29] Schle-

28. Noam Chomsky, "Vietnam, the Cold War and Other Matters," *Commentary* (Oct. 1969), p. 18.
29. Lionel Abel, "Vietnam, Cold War and Other Matters," *Commentary*, (Oct. 1969), p. 19; and John R. Silber, "Soul Politics and Political Morality," *Ethics*, Vol. 79, No. 1 (Oct. 1968), pp. 14-23.

singer in turn accuses Chomsky of foreswearing "reasoned analysis" and of fabricating evidence, while Chomsky replies by denying this and accusing Schlesinger of deliberate and gross misrepresentation, invention, and an "inability to get the simplest facts straight."[30] There is, in short, the strong conviction on the part of the parties to the dispute—if indeed we can take their claims at face value—that there is a plain appeal to fact which would decisively establish their respective cases. Is this just the hyperbole of men caught in a grim ideological battle or is there some appeal to fact—not overladen with ideological encumbrances—which, if we would but dispassionately observe and coolly and intelligently infer from our observations, would establish one party to be right and the other wrong?

Let me begin by trying to ascertain what Chomsky's liberal and conservative critics take to be the plain matters of fact which show beyond a shadow of rational doubt that Chomsky's claims are mistaken.

Flew, in discussing Chomsky, alludes to certain factual considerations which he believes, if taken due note of, make it highly implausible to speak of America as an aggressive, violent, imperialistic nation.[31] Flew argues that what Chomsky takes to be American imperialism, seen in another light, is not imperialism at all, but a defensive stance taken as a response to Soviet revolutionary imperialism. Here we seem at least simply to have two general interpretive points of view in accordance with which we look at the facts. But surely it is plausible to treat (as does Flew and indeed Chomsky as well), "The Soviet Union is an expansionistic revolutionary imperialism" as an empirical hypothesis. What happened in Eastern Europe, which Flew says Chomsky for the most part ignores, is evidence for it or against it. That the Soviet Union imposed Communist regimes on Poland, East Germany, Czechoslovakia, and Hungary, and tried to destroy Tito and re-

30. Arthur Schlesinger, Jr., "Review of *American Power and the New Mandarins,*" *loc. cit.,* pp. 4-5. And Noam Chomsky, "Vietnam, the Cold War and Other Matters," p. 22.

31. Antony Flew, "New Left Isolationism," *The Humanist* (Sept.-Oct. 1971), pp. 38-40.

place him with leadership obedient to Moscow, counts for that hypothesis. The failure of this to be so counts against it. However, even here we have something which is very tricky, for what we are talking about is very interpretive and hardly brute-fact-identifiable. Notice that it is no mean trick to identify whether certain leaders are obedient to Moscow; they may instead act in fraternal solidarity with Moscow because they have the same beliefs and ideological convictions. But, all the same, in principle at any rate, do we not know what it would be like to specify "brutish data," if not exactly "brute data," which would enable people to confirm the obedience-hypothesis and disconfirm the fraternal-solidarity hypothesis? If we found a tape, for example, in which unknown to them the East European leaders' inner circle conversations were recorded, and on this tape the leaders said things such as "They didn't at all like policies X, Y, and Z of the Soviet Union and indeed would not have gone along with them but for the fact that they would like to keep their jobs and summer villas," then we would have evidence against the fraternal-solidarity hypothesis. If we accumulated much evidence of this sort—evidence which anyone who understood the language could gather and understand—then we would have good evidence against the fraternal-solidarity hypothesis. Moreover, it is at least plausible to claim that such statements of evidence are often normatively neutral empirical statements of fact. If we had many and varied statements of this sort, not only would it be the case that the obedience-hypothesis was confirmed, if there were no other hypothesis in the field, but we would have some evidence for Flew's Soviet revolutionary-imperialism hypothesis, though, of course, not very conclusive evidence, for the domination of Eastern Europe can be explained not only by the revolutionary-imperialism hypothesis but also by the Buffer-Zone hypothesis, namely, that having been invaded three times in modern history by Western powers, Russia, in defensive reaction, wishes to protect itself by having buffer states between it and the great Western powers. But again, as with the obedience-hypothesis, as over against the fraternal-solidarity hypothesis, what private, recorded conversations were taken, what orders were issued to military commanders and what was done *vis-à-vis* neighboring states such as Finland and Greece are indeed confirmatory or disconfirmatory of the revolutionary-imperialism hypothesis. And, indeed, one of the actual hot points of dispute about the origin of the Cold War and implicitly about Flew's revolutionary-imperialism hypothesis turns on how the Greek Civil War started and continued. Was it mainly internal to Greece, arising out of the discontent of the Greek people with little Soviet prompting; or did agents enter Greece from the Soviet Union under direction from Stalin to start an uprising? There are obviously several intermediary stages and while all of these activities are indeed characterized in such a way as to admit of divergent interpretations, still there are empirical limits or constraints here. Did Stalin tell X, Y, and Z to enter Greece and try to start a revolution or didn't he? Did he give them arms or not? It is implausible to speak of a hermeneutical circle here, or of needing to rely on insights or intuitions. We have something very much like "brute data" here. The difficulty is the straightforwardly empirical one of finding out for a wide range of politically relevant cases what the rather brute data are.

This is particularly difficult for some contingently well-hidden but conceptually unbaffling or even unproblematic instances.

Against Chomsky's proposition that America is presently the most aggressive nation in the world, Flew counters that the Soviet Union is still more aggressive and offers as evidence the American response to de Gaulle's withdrawal from NATO as compared with the Soviet Union's crushing of the Dubcek government. However, this evidence, even if taken as Flew takes it, might seem insignificant when compared to U.S. behavior in Indochina, Central America, South America, Greece, and Indonesia and their posture toward China and Cuba. Moreover, it could be at least plausibly argued that de Gaulle out of NATO posed no threat to the U.S.—when the chips were down he came running to the U.S. anyway—while in the relaxed situation in Czechoslovakia, West German and American agents came into the country and were not adequately guarded against by the Dubcek government, so that a real threat to socialist institutions occurred. That either the Russians believed this or that there actually was such a threat, would account for the differing receptiveness to opposition by the U.S. and the U.S.S.R. in the above situations. Remember that the U.S., until it had to, was of no mind to tolerate Cuba and imagine—to take a comparable example to Czechoslovakia—the United States tolerating Quebec as a revolutionary socialistic country backed by China or the Soviet Union.

However, to Chomsky's liberal and conservative critics, this very line of argumentation will seem, as it did to Flew when he read an earlier draft of this essay, already to skew things unfairly in Chomsky's favor. Many conservatives and liberals, still very much caught up with Cold War ideology, will not take at face value the claim that the leadership in the U.S.S.R. thought its institutions threatened, feared that Czechoslovakia might turn to the West, and believed that Western agents were at work. Rather they interpret the situation as the Russians objecting to liberalization, free speech, free inquiry, and the like. Some will even see my use of the hypothetical case of Quebec as a bit of apologetic desperation resulting from the fact that there is not much on the American side which is actually parallel. Bosch in the Dominican Republic and Allende in Chile, they will argue, is the closest parallel to the Russian invasion of Czechoslovakia.

What is evident here is how strong the hermeneutical account is. We not only see with this case different data being used, differently understood and differently placed, but we also see "the same data" being given quite distinct evidential significance.

It could be objected—to make a related but more general point —that I have not faced the fact that even if we had taped recordings of secret meetings and the memos of high governmental officials, we still would not have something that would help us, together with similar data, to break out of the hermeneutical circle. This is precisely the kind of information on the interpretation of which people with different ideological perspectives will disagree. If we found such tapes with Kennedy or Johnson saying they were doing it all to preserve freedom and to further the prosperity and long-term happiness of the people of Asia and the world, Chomsky would regard this as simple self-deception of an ideological kind. Differences of point of view show themselves in the interpretation of "hard data," and in decisions about relevance and evidential significance.

Surely this is so and it inclines one toward a hermeneutical account. Yet there are data here which are there for either side to take account of. The number and type of bombs dropped on Vietnam, the number of people killed, the number of people in prison, the movements of populations, the existence of American armed forces on foreign soil, and the like are facts there for any account to come to grips with. It is not that the data exist for one account with one interpretive framework but not for another, though it is indeed true that different interpretations would often attach a different weight to commonly acknowledged data and that people tend, hopefully usually unwittingly, to ignore data embarrassing for their own interpretive accounts. But it is just the facts about the numbers and types of bombs and their targets and the like that would no doubt lead Chomsky to speak here of Kennedy's or Johnson's self-deception, if we were to come across such a tape. But this data would not be the creature of a hermeneutical framework or a cluster of constitutive rules and practices, but would be there, in theory at least, for anyone to take account of.

It is indeed true that anyone who did not understand the language in question or did not understand what was meant by 'bombs', 'fragmentation bombs', 'napalm', and the like would not understand the claims and counter-claims being made. But this is a trivial observation, for similar things could be said about an understanding of anything. Only if 'constitutive rules' and 'constitutive practices' contrast with something which is not such do these conceptions, crucial to the hermeneutical account, have much significance. If no one had ever had a conception of a fragmentation bomb, then fragmentation bombs would indeed not exist, but there is no logical sense in which their existence depends on constitutive rules or practices in the way chess or basketball does.

The hermeneutical account works well when we are thinking of social arrangements such as Christianity or capitalism, or social practices such as praying or charging interest. But that a fragmentation bomb explodes in a certain way, that napalm burns in a certain way, that people lived for over a year in caves all day and tended their vegetable gardens at night, are facts which do not depend for their existence on the adoption of an interpretive framework. They are unfortunately part of the "furniture of the world" to be taken account of by any account which would square with the facts, though different interpretive viewpoints may well attach different significance to them.

However, one or another account may be shown to be mistaken because certain of its claims have been disconfirmed. We would have strong disconfirming evidence of the claim that America pursued its Viet Nam policy in the way it did primarily to protect freedom and democracy if we had a candid and reasonably lengthy tape recording of a private conversation between Nixon and Kissinger in which they both said or plainly implied that talk of preserving freedom and democracy in Viet Nam was just so much blather for public consumption and that what they were really interested in was preserving American power in the interests of business enterprise. A liberal account which ignored such evidence would plainly be mistaken.

People, given such reports, might speak of self-deception on Nixon's and Kissinger's part, but it is not difficult to imagine details of such a secretly taped private conversation which would make such a claim perfectly absurd. ('Perfectly absurd' is indeed itself a conception which takes an interpretive reading, but again there is an appeal to the facts about what is perfectly absurd.) There is a complex interplay between interpretation and data, but there is an interplay and we are not imprisoned within an interpretive framework.

In his "Scholarship and Ideology," Chomsky makes an argument which could serve as a realistic example of the distinction I am making between what is a matter of interpretation and what is at least a putative fact, hardly enmeshed in any hermeneutical circle. In discussing the work of the American political scientist Robert Tucker, Chomsky remarks:

> Tucker's interpretation of Kennedy's remark presupposes that American hostility towards Castro was a consequence of his turn towards the Soviet Union, which is untrue. Perhaps one can argue

that American hostility was not a determining factor in this move, but that it preceded it is beyond argument.[32]

Here Chomsky in his practice nicely illustrates what is a matter of interpretation and what is not. What is "beyond argument" is that Castro turned to the Soviet Union and oriented his policy toward the Soviet Union *after* American hostility to his government developed. That this is the case is just a fact there for any interpretive account to come to grips with. But it is another thing to claim that American hostility *brought about* this move. Such a claim involves making an interpretation and its truth cannot be determined without committing oneself to an interpretive framework. In this important way it differs from the first statement about Castro.

Taylor would surely say that the conceptions "turning to a certain power" or "orienting one's policy in a certain direction" are rather complicated notions involving an understanding of how certain constitutive social practices work. In this way, Chomsky's case does not count against an interpretive account, but in another important way it does, namely, that it is just a fact that Castro turned toward the Soviet Union in this way after he received a cold reception in the United States and American hostility became evident. That this is so is something which is not in dispute and requires for its acceptance no contestable intuitive understanding or grasp of the situation. It is something which is just there to be empirically verified.

Indeed, in arguing about whether the U.S. or the U.S.S.R. is the most aggressive nation in the world and the greatest threat to world peace, we are involved in something very interpretive. Here we indeed have rival interpretive accounts, and we do in effect appeal rather impressionistically to our intuitive or impressionistic idea of what is most plausible to believe. But it is also the case, as with the obedience-hypothesis versus the fraternal-solidarity hypothesis, that minimally interpretive empirical states of affairs would confirm and disconfirm the rival hypotheses. Did

32. Noam Chomsky, "Scholarship and Ideology," *The VAG Magazine* (Winter 1973), p. 32.

West German agents, agents of industrialists, C.I.A. agents, and the like go in and try to alter radically certain Czech institutions or did they not? What did Brezhnev and his intelligence officers actually believe about the situation? All these things and myriad things like them are for the most part establishable by observation with a minimum of interpretation, and they can count for and against the hypothesis that the Soviet Union is the most aggressive world power.

In this situation it is not the case that we have a practice-defined and created conception of social reality keeping us in an interpretive and norm-laden circle. Rather, it is the case that what we have is a veritable plethora of fairly straightforward empirical considerations, some hard to actually establish and others, even when they are not hard to come by, hard to weigh in such general judgments of American capitalist imperialism versus Soviet revolutionary imperialism. But this does *not* establish that always and forever, we are and shall be, forced to rely, as Taylor says, in the last analysis on insight. There can be an increased, more systematic and more comprehensive scrutiny of putative empirical facts: brutish if not utterly brute data.

In trying to tot up American aggressiveness to ascertain whether the second of Chomsky's propositions listed above is true—whether or not the United States is presently the most aggressive country in the world, the greatest threat to peace, and a fertile source of criminal violence—other critics cite different putative disconfirming evidence. In fact John Silber believes he has disconfirming evidence of such a conclusive kind that he is confident that Chomsky's claim can be shown to be "patently false" and he even doubts whether Chomsky really believes what he is saying here.[33] The evidence that Silber cites for what he takes to be the patent falsity of proposition 2, as well as proposition 1, is the United States' behavior toward Japan after the Second World War and the refusal of the United States to make an atomic attack on the Soviet Union after the Second World War. Silber contends that if the United States government were as aggressive

33. John R. Silber, "Soul Politics and Political Morality," *Ethics* (Oct. 1968), pp. 14-23.

and barbarous as Chomsky claims, then it would "never have offered the generous terms o´ the Japanese peace treaty" and the
United States "would certainly have followed the advice of Bertrand Russell in the period from 1945 to 1950, while it [the United
States] still enjoyed a monopoly in atomic weapons, and waged
a preventive war against the Soviet Union."[34] Silber concludes
that its forbearance when it had an atomic monopoly provides
"clear evidence of its peaceful intent and of its lack of interest in
dominating the world by force."[35] Now whatever we should conclude from this, it is fairly evident that we have something which
is very interpretive: our "clear evidence" here is not anything
like brute data. Moreover, it is also true, and again supportive
of an hermeneutical account of social science, that someone inclined to a Chomskyian view of the matter could at least plausibly interpret the American behavior in a quite different light,
namely, that the United States, having learned the lessons of the
Allied Powers in the First World War, was not about to prepare
the ground for World War Three or lose what could be a good
hold on defeated nations with considerable industrial potential
(Japan and West Germany) by making a vindictive peace treaty.
That is not the way to make such parts of the world safe for
American capitalist expansion and take-over. And the failure to
destroy the Soviet Union by atomic bombs does not show that the
United States is not the most aggressive nation on earth; it shows
rather that even its aggression knows bounds. Moreover, but somewhat more peripherally, it is not perfectly evident whether or not,
between 1945 and 1950, the decision-makers in the United States
really believed their own propaganda about Russian expansive-
ness and might. If they did not, they may have very well concluded that the cost of occupying such a devastated, and consequently ungrateful, country after such an atomic strike might be
just too high. Whatever the exact motives here, the behavior of
the United States in that instance does little to show that it is
not, when balanced against the evidence from other areas cited

34. *Ibid.*, p. 19.
35. *Ibid.*

by Chomsky, presently the most aggressive, violent, and imperialist power in the world.

However, do we not remain here—no matter which side we take—on a highly interpretive level? Only contingently, I think. That is to say, either interpretation seems to me to be "brutish data" *verifiable*, though this does not mean it is brutish data *verified*. Again, if we discovered records of candid and secret policy discussions between the President and his top advisers in which it was agreed that the best way (1) to make Japan an adjunct to American capitalist enterprise and (2) to keep Japan as a willing ally in the U.S. orbit was to make generous peace terms with her, the second claim would be confirmed. We could also readily imagine scenarios in which things were said which would confirm Silber's contention. In either case, we have "brutish data" verifiable claims. The same thing should be said *vis-à-vis* a preventative atomic war with the Soviet Union. The crucial point is that we can readily conceive of very brutish facts which would confirm or disconfirm either hypothesis. The trouble isn't as much the hermeneutical circle, as the difficulty in getting enough empirical facts. We know what it is we would have to observe to confirm or disconfirm certain hypotheses, but we are seldom in a position to make the observations, and what comes back to us, as having been observed, is often suspect as having been subject to deliberate ideological distortion. The mass media and indeed the government reports are not wholly reliable as repositories of truth. They are hardly institutions committed to the disinterested search for truth. But this is not "a principled blocking of hard data" or rather (and more accurately) it is not the recognition that nothing really counts as "hard data" in situations where it is needed or at least wanted for sociological understanding. Rather, what is involved here is the quite *contingent* fact that we often cannot get at the facts. This consideration, together with the fact that what is at issue is sometimes at least very complex, often makes "political truth" elusive. Frequently, in trying to make up our minds what to believe, all we have to go on is the unreliable mass-media and the official sources. But this is not a principled, conceptual roadblock emanating from the very nature of social

reality. Sometimes in practice and always, or at least typically, in
principle there are rather straightforward observations that could
be made which would confirm claims or disconfirm claims about
what is the case here. The most difficult interpretive problem
comes over balancing up the relative weight of different observa-
tional claims in deciding what to say and believe in such situations. But this does not show that we must be thrust back here
upon a reliance on insight with no decisive tests, because the social reality we are talking about is constituted by certain practices
embodying certain norms.

In trying to ascertain what the situation is, there are myriad
phenomena which are not simply the creatures of practices, such
as how many guns and tanks went from one border to another,
how many Americans versus how many non-Americans hold jobs
at a certain salary range in the so-called multi-national corporations, and how many missiles do the Americans have and where
are they placed, and how many missiles do the Russians have and
where are they placed. In trying to make the complicated claims
that Chomsky and his critics make, it is true enough that interpretations must be made, but it does not appear that we are inextricably caught in a hermeneutical circle from which we cannot
break out. There are non-interpretive phenomena which test,
with varying degrees of decisiveness, depending on the nature of
the particular claim in question, at least some of our claims about
social reality. We may very well not be able to make *exact* predictions in the social sciences, and insight in knowing what to
ask is indeed very crucial, but in the confirmation or disconfirmation of our claims about social reality, what goes on is not so
thoroughly screened as Taylor suggests by conventions from
"physical reality"—brute-data-identifiable facts. Since this is so,
it is not true that we cannot, if we will be honest intellectuals and
take care, confirm or disconfirm even such controversial claims as
Chomsky and his critics make. I have not tried to show here who
has (if anyone) correctly ascertained what are the plain facts in
this situation. I have hardly even rehearsed, particularly on Chomsky's side, what might be taken to be the plain facts. But what I
have been concerned to argue is that even over such complex

social questions as these, there are plain facts there to be uncovered to confirm or disconfirm the conflicting interpretive claims. We are not caught in a situation where we must endlessly make interpretive readings of interpretive readings of interpretive readings with no possible appeal to brutish-fact observables to confirm one claim and disconfirm another.[36]

36. The question might be raised as to whether I have not, in what I have shown about the role of verification, eliminated the need for interpretation— shown how it is theoretically eliminable. In short, I have shown that Taylor is just wrong about interpretation. However, I am not prepared to make such sweeping claims. It seems to me, as I tried to show, that Taylor has established that certain social practices are in part at least constitutive and that there are crucial classificatory and conceptual claims in the social sciences in which interpretive judgments are unavoidable. I was only concerned to reduce his claims about the untestability of social science claims. I would like to thank Virginia Held, Tom Nagel, Antony Flew, and Robert Ware for their useful criticisms of earlier versions of this essay.

Notes on Contributors

Hugo Adam Bedau is Austin Fletcher Professor of Philosophy at Tufts University. He has also taught at Dartmouth, Princeton, and Reed. He has edited *The Death Penalty in America* (2nd ed. 1967), *Civil Disobedience: Theory and Practice* (1969), and *Justice and Equality* (1971). He is the author of many articles in the areas of social, political, and legal philosophy, and was Chairman of the Society for Philosophy and Public Affairs during 1973.

Marshall Cohen is Professor of Philosophy at the City University of New York. He has also taught at Harvard University, the University of Chicago, and The Rockefeller University. He is the editor of *The Philosophy of John Stuart Mill* (1960), of the journal *Philosophy and Public Affairs,* and has contributed articles to literary and legal as well as to philosophical journals.

Richard A. Falk is Albert G. Milbank Professor of International Law and Practice at Princeton University. He is the author of *Law, Morality, and War in the Contemporary World* (1963), *The Role of Domestic Courts in the International Legal Order* (1964), *Legal Order in a Violent World* (1968), *The Status of Law in International Society* (1970), and *This Endangered Planet* (1971). He has been an editor of fourteen volumes in the area of world order studies and has written articles for a variety of journals. He is director of the North American Section of the World Order

Models Project and co-director with C. E. Black of a continuing project on the Future of the International Legal Order.

Peter A. French is an Associate Professor of Philosophy at the University of Minnesota at Morris. He is the author of *Exploring Philosophy* (1970) and editor of *Individual and Collective Responsibility* (1972) and *Conscientious Actions* (1973).

Stanley G. French is Dean of Graduate Studies at Sir George Williams University, Montreal, where he was formerly Professor of Philosophy. He has contributed articles on Hume, Kant, and topics in ethics to *The Journal of Philosophy, The Monist, Dialogue,* and other journals.

Alan Gewirth is Professor of Philosophy at the University of Chicago. He is the author of *Marsilius of Padua and Medieval Political Philosophy* (1951), and *Moral Rationality* (1972), a co-author of *Social Justice* (1962), and editor of *Political Philosophy* (1965). He has published articles in philosophical journals on Aristotle, Descartes, the social sciences, and in the areas of logic and moral and political philosophy. He was President of the American Philosophical Association, Western Division, in 1973-74.

Andres Gutman is a doctoral candidate in philosophy at the University of Toronto, working in the area of political-economic theory.

Joseph Margolis is Professor of Philosophy at Temple University, Philadelphia. He is the author of *Psychotherapy and Morality* (1966), *Values and Conduct* (1971), *Knowledge and Existence* (1973), and has contributed to many philosophical journals. He has edited four anthologies of philosophical articles.

Sidney Morgenbesser is Professor of Philosophy at Columbia University. He has been an editor of *Philosophy of Science* (1960), *Free Will* (1962), *Philosophy of Science Today* (1967), and *Philosophy, Science, and Method* (1969), and is an editor of *The Journal of Philosophy*. He has written articles on philosophy of science, the social sciences, and social philosophy. He was a founder of the Society for Philosophy and Public Affairs.

Kai Nielsen is Professor of Philosophy at the University of Calgary, Alberta. He has also taught at New York University and Amherst College. He is the author of *Reason and Practice* (1971), *Contemporary Critiques of Religion* (1971), *Ethics Without God* (1973), *Scepticism* (1973), and of many articles. He is an editor of the *Canadian Journal of Philosophy* and was an editor of *Philosophy and Political Action* (1972), the Society's first volume of essays.

Richard Wasserstrom is Professor of Law and Philosophy at the University of California, Los Angeles. He has been an attorney in the U.S. Department of Justice, and Dean of the College of Arts and Sciences at Tuskegee Institute. He is the author of *The Judicial Decision* (1961), of articles and reviews in legal and philosophical journals, and editor of *War and Morality* (1970) and *Morality and the Law* (1971).

Beverly Woodward is a consultant for the Institute for World Order. She has been a Fellow of the University Consortium for World Order Studies and Visiting Research Associate at Princeton University. She has published articles in *Commentary, Dissent, Peace and Change,* and *Win,* and taught philosophy and political science at Southeastern Massachusetts University.

Index